PROBLEMS AND PERSONS

PROBLEMS AND PERSONS

BY

WILFRID WARD

Essay Index Reprint Series

 BOOKS FOR LIBRARIES PRESS
FREEPORT, NEW YORK

First Published 1903
Reprinted 1968

LIBRARY OF CONGRESS CATALOG CARD NUMBER:
68-29254

MANUFACTURED
BY
HALLMARK LITHOGRAPHERS, INC.
IN THE U.S.A.

CONTENTS

	PAGE
INTRODUCTION	vii
ANALYTICAL SUMMARY	xxi
I. THE TIME-SPIRIT OF THE NINETEENTH CENTURY . .	1
II. THE RIGIDITY OF ROME	66
III. UNCHANGING DOGMA AND CHANGEFUL MAN	99
IV. THE FOUNDATIONS OF BELIEF	133
V. CANDOUR IN BIOGRAPHY	184
VI. TENNYSON	196
VII. THOMAS HENRY HUXLEY	226
VIII. TWO MOTTOES OF CARDINAL NEWMAN	260
IX. NEWMAN AND RENAN	283
X. THE LIFE-WORK OF CARDINAL WISEMAN	301
XI. THE LIFE OF MRS. AUGUSTUS CRAVEN	334

INTRODUCTION

Most of the Essays here given to the public have appeared in the leading reviews in the course of the past eight years. They are here republished, with additions and alterations, in some instances considerable; and the incidental references to persons and facts are brought into accord with the date of their present issue. Three of them—the first, fourth, and eleventh—now appear for the first time under the author's own name, having been originally printed in the *Quarterly* and *Edinburgh* Reviews. One—that on the "Life-Work of Cardinal Wiseman," based on a lecture delivered in Cambridge in 1897,—has not hitherto been published.

There is a certain continuity and unity in those Essays which deal primarily with Problems rather than with Persons. And the desire, expressed in some quarters, that a line of argument which has cost considerable labour in its elaboration should be exhibited in a volume rather than in scattered periodicals, has been one reason for the present publication.

The Essays to which I refer are the first

four—on the "Time-Spirit of the Nineteenth Century," the "Rigidity of Rome," "Unchanging Dogma and Changeful Man," and the "Foundations of Belief,"—together with portions of the eighth and ninth Essays, on "Two Mottoes of Cardinal Newman," and on "Newman and Renan."

In the first of these I endeavour to give some account of the bearing on our way of regarding the universe, of the far-reaching development of scientific knowledge in the nineteenth century. The "new framework" in which the century has placed our knowledge—to use Mr. Balfour's phrase—is regarded in my first Essay as consisting chiefly in the evolutionary view of the world and of society. We no longer regard the universe statically; we view it dynamically. We view its phenomena in relation to their causes and their antecedents, and to their probable future developments. We endeavour to ascertain those laws whereby it has come to be what we know it, and will eventually become other than it is. We have come, especially, to contemplate mankind as a developing social organism. And concomitantly we view human knowledge as developing with man himself. This process is likewise an organic growth. Minds react on each other, and common consent at certain points ratifies the combined achievement of many different, including at some stages divergent, intellects.

Such a general view, together with its bearing in particular on what is known as the "religious consciousness," is dealt with in the last part of the fourth Essay. But that Essay is preceded by two which present the actual religious problem in more concrete form.

It would be idle to deny that the "new framework" in which we have set our conception of the universe, has incidentally thrown theology into some confusion in all religious communions. Forms of theological expression fashioned at a very different phase of civilisation from our own, often contain the record of views which the present age has outgrown. Rejecting some of their more obvious implications, men may find themselves out of joint with the *formulæ* themselves, and feel more or less alienated from the communions which preserve them. This war between the implications of traditional theology and the accepted conclusions of the time-spirit, has made many persons uncertain how much they do believe of the faith of their fathers and how much they do not; and the doubt is sometimes accepted by themselves as tantamount to general religious disbelief. On the other hand, the generalisation of the evolutionary process brings home to us the fact that each successive age has really had to do a similar work of discrimination; that the theology of no age has been unalterable or final, although the slower

pace of its evolution in the past has prevented
this fact from being unmistakably apparent.
Its full realisation supplies, I maintain, the
key to a solution of our present difficulties,
and should eventually prove an antidote to
doubt.

If, in other words, the finality of the theology practically accepted by our ancestors is
disproved, and if the effect of this disproof on
very many minds is to disturb the faith of our
generation in Christianity by dislocating its
accustomed intellectual setting, the restoration
of faith must be looked for, so far as the
difficulty is a speculative one, in the con-
comitant view of this dislocation as being a
necessary part of the process of development,
to which theology, like all other sciences, is
subject. For gradual displacement, and substitution of new for old, is a necessary
part of the process of organic growth. Nevertheless, just as the thinking subject remains
the same while his organs of self-expression conform to the law that "to live is to
change," so an underlying supernatural truth,
ever the same, must be postulated as the living
principle of theological evolution—as the Reality
of which successive theological developments are
the part-expression. The old idea of fixity, which
did not look beyond the tangible *formulæ* with
their supposed unchangeable analysis, is parted
with. But another principle of persistency

is disclosed in theology, as the lesson of religious history is more and more realised— the persistency of certain central religious ideas, reappearing in more and more purified form under the influence alike of an exacter knowledge of the world of fact, and of the criticisms of the intellect and moral sense; and the persistency of the law of development. According to this view, the story of Christian theology is seen to exhibit, in some degree, the more general law which underlies the development of monotheism from the polytheistic mythologies, and the purifying process whereby the Deity came to be conceived less and less as a tribal god, with quasi-human purposes, more and more as the embodiment of sanctity, and the just Ruler of all mankind.

Thus the evolutionary view, which broke up the old supposition as to the fixity of theology, brings its own compensation. A fixed theology, viewed as final, with no thought either of its sources or of its possible future modifications, was the analogue to a view of the universe which failed in other departments to grasp evolution as a fact. An avowedly living and developing theology, on the other hand,—a theology viewed as consisting of ideas capable of organic growth, the symbolic expression of a living and lasting Divine truth,—is the analogue to a science which contemplates and investigates the laws of evolution in all other departments.

The advent of Christianity becomes, according
to this account of the matter, a stride in the
development of religion, much as the first appearance of consciousness, and of reason, as
developments from the unconscious and the
nonrational, were strides in organic evolution.
But in both cases, as I argue in my fourth Essay,
the stride is a manifestation of the Power behind
evolution, and not part of a merely mechanical
process.

The conception of the Christian Church as an
organism, one from its beginning, to which God
has entrusted a "deposit of faith," defined in
the first instance only in its bold outlines, to
be used, and where necessary to be made more
concrete in course of time, with a view to check-
ing modes of thought calculated to corrupt the
Christian idea, and so to kill the organism of
which that idea was the life, is obviously in accord
with the philosophy of evolution.   This general
view is also, of course, the acknowledged groundwork of Catholic theology, in so far as it has
always maintained that successive definitions are
but the express declarations, generally called for
by some new heresy, of what has been contained
implicitly from the first in the *depositum fidei.*
A view of theology as developing, underlies also
the religious position of many thinkers who are
external to the Catholic and Roman Church.
It is formulated by Auguste Sabatier in his
" Esquisse."   It is visible in Harnack's

" Dogmengeschichte." It is largely in harmony with the thought of Professor Caird ; and, to take writers in a different theological camp, it is in accord with the historical view of the Church to be found in ·the pages of " Lux Mundi." So far the argument in this volume may, to a considerable extent, appeal to many Englishmen.

The character of the Church as a corporate, abiding, and growing organism has, however, it can hardly be questioned, been preserved by the Catholic Church in union with the Apostolic See, with a definiteness and consistency which it has not shown elsewhere. On the other hand, the popular charge of " rigidity " and narrowness against the Church of Rome, of an incompatibility of its theology with advancing thought and knowledge, has to be considered. This view leads many to find a truer, if less distinct or symmetrical, realisation of the ideal Church—the organism wherein the Christian idea is preserved, which grows and assimilates in the expression of that idea the culture of each successive era—in some other form of historical Christianity. I endeavour to meet this objection to the *prima facie* claim of the Catholic and Roman Church in my second Essay.

The view indicated in that Essay is that the rigidity apparent in our prevailing theology in modern times, in so far as it may have been seriously hostile to intellectual growth and assimilative activity, has been largely due to the abnormal state of Christendom caused by the revolt of the sixteenth century. A choice had to be made between the positive destruction of the Church as one organism, and the safe-guarding of its existence by a symmetrical and controversial theology and a uniformity of discipline which were needed for the emergency, just as military discipline and the prompt but autocratic action of a court-martial are needed in time of war. According to this view, then, such rigidity and narrowness as may have been excessive, so far as the necessities of thought were concerned, have been inevitable and should be temporary. There has been ebb and flow of this tendency since its first appearance. It is now gradually giving place to more normal conditions.

The essential *semper eadem* of Catholic dogma, on the other hand, which some would identify with an unplastic rigidity, has, as I argue in the third Essay, been ever compatible with the assimilation of contemporary culture. This assimilative principle, though not adequately formulated, has been always acted upon. And it may well be now applied to the more rapid and conscious developments in theology which the age of science demands, as it has been applied in the past to the slow and unconscious developments of the pre-scientific period.

Semper eadem, for the future, need mean no more than it has meant in the past. The very theology whose imposing structure now, for some minds, is an obstruction which bars the way, contains the record of diverse phases of intellectual development in different ages, during which the original revelation, at first committed to unlettered disciples, found its organic expansion in forms of intellectual expression still ratified under "the seal of the fisherman."

This line of thought, which is further examined and explained in the eighth and ninth Essays, does not impair the sacredness of the definitions which have been called for by successive emergencies, or of the truths which these definitions were needed to protect. But it does present a view which makes the acceptance of the definitions possible without the acceptance of certain implications which may have been in the minds of those who framed them—implications based on conditions of culture and a conception of the universe which are not our own. Thus we have the clue to what had startled many of our contemporaries, and we view theology with an eye directed by history to discriminate between the lasting dogmatic truth it guards, and the bulwark itself, whose shape is that belonging to the date of its construction. We realise that we may accept old propositions as sacred and true, but with a

new explication in those incidental features
in which they bear traces of an older civilisation. Thus—to take the instance most urgent
on our thoughts — the definition that God
is the "Author of Scripture" was long
understood by the majority of Christians as
precluding inaccuracy of scientific detail in
Holy Writ. The proof of Copernicanism was
the beginning of a more critical examination
of the implications of the Divine authorship in
regard to the secular and scientific facts referred
to in the Bible—an examination which will
receive valuable aid, it may be hoped, from the
Pontifical Commission on Biblical Studies now
sitting in Rome. The old inference, "God
cannot be the Author of error, therefore there
is no error in the Bible," is now seen to
contain an ambiguous middle term. For there
may be error attaching to the contemporary
human culture used by God as the necessary
medium of His teaching at a particular time;
and He was not, in using it as a means of conveying fresh spiritual truth, the Author of the
error in human knowledge which He was
thereby diminishing.

Such a line of thought as the foregoing is
placed before the general English reader with
little hope of winning his assent to a view
of Roman Catholicism which involves as a pre-
requisite so many further considerations than I
have dealt with. It is urged, however, with

greater hope of its acceptance on the large number to whom the great historical Church would still appeal with overwhelming force as almost its own evidence, were it not for the shadow cast on the claim of Catholic theology by the supposed opposition of its authorised exponents to a frank and open-minded consideration and acceptance of the contemporary conquests of the human reason.

And in this connexion these essays may be regarded as a contribution to that movement of thought among Catholics in France, Germany, and America, as well as in our own land, which has been for some years urging, as of vital importance, that the positive sciences should take their full share in the further development of theology in so far as theology touches incidentally those facts of which secular science takes cognisance. To blend theology with these sciences is a no more unpromising task now than it once seemed to adapt to the philosophy of Aristotle—the *bête noir* of the early Fathers—the sacred science of which the Fathers themselves were the most authoritative exponents. In both cases it has been a question of new prominence to be given to sources of knowledge hitherto unknown or disregarded. In the thirteenth century the deductive reason and the Metaphyics of the Stagirite took up quite a new position in detailed theology : and in our time the positive sciences, physical and critical, claim a prominence and influence equally new. The celebrated Toulouse address of Archbishop Mignot recently crystallised, with the lasting clearness resulting both from the ability of the discourse itself and from the Archbishop's great official position, the main contention which has long been the characteristic feature of a movement of thought remarkable from its simultaneous manifestation in thinkers of very different antecedents. Some of its protagonists have pursued their own special studies, in history or Biblical exegesis, and presented the trend and results of those studies with the double guarantee afforded by their antecedents, as at once acute and learned critics and convinced Christians. My own principal endeavour here has been to point out that there is abundant room already provided by acknowledged theological principles for such developments in Catholic theology as these results may render necessary. The fault in the more conservative theologians has been (if my contention is true), that they have not seen the full capabilities of their own principles, but have identified their utmost reach with the very limited application of them which past circumstances have demanded.

Thus the scare which has been raised, that Catholicism, as being the ancient and unchangeable faith, must be destroyed by the introduction of intellectual views in themselves novel, is maintained by me to be quite contrary to the teaching of history. The traditionally conservative tendency of the Church is, I argue, the providential breakwater against the permament admission into theology of premature or immature theory, and the security for its development along uniform lines in place of exhibiting a plastic, opportunist changeableness, inconsistent with the real depth and unity of the Divine truth of which the Church is guardian. But assimilation by Catholic theology of the serious and mature achievements of the human intellect, though gradual, has been in the past, and is likely to be in the future, extensive and thorough. This view is indicated in various ways in the third, eighth, and ninth Essays. I propose its detailed application to the present outlook as the chief intellectual remedy for the epidemic of doubt which is arising from the threatened divorce between the view of the world long associated with Christian theology, and that suggested by the modern developments of the positive sciences.

What medicine, however, can do more than give its full opportunity to living nature, by getting rid of impeding disease or disorganisation? My endeavour is, therefore, limited to pointing out those defects of method which cramp the capabilities of theological principle, and drawing attention to the essential largeness of the capacities of Catholicism viewed historically. The full realisation of these facts will be, it may be hoped, an antidote to any want of faith or of vigorous thought among Catholics themselves. But it is for the exercise of this faith and of this vigorous thought gradually to do the real work, and to adapt our theology in detail to the twentieth-century culture as Albertus Magnus and St. Thomas Aquinas adapted it to the then almost equally novel conditions of the thirteenth.

To two friendly critics—now, alas! no longer with us—I am under special obligations in connexion with the two longest Essays in the volume. The Essay on the " Time-Spirit of the Nineteenth Century " was read in proof by Lord Acton, and has profited by his valuable criticisms and suggestions. That on the " Foundations of Belief " owes a similar debt to Mr. R. H. Hutton.

It remains for me to thank the Editors of the various periodicals in which portions of this volume have already been published, for their kind permission to include those portions in my book.

WILFRID WARD.

ANALYTICAL SUMMARY

I.

THE TIME-SPIRIT OF THE NINETEENTH CENTURY.

PAGE

Achievement of the nineteenth century—In part the completion and practical application of the work of its predecessors—What has been its special and original contribution to our knowledge?—Mr. Balfour's views on the subject criticised—But he touches the really characteristic feature of the century when he speaks of it as contributing a " new mental framework " and a " new point of view " to our knowledge of the universe—This contribution is not due merely to the extraordinary development of physical science, but still more to the application of scientific method to a sphere far wider than the physical—The advance in biblical exegesis, archæology, and historical criticism as noteworthy as in physics—This advance has been due to the researches of specialists and to hypotheses designed to account for facts they have accumulated   1

The most characteristic activities of the century have been the application to the Universe in *time* of the inductive method applied by Newton to the Universe in *space*—The Baconian or inductive method was first applied to persisting or recurrent phenomena from the falling of a stone to the movements of the planets—Now we are applying it to the phenomena and laws of evolution ; to geology, biology, the evolution of species, documentary history—The process to which it is applied begins with the derivation of the "million million of suns" from the primitive nebula, according to Kant's theory—The method of induction and hypothesis is applied to the whole course of inorganic and organic evolution, culminating in man and the phenomena and laws of his social evolution—The idea of man as a developing social organism is that which is most characteristic of the nineteenth century—It was glimpsed before the dawn of the century —It is to be found in writers whose starting-point is most diverse

PAGE

—Condorcet, Kant, Burke, Bonald, Spencer, Hegel, Comte, De Maistre, Lamennais, Newman—The conception of evolution is itself evolved—It comprehends as parts of an organic whole the very varying lines of thought which gave it birth 5

The "new framework" supplied by the idea of evolution came at a time when, the mediæval synthesis being destroyed, knowledge had lost its unity—An unsynthetic specialism, and individualism without any unifying framework, were the notes of the eighteenth century—The old mediæval framework was best defined in St. Thomas Aquinas' "Summa," and best illustrated in Dante's "Divina Commedia"—Under pressure of the intellectual movement of the thirteenth century, Aquinas attempted that speculative unification of knowledge which St. Bernard had, a century earlier, dreaded as rationalistic in tendency—The faith underlying his synthesis was guarded for the many by the great principles of practical union embodied in the Holy Roman Empire and the Holy Roman Church—In the thirteenth century alone both the intellectual and the practical syntheses were fully operative 10

Two great facts of history imparted a glory and practical force to the old synthesis : (1) The wonderful spread of Christianity following upon the victory of the meek Christian over his oppressor; (2) the existing mediæval Christendom, suggestive of the *Civitas Dei*— Testimony of Harnack as to the general sense of ideals realised in the Middle Ages—The Church was like the sun in the heavens—Her "white robe" covered the land—In the eyes of the childlike and uncritical intellect of the Middle Ages, God was visibly building up on earth the *Civitas Dei*—To aid in this work was the inspiring motive of the Crusades 12

This visible *Civitas Dei* was the "tower" which "men hoped would reach the heavens"—But it tottered and fell—And the builders came to speak different tongues—Failure of the Crusades to realise their ideal—Failure of the Holy Roman Empire— Decline of the Papacy after Boniface VIII.—The "white robe" of the Church torn—Physical science and the spirit of doubt— "Unclothed pagan nature" in the Renaissance—Luther and the Reformers "confound the old common speech"—Corruptions and promises apparently not realised on the part of the Church gave

PAGE

the " protesting " individual his foothold —The claim of theology to
judge science expired with the Galileo case   18

A fashion of individualism succeeded—In physical science it
proved constructive, because individual effort and research issued in
general agreement—It was otherwise in metaphysics and theology—
Bacon's movement issued in the victories of modern science, Locke's
culminated in Hume's barren negations—Theology stood apart,
deserted like Lear by its former subjects—It neither resigned its
claims nor assimilated the new knowledge—To the most typical
intellects of the day it appeared doomed and discredited   20

But the assailants of theology soon found that they had no unity
beyond opposition to their discrowned ruler—History, metaphysics,
and sociology failed to construct anything to replace the theological
edifices they had destroyed—The phenomena of life appeared meaningless and disconnected—Leslie Stephen's account of the situation
—Illustrations in the works of Shaftesbury, Bolingbroke, Mandeville, Voltaire, Gibbon—Individual liberty of thought prevailed—
The *securus judicat* of the Church was rejected, the *securus judicat*
of modern science was not yet attained—The individual could
think as he pleased   24

The crisis of the French Revolution suddenly revealed the difference between the barren speculative individualism in sociology and
theology which had failed, and the individual effort which had been
so fruitful in science—In the one case there was defiance of law and
indifference to synthesis, in the other obedience to law and the
attempt at synthesis—Individual freedom was properly not an end
in itself, or opposed to the recognition of authority, but a means
to the recognition and creation of the best expert authority—This
had been recognised in science, but was ignored in sociology—
The successes of science and the destruction of religious and
social life at the Revolution revealed with startling clearness the
discrepancy   29

Two paths were then open for the reconstruction of society : the
" reactionary " and the scientific—The German Romantic School

PAGE

together with De Maistre and De Bonald took the one, such men as
Niebuhr and Ranke took the other—Both lines of thought are now
yielding to a combination of the two   31

Connection between the two movements and their interaction—
What the Catholic writers designed as an aureole to be thrown
round the past history of Christendom served the scientific
historians as a limelight—It made the past stand out with new
vividness—Share of Comte and Hegel in the movement   33

Mr. Balfour's phrase "non-rational" helps us to understand
the difference between the critical methods of the eighteenth and
nineteenth centuries—What the eighteenth dismissed as irrational,
the nineteenth has regarded as material, to be sifted and appraised—" Notre œuvre est d'expliquer ce que le XVIII. siècle avait
mission à nier "—An attitude of provisional sympathy (unlike that
of the Voltairian scoffer) is necessary to appreciate and understand
the past—Instances of the new temper and method   36

What will prove to be the bearing of the new scientific synthesis on religion?—Mr. Balfour holds that it will be favourable
—His prophecy on the subject   42

In the mediæval synthesis we must distinguish between (1) its
dialectical method and philosophy, (2) the faith accompanying it,
and (3) the imaginative force which impressed it on mankind—The
greatest change effected by the new synthesis so far as religion is
concerned is in this imaginative force which was formerly the pervading presence of the great victorious mediæval Church, and is
now the confidence inspired by the victories of science—But, we
may ask, Will Christianity prevail as a faith consistent with the
new philosophical method and synthesis?—Will it prevail again as
it did with the Greek apologists whom it subdued by the beauty of
its message in days when no world-wide Church existed?   43

Knowledge in secular science is no longer looked for amid the
rays of light surrounding the chair of the *doctor ecclesiæ*—And
the independence of modern science has expelled incidental visions

PAGE

which had been bound up with religious faith—But apart from this the trend of events is in the direction of the fulfilment of Mr. Balfour's prophecy—The "Divine Child" is once again sitting among the doctors of science, asking questions and touching their answers with light from another world—We dream of a religious philosophy which shall combine the benefits of individualism (admitting free scientific inquiry) with the fulness of that organic life which the Catholic Church has ever preserved—Symptoms of this desirable combination among both Protestant and Catholic thinkers.   48

Evolution is essentially optimistic—This leads us to expect the fulfilment of Balfour's prophecy—For the ethical element in man has appeared in the course of evolution—And its highest development can only be found in and by means of religion—The Christian ideal of the relations between the human spirit and God completes the evolutionary scheme—For Comte the highest in man sums up the best which evolution has yet attained—For Spencer the Unknown represents the cause of that best, and the further goal— Comte's object of worship (the best we know) and Spencer's Unknown cause are combined in Christian Theism—God is the Being unknown as He is in Himself, Whom our highest ideas inadequately symbolise : and man's highest qualities are the imperfect revelation of the Absolute   54

Apparent exceptions to the preceding estimate of the nineteenth-century temper—Narrow outlook of some modern historians—Their failure to look at the relation between the various facts in the field of history—Their indisposition to study causes or the movement of ideas—These characteristics are partly due to the enormous multiplicity of facts now known—Our thinking powers unequal to dealing with so heavy a burden—The age has been described as being "bankrupt in ideas"—This phase is, we may hope, temporary—The evolutionary view (which regards history as an onward movement of forces) is not really questioned, though the effort of applying it may be at times too great—Men shrink from dealing speculatively with so vast a mass of material—But the specialists will not ultimately be false to what Renan describes as the essence of the historical development of the nineteenth century .   56

II.

THE RIGIDITY OF ROME.

PAGE

Dr. Jessopp's comparison of the Catholic Church to the Celestial Empire crystallises a popular impression among Englishmen—The idea of reunion between England and a Church of Rome so conceived is absurd—The similarity between Rome and China is in reality superficial—China owes its exclusiveness to its self-contained genius, Rome to its adaptability—Rigidity and exclusiveness were in the Roman Catholic Church largely an attitude assumed to meet a special emergency—Such an attitude was the only means whereby the revolt which began in the sixteenth century could be withstood   66

Dr. Jessopp's account of China helps us to appreciate this difference—China has (he says) in time of peace and liberty derived its strength solely from its own resources—The Catholic Church, on the contrary, in its rites and theology, has assimilated ideas and customs from every civilisation with which she has been in contact—Instances given by Cardinal Newman—The Catholic Church has been in later times exclusive, not from choice or in time of peace, but from necessity in time of war 69

This state of war has also caused in England a mental estrangement which has made the English critics of the Church fail to understand her real genius—The difference of intellectual tradition casts a reflected light on the dogmas, which are popularly interpreted in the sense least acceptable to Englishmen—But if the difficulties on both sides have been due to a state of war which is passing away, and if power of assimilation is characteristic of the Catholic Church, there is hope for a change for the better in their future relations—The change would have to include two elements : (1) increasing individualism among Catholics and with it the share of Catholic thought in contemporary intellectual movements ; and (2) a consequent recognition among those outside the Catholic Church of her power and genius 72

This view further explained—The Catholic Church at Trent accepted the state of siege—The policy of compromise was set aside, war was declared—In time of war court-martial supersedes trial by jury—Arts, science, and literature no longer flourish—Museums are turned into barracks—Everything is sacrificed for military efficiency—A, similar transformation was effected in the Church—When the siege is raised its traces remain for a time together with some of the habits which war has generated—The transformation I speak of was illustrated in the substitution of seminaries for universities ; in the military drill and *esprit de corps* of the Jesuits ; in the increasing rigidity of dogmatic *formulæ* and of the prevalent theological teaching under pressure from the Reformation—The Church could not assimilate contemporary thought which was actively hostile to her—She had therefore to protect her dogmas from assault, sheathing them in iron-bound *formulæ*—The freedom of Catholic opinion which characterised the Middle Ages was sacrificed for polemical concentration against Protestantism—Authority became all in all—The typical Jesuit was the antithesis of the typical Protestant—The law of self-preservation tended to make the Catholic Church slow in accepting even what was true in speculations advanced by her declared foes 75

The siege lasted upwards of two centuries and a half—At the end of the eighteenth century the Church was supposed to be defeated—Then came a great Catholic revival—Chateaubriand and the German Romanticists—A general conversion to Rome was anticipated by A. W. Schlegel 85

A revival of Catholic ideals took place also in the Church of England—But when Anglicans call on the Papacy to abate its pretensions as the representative of Catholicism, we are tempted to smile —Who preserved the Catholic ideals, now fashionable, in the years when they were treated by the world at large with scorn ?—The soldiers of the Church of Rome may have been decimated in the struggle, but the victory of Catholic ideals is the victory of the cause for which they have fought and fallen—Catholics cannot easily accept the view that the Anglicans who persecuted their ancestors for their faith, belonged to a communion which potentially held the doctrines they killed others for holding 87

Reunion cannot be hoped for—Divergences and misconceptions are on both sides too deep—But the state of war should cease—A policy of *rapprochement*, though not of reunion, is possible—Personal intercourse and common work for religion will do more than mere discussion towards mutual understanding—Pope Leo's Letter *ad Anglos* in 1896 recognised that the state of war is passed—Let Catholics and their countrymen work together for religious education, and against agnosticism and secularism—This will gradually effect a change of attitude on both sides—The polemical spirit substitutes heat for light—To work together in sympathy may lead to a truer mutual appreciation unclouded by prejudice   90

III.

UNCHANGING DOGMA AND CHANGEFUL MAN.

The late Dr. Mivart represented every discovery of science as attended by the "groans of a strangled theologian"—He regarded new theological positions developed by the advance of thought as simply reluctant acts of obedience on the part of theologians to the scientists and critics—He failed to understand that earlier statements may be in their nature partly provisional—He sees in their modification no law of theological development, no underlying identity of dogma—Thus one change is to him just like another—No principle is maintained by him which would prevent the giving up of belief in what is essential to the identity of Christian dogma—as, for instance, in the doctrine of the Incarnation   99

This attitude throws confusion over a really critical problem, namely, that of showing that Christianity *is* a revelation of unchanging Divine truth, though long inevitably taught through the medium of an inaccurate science—On this view the claim of men of science to dictate to theology is as unsound as the old claim of theologians to teach science—The *via media* I suggest is the view that theology and science are mutually corrective in giving a true knowledge of the Universe   101

My object here is to show that the gradual changes (of which Mivart speaks) which science has wrought in the beliefs of Catholics have been reconcilable with the maxim that Catholic dogma is *semper eadem*—If this is so, other changes, equally reconcilable with that maxim, may be now seen by individuals to be possible or necessary—These changes would be effected by a further application of the very principle which has effected changes in the

PAGE

past—That principle has been expressed by Newman—A belief retained in new relations and circumstances " changes with them in order to remain the same "—So the living body changes as a condition of the same individual continuing to live—It is man with his modes of intellectual expression and analysis who changes—The dogma is the same—Instances of this in the past—We do not believe with St. Gregory that hell is in the bowels of the earth—We do not believe with St. Thomas that the Aristotelian physics explain the *Resurrectio carnis* 103

The change is in our apprehension and interpretation of mixed propositions in which truths known by science and reason are mingled with truths known by faith—The former change, as science advances, and the explanation of the propositions changes with the changing element—Dogma is often expressed in terms which to some extent, at least by implication, include science—There is change not in the *meaning* of dogma but in the explication of dogmatic propositions—Theology is jealous of the phrase " change of meaning " in dogma lest it should seem to imply a change of meaning in Divine truth—With dogma, as with Scripture, there is theologically no error and no change—But there is a change in the concrete beliefs whereby we represent to ourselves the teaching of Scripture or the consequences of dogma—Such changes are the application of a principle which is itself *semper eadem*—This is the principle of development 106

This principle was never entirely forgotten even in the days of Galileo—But people, while ready to apply it to the past, are often unwilling to accept its fresh consequences in the present—It was well formulated (in this connexion) in 1888 by Monsignor D'Hulst—His phrase, " le sens indecis du dogme "—Dr. Mivart fails to see that the whole history of Catholic definitions presupposes a "sens indecis du dogme" which is further determined by each new definition— Religious philosophers, from St. Thomas to Cardinal Newman, have ever insisted on the position rejected by Mivart, as fundamental—All propositions relating to God are analogical—We cannot fully define their sense, as the conceptions they involve are beyond human comprehension—" Dogmas are symbols of a Divine fact " 108

The element of mystery in dogmas is thus responsible for the changes in their concrete representation—When the unknown factor

PAGE

is a Divine truth beyond our apprehension the dogma is made gradually more determinate by theological propositions or definitions excluding heretical perversions—When the unknown factor is scientific or historical, truth it is made more determinate as such truths are known more accurately—Instances of both classes of development . 113

    The doctrine of the inerrancy of Scripture has been developed in both of these two ways—The *communis sensus* of Catholics in Galileo's time was that this doctrine was inconsistent with the truth of Copernicanism—No one thinks so now—The change is due to two causes : (1) the proof of Copernicanism ; (2) the concomitant reflection by theologians as to the limits of the theological doctrine even as already taught—It gradually became clear that the stringent interpretation which made it inconsistent with Copernicanism had not been consistently advocated by authoritative writers—Again, the meaning of the doctrine can best be reached by considering the defined dogma from which it is derived, that God is the " Author of the Scriptures " —" He cannot " (it had been argued) " be the Author of error, therefore there is no error in Scripture "—But to utilise, in teaching truths, erroneous scientific ideaswhich are current, is not to be the " Author of error "—The " error " already exists, and could only be dissipated by a revelation (which has not been granted) of secular fact or secular science—If I teach my child history by a picture-book, though the child may take inaccurate details in the pictures as literally true, I am not the author of the child's error—I am diminishing its ignorance by new though not wholly accurate knowledge—So also to use in teaching a rude people the *communis sermo*, the accepted ideas, scientific and historical, is not to be the author of error . . 120

    Father Robert Clarke's illustration of this principle—His position as one of the Pontifical Commissioners on Scripture—Once we admit that a revelation of Divine truth was given, but no revelation of secular knowledge, it becomes clear that truth had to be expressed through the inaccurate medium of prevalent ideas—Only fresh revelations could have prevented this necessity, including scientific revelations—The inevitable complexity of theology which like the statute-book preserves the record of all past controversies—All sciences are progressive, and are at any given moment inaccurate in some of their conclusions—Yet in the long run they right themselves, and pursue a definite line of development 123

PAGE

People will ask, Where are the changes in current theological opinion to end?—We may answer that, in the first place, many of the changes are not changes in practical belief—Copernicanism itself brought no change in the beliefs affecting everyday life—To change our physical analysis of the Ascension, our ideas concerning the locality of heaven and hell, is not to touch any fundamental belief as affecting ourselves practically—That our knowledge of the physical Universe is ever, with the advance of our scientific knowledge, deepening and changing in the sense of growing, does not make us sceptical of the reality of that universe—And so it should be with Divine truth—That it is intellectually inexhaustible should throw no doubt on its reality—But, moreover, the limits to changes of explication are clear in what is most important— Central truths not touching the field of science in their explication (as the Trinity and Incarnation) must ever remain certain, though inexplicable—Others, as the Resurrection and the Virgin birth, remain, not as scientific explanations (which they do not profess to be), but as facts encompassed with physical mystery—They are witnessed to by the Church as facts, and our belief in them stands or falls with our belief in the Church 128

People will object to the subtlety of the foregoing theory—How can it suit the "man in the street"?—I answer that the *theory* of knowledge (even of our knowledge of a chair) is in all departments infinitely subtle—For *practical* belief in a chair the man in the street has his senses—In religion he has the Church—In both cases the theory is subtle, but the practical belief is simple to him who trusts the normal informant, the information of his senses, or the information of the teacher who reports the general outcome of theology—The senses cannot teach him all that science gradually learns, nor does the priest teach him all the most recent developments of theology— But both teach enough for daily needs—for the average life of action, physical or religious 130

We cannot now tell what the compound between the changing and the changeless elements will be in our grandchildren's time—Our present task is to continue, in view of the existing outlook of secular knowledge, the task of our ancestors in the faith who maintained in each generation living relations between the unchanging dogma and the civilisation of their own time—The Church ever, like the living man, asserts its individuality, and influences the world by means of that strength which it draws largely from the world itself, namely, from the surrounding culture which it has assimilated . . 132

IV.

THE FOUNDATIONS OF BELIEF.

PAGE

Mr. Balfour's primary object of attack is Naturalism—He identifies it with Empiricism—Yet if we look for Balfour's intellectual ancestors we shall find them among Empiricists—Empiricism began, with Locke, in the appeal to facts as opposed to mere speculation— but Locke was no agnostic or sceptic—Balfour shows a similar aversion to "brain-spinning" and dogmatism—He too refuses to acquiesce in agnosticism or scepticism 133

How is it, then, that the Empirical philosophy is one of Balfour's chief objects of attack?—In the first place, it is because the later Empiricists became speculative dogmatists — Hume arbitrarily limited Locke's derivation of all knowledge from experience to his own view that all our knowledge is of phenomena—He trans- formed Empiricism into Naturalism—He added to it, moreover, the dogmatism involved in his argument against miracles—Hume was succeeded by Mill and Spencer—These writers were as dogmatic in what they excluded from the knowledge they accounted valid as were the Mediæval Schoolmen or the defenders of innate ideas in what they included—Thus the system which took its rise in a scientific opposition to the arbitrary dogmatism and speculation which divert attention from facts, has issued in a new speculative dogmatism — "Association" and "evolution" have been regarded as all-solving principles 135

Mr. Balfour recalls the Empiricists to their true principles—He points out that their arbitrary theory of knowledge leaves large tracts of the human consciousness unaccounted for—For example, Mr. Spencer's explanation of conscience will not account for the sentiment of moral approbation on the sense of sin—The naturalistic account of æsthetic is similarly inadequate to the facts of consciousness 137

In point of fact, Empiricism and Induction, although belonging to a movement of thought which was an intellectual advance, were

PAGE

accompanied at one time by the neglect of important truths hitherto recognised—Both Locke and Bacon undervalued the rational elements in knowledge, in consequence of their horror of the *intellectus sibi permissus*—Dean Church's testimony in his " Life of Bacon "—Bacon's theory as formulated by himself was wholly barren—He did not understand the rational process which led to the hypotheses of a Newton or a Darwin, with its tentative trust of the highest semiconscious reasoning—What Newton's method adds to Bacon, Mr. Balfour's method adds to that of the extreme Empiricists—It adds to passive observation the active interrogation of consciousness and the framing and testing of assumptions—He asks whether the naturalistic evolutionists' assumption of a reasonless concourse of atoms as the ultimate origin of the human reason can account for that correspondence of the human mind with objective truth which we presuppose in our reasoning—A negative answer is inevitable—His criticism of Naturalism is more definite than his more affirmative positions—Theism and Christianity are accepted by him as necessary to the "satisfaction of a need"—This ground is represented as similar to that on which we believe in the existence of an independent external world 139

The destructive side of Balfour's argument—His disparagement of "reason"—While he believes in a Rational Source of the human reason, it is not clear that he finds in the scrutiny of that reason sufficient ground for his belief—Empirical methods are in some passages regarded by him not only as partial but as misleading—Psychological analysis is regarded as issuing in an *impasse*—We have here not a method developing and completing Locke's method, and making it issue in a higher estimate of human reason than Naturalism contemplates—Just the contrary—Instead of finding the human reason so wide in its sweep that it suggests a higher Reason as its Source, Mr. Balfour represents human reason as self-contradictory in instances where we can observe it—Instead of regarding the unanalysed insight of the rational spirit, visible especially in men of genius, as a form of rational perception outstripping and supplementing the logical processes, he presents to us non-rational instincts contradicting logical analysis—Thus we are led to mistrust our own higher unanalysed inferences—Instead of coming to believe in an ultimate rational cause by a process higher than mere analysis though less capable of verification (much as sight gives information of a far vaster world than touch, though its information is harder to verify), we invoke in our despair a Divine guarantee for non-rational beliefs—We have only the "guess of a worm in the dust and the shadow of its desire" 143

PAGE

Mr. Balfour's disparagement of reason is based on an insufficient
examination of the psychological processes—A truer analysis, on
very similar lines, was made by J. H. Newman more than half a
century ago, in the " Oxford University Sermons "—His view was that
the human intellect "embraces more than it can master," and "is
swayed by a body of proof which it recognises as a body and not in
its constituent parts "—Thus an *impasse* in the process of analysis was
not regarded by him as discrediting the reason, but as an instance
of the inequality between the mind's powers of " embracing " and of
"mastering "—According to Newman, unanalysed proof *is* proof and
is rational ; according to Balfour, it is " non-rational "—The judgment
" I was born," or " England is an island," is rational according to
Newman, though it depends upon reasons in part consisting of
forgotten experiences and in part not susceptible of analysis by the
individual   145

Mr. Balfour's chapter on the " Philosophical Basis of Naturalism "
shows that he has not fully mastered the theory he criticises—His
inadequate account of the theory that knowledge of the external
world is an inference from sensation—He seems to think that it is
supposed, by those who hold it, to be a *present* inference from present
sensation—He speaks of men of science observing their " fleeting
impressions "—This is surely inaccurate : it is the system whose
coherence has been revealed by constant *past* experience which men
of science observe—The present experience is only the means of
reminding ourselves of that system—The present sensation is interpreted by the product of past experience, and itself only touches
isolated aspects and instances—Berkeley was quite willing to call
that system "things"—Scientific investigation is (on this hypothesis) not undertaken (as Mr. Balfour says) to "account for" our
impressions, but to extend the knowledge (relative though it be)
which the simplest experience has begun—The conclusions of science
are not (as Balfour's words imply) less relative than other sensible
knowledge—They are on the same plane of relativity—To realise
this should not lessen our interest in physical science—It did not do
so in Kant or Berkeley—It is similar to the discovery of the relativity
of pre-Copernican astronomy—Plane astronomy is "true," though
we now know its statements to be relative—Balfour uses the word
" truth " in two senses—A conclusion may be exact and yet not
absolutely " true," because it may belong to a relative plane of knowledge—Balfour, viewing the inference from sensation to an external
world only as an inference made at the moment of present sensation,
naturally enough finds it shadowy and dismisses it as valueless
—Newman, viewing it in its true strength as based on a complicated
record of experiences the memory of which is not fully present to

PAGE

the mind in explicit form, finds the analysis valuable though incomplete—It is to him like a doctor's soundings which by the examination of a few critical points give fair ground for general conclusions as to the healthy state of the body—The assumption is that the rational nature makes for truth as the vital functions make for life—If either are in a healthy condition they may be trusted to do their work aright 151

Balfour's account of the functions of authority—He rightly points out the limited power of the individual's " free speculative investigation "—But even Descartes recognised the value of authority in his " morale par provision "—Balfour's recurrent fallacy from failing to keep distinct in his speculation the reason of the individual and the reason of the race—His criticism of the current exaggerations of the importance of reason as a cause " producing and maintaining beliefs, customs, and ideals which form the groundwork of life "—His illustration adduced in proof of his position has no appositeness at all to the question, What share does Reason take in the aforesaid beliefs ?—It only applies to the share of the reason of *one individual*—In point of fact, beliefs forming the groundwork of life are very largely due to reason in the race, though by the individual they are received through authority—The reasoning of one generation issues in conclusions which the next generation arrive at, not by argument, but as part of the authoritative groundwork of life accepted by all—The XIXth century railway traveller thus enjoyed the fruits of Watt's reasoning 159

Balfour proceeds to distinguish beliefs accepted because they are taught by " an Authority " which is trusted on rational grounds, from beliefs due to " Authority " rather than to " Reason "—but this distinction would very seriously diminish the list of beliefs he had at the outset ascribed to Authority—Authority is seldom trusted blindly—There is some reason for trust (latent or explicit), varying with individual culture—Here again his analysis has failed to get to the bottom of the question he raises—He perceives that authority acts latently when we think we are influenced only by reason—He fails to recognise the converse, that there is generally latent reason at the bottom of our trust in authority—I may trust my banker as to my investments with no explicit thought beyond that of my own habit and my father's of being guided by him—But if I see in the papers that one of my investments is endangered, I question its wisdom—Thus I come to see that there was a latent reason for my habitual trust, namely the presumption that the banker's information on such subjects is accurate—Nearly all cases of trust in Authority in adults have a similar latent ground in reason—Man's superiority to the brutes lies then, I would suggest, not, as Balfour says, in "influencing and being influenced through the action of Authority," but in an intelligent recognition of the functions of Authority as an instrument of Reason, and in a capacity for acting on that recognition —Not blind submission to Authority, but a sense of the weakness and inadequacy of private judgment, of the individual reason *in isolation,* is the important lesson to learn—Vicomte de Bonald on the individual reason and the universal reason 164

Bonald's conception of collective wisdom and sanctity in mankind gives the necessary supplement to Balfour's views—Reason and Authority constantly interact—The insight of saint or seer affects the whole society—The resulting Wisdom which comes to permeate the body corporate appeals as an authority to the faith of the unreflecting—This was the ideal of the Mediæval Church—It really illustrates Balfour's statement that there is hardly such a thing as unaided reason for the individual—We have also to consider the wisdom of all times —" Psychological climates " do not succeed each other at random, but there is an underlying cause of advance from one to another— Extending our view to the religious beliefs of the human mind *semper et ubique,* we find new force in the argument from " needs "— The " need " for religion as disclosed in history is a far stronger argument than the need in an individual 173

But if we look at the past development of religious ideals in human consciousness, we are led to look back still further at the development of conscious life from its first rudiments—We can trace it from the lowest forms of life in which there is presumably hardly any consciousness of the not-self, to the first rudiment of sight, that sense which in developed form gives some knowledge of the universe known to astronomers—The advance from the earth-worm to man is the gradual unfolding of the sensitive consciousness to a reality outside the living organism—Francis Balfour on the gradual advance from the first sensitiveness to light to an eye capable of true vision—At each stage in the development of consciousness the germ of what eventually proves to be important knowledge is mysterious and uncertain—The rudiment of sight, that sense which gives man such definite knowledge of his fellows, probably gave but the vaguest consciousness of an external object to the star-fish—We can fancy at this stage the advocate of Naturalism who regarded the new and dim knowledge as illusive, and the transcendentalist who was convinced of the " beyond " to which it pointed—This latter view was

PAGE

afterwards verified by the further development of sight—The
transcendentalist is thus eventually justified—The religious consciousness similarly gives to man some dim presage of a world
beyond, as rudimentary sight gave a dim presage of the world of the
fixed stars—Does not the past course of nature raise a presumption
that this dim presage does point to a further stage in the
path of conscious knowledge towards Reality?—And the evolution
of the primary religious ideas confirms this view—Note the advance
from Theism as conceived in the Vedas to Christian Theism, which
is that of the Psalms—It is an advance in personal relations with
and apprehension of the Deity—A further indication of the nature
of the Reality to which the religious consciousness is pointing . . 177

The strength of Balfour's position depends on his faithful adherence to the quasi-inductive method on which it is founded—
Where his observation has been accurate his results are valuable
—The complete opposition between "reason" and "non-rational
instinct" is based on inaccurate observation — It ignores the
highest latent rational process which is above and not below reason,
and is characteristic of genius—Thus Joubert feared to go wrong in
religion if he differed from the saints, who are the men of religious
genius—According to this line of thought, Balfour's justification of
religion, that it satisfies a "need," is equivalent to its satisfying the
highest intellectual and moral insight—It is thus rescued from the
semi-sceptical interpretation, which would identify it with the satisfaction of a blind desire—The need becomes identical with a
"rational necessity" as seen by the human reason at its highest
point of development 179

V.

CANDOUR IN BIOGRAPHY.

The theory of biography advanced by the author of the life of
Cardinal Manning—"Publish everything"—"To idealise is to be
untruthful"—"Omission means want of candour"—How far is this
theory true? 184

Undoubtedly the careful student will form the truest possible
estimate of a character by seeing the whole of the available documentary evidence—And in the long run the judgment of the public
is likely to be formed by the verdict of the most careful students—

PAGE

But a biography is not a mere collection of documentary evidence
—It is a narrative illustrated by selected documents—The sifting
of evidence is supposed to have been done by the biographer—The
biographer chooses from the material at his disposal what best
illustrates the conception of the character which he has himself
formed from the study of the whole of that material—If Carlyle and
Macaulay had both written lives of Boswell, the letters they would
have chosen would have been largely different—To the former he
was primarily a reverent disciple, to the latter primarily a prying
and toadying busybody—A biography is not a mere accumulation
of evidence ; it is a picture—In a picture minute differences may
completely change the whole effect—Proportion is everything—So,
too, in biography—Treat an occasional fault as though it were a
besetting sin, and the biographical picture is quite false—Thus true
items of evidence may be so combined as to give a false representation   185

The caricaturist combines true elements in false proportion—
He may make the whole face suggestive of one peculiarity—
The Jew is the embodiment of a nose, the vacant fop of the
absence of chin—And so does the biographical caricaturist seize
a leading feature and develop it so much out of proportion that
all else seems subsidiary—He makes a Macchiavelli or an Iago
of one who had really many qualities evenly balanced—He really
commits, in an opposite direction, the same fault as the idealising
biographer who develops out of proportion what is good and beautiful—Each feature in such a caricature can be defended as true, yet
the effect of the whole is, from the false proportions, grotesquely
misleading   188

A one-sided view of a character held with conviction by the
biographer will produce at once the most vivid and the most misleading picture—One who only saw Dr. Johnson once, when he was very
rude and the worse for liquor, would very likely, if he wrote his Life,
produce from true facts a totally false likeness, drawn with the vividness of the mental picture which that one occasion had stamped on
his memory—He would select as most typical what represented
excesses which were in reality extremely rare—And it might take
years for the *evidence* which even his book contained to correct
the picture it would present, which reversed the true proportions—
Meanwhile reviewers would popularise the misleading picture, and
a generation would have quite a false idea of Johnson—Hence the
wise custom of choosing for a biographer one who appreciates
those qualities which make a man's biography worth writing . . .   191

VI.

TENNYSON.

PAGE

Huxley's account of the quality of Tennyson's conversation—He said that the phrase " Doric beauty " summed it up—Yet the first sound of voice and accent suggested the poet's own " Northern Farmer "—My own first recollections of Tennyson 196

His shyness on first entering a room—The ante-room at Farringford—" How d'ye do? " followed by dreamy silence—To tell him a good story brought him back from dreamland to earth—To read some of his own lines in a way which he disapproved also broke the spell , ... 197

His morning walk—Parties of six or eight—Our walks *tête-à-tête* in later years—The unloosening of his dogs before starting—Crossing the " careless-ordered garden "—The " crucified " tree—The rabbits and the chalk-line—His keen eye for trees and plants—His impatience with his companion—" You are as bad as your father, who noticed nothing "—" You once took a lily of the valley for a snowdrop "—The sound of a cuckoo's voice makes him recite a Lincolnshire rhyme—His unflagging conversation—His rapid pace—His glee at outwalking Professor Jebb—He climbs a gate and runs down a hill at the age of eighty-two 198

Douglas Jerrold's comment on " Sordello "—" I can't understand a single line "—Browning (according to Tennyson) had no " glory of words "—" He makes ' impulse ' rhyme with ' dim pulse ' "—Browning's love of society—" He will die in a white tie "—Tennyson on Arthur Clough—Tennyson's conversation with George Eliot at Aldworth—Absurd accounts of it in the papers—" They said that I disputed with her till I was red in the! face, and then roared, ' Go away, you and your molecules ! ' "—The conversation was really " sweet as summer "—George Eliot not quite as true to human nature as Jane Austen—The character of Adam Bede idealised—Austen to Shakespeare as " asteroid to sun "—Jane Austen's perfect " stippling "—A meeting with Macaulay—Jowett's account of Macaulay's conversation as " a lecture to an audience of one person "—Macaulay and Carlyle—" Carlyle was at his best ' rollicking at the Asburtons' ' "—" Carlyle used to say, ' Our Cromwell is being born somewhere ' " 201

PAGE

Gladstone's attempt to rule "with a silk glove"—"You must have an iron gauntlet"—Gladstone and Disraeli—Disraeli's contemptuousness—Contemptuousness a sign of littleness—Tennyson quotes Wordsworth on "contempt"—The revolution of 1848—Tennyson's story of Edward Lear in Sicily—The Italian waiter full of *chianti* and of patriotic fervour—Refuses to find Lear's luggage and keys—"No keys, no luggage, no anything now"—"All is love and liberty. *O che bella rivoluzione!*".   203

Tennyson's experience as a vegetarian—At first he gained "lucidity of mind"—In ten weeks he became "almost foolish"—His first chop brought a glow as though it were brandy—His account of this episode in the dedication of "Tiresias"—The excellence aimed at in that dedication was that of being "belle comme la prose"—The "fools of the *Edinburgh Review*" called it "prose in rhyme"—Tennyson's simplicity in discussing his own forthcoming poems—Occasional lapses into the grotesque in a first draft—He changes a line in "Vastness" which at first ended with the words "sober and clean"   205

His earliest speculative poem, "The Two Voices"—His metaphysics suggestive of Kant, Malebranche, and Berkeley—His method of presenting two veins of thought, one of doubt, the other of conviction—"De Profundis," "Vastness," "The Ancient Sage," "Despair"—His attitude that of "an infant crying for the light"—Intense candour and truthfulness—He carried into pyschology the accurate observation he showed in watching external nature—Instances of his scrupulous accuracy—His love of accumulating facts—Ball's "Astronomy"—His imagination like a limelight which makes facts more vivid and never blurs them—Parallel quality in his Metaphysics.   206

Metaphysics regarded by him as an antidote to materialism—They show that "you can't escape from mystery by escaping from religion"—Relativity of greatness—The clod in a ploughed field seems to a woodlouse what a Swiss mountain seems to us—The human eye and the Milky Way—He points with his stick at the evening star—"Our earth would look like that from the star itself"—"Roaring London, raving Paris, in that point of peaceful light" .   212

PAGE

Misuses of the word " God "—Vindictive Deity of the Calvinists
—The Calvinistic friends of his youth—" Alfred, whenever I look at
you, I think of the words of Scripture, ' Depart from Me, ye cursed,
into everlasting fire ' "—Argument between the Calvinist and the
liberal clergyman—" Your God is my devil "—The " magnified
clergyman " idea of God—God is called the " Nameless " in " The
Ancient Sage "—God touches man at one point, namely, the conscience—A man without religion only ' half a man—Free will is
limited, as a bird's movements are limited by its cage—The
Buddhist Nirvana 215

Tennyson's admiration of A. R. Wallace—Wallace showed that
the brain is in excess of man's physical needs, and therefore cannot
be explained by natural selection—Evolution solves the mystery of
man's dual nature—He inherits much from brute ancestors . . . 217

Tennyson's reading and analysis of the " De Profundis " poem . 218

VII.

THOMAS HENRY HUXLEY.

Necessity of the " personal equation " for a true interpretation of
a great writer's words—My first intercourse with Huxley by letter
confirmed my impression that he was unapproachable and a man of
war—My subsequent change of view—His account of his relations
with my father in the days of the Metaphysical Society as " the
friendliest of foes "—The " circular voyages " of the Metaphysical
Society—It was a rudderless craft of which the oarsmen were pulling
in opposite directions—W. G. Ward described by him as a " philosophical Don Quixote " 226

My own first personal impression of Huxley—The expected
elements of pugilist, pedant, and scoffer were conspicuous by their
absence—His personal charm and brilliancy—His appearance
—His conversation clean-cut, terse, and enlivened by illustrations—
Contrast between his conversation and that of Newman and
Tennyson — His dignity — Over-positiveness — Intolerance—The

PAGE

"Grand Inquisitor" of Science—The definitions of his scientific
Church—His conversation dialectical in form—He was, on the
whole, a *just* advocate, but always an advocate—"That is my case,
my lord," would have come naturally at the end of his remarks—His
appreciation of a "foeman worthy of his steel"—His admiration of
St. Thomas Aquinas—His commendation of the intellectual drill of
the priests at Maynooth 230

My first talk with Huxley about the Metaphysical Society—
Huxley described how he was feared at first as a "firebrand"—
Expected repetition of the sad history of the "Kilkenny cats"—
Agreeable surprise of the members—"We loved each other like
brothers"—The society "died of too much love"—The result was a
curious mixture in Huxley's feeling towards theological opponents
—The "ecclesiastical obstructives" had long dwelt in his mind as
the very types of bigotry—And he was alive to their moral reprobation of his views—But at the Metaphysical Society great friendliness
and undoubted ability in the adherents of ecclesiasticism begot a
feeling somewhat inconsistent with his earlier feeling—Both feelings
lasted — But the earlier feeling lost much of its bitterness — "We
wicked people"—His enjoyment of meeting a priest or clergyman—
He "receives the *pallium*" from Archbishop Benson—His meeting
with Dr. Steffens of Freiburg 235

He encounters Henry Smith in York Minster—"You did not
expect to see me here?"—"Yes, I did. But on the pinnacle"—His
letter to me when he was made Privy Councillor—"I was born to
be respectable"—His dislike of being identified with the Voltairian
scoffer or destroyer of religion—His claim to brotherhood with
Descartes—His tendency to identify outspoken candour with love of
truth—He had little appreciation of the utility of reserve—His
account of the reason of Kant's obscurity of style in his speculative
writings : "He did not wish too many people to understand him.
He would have been persecuted" 239

The Romanes Lecture—Its concessions to the "right" wing of
thinkers were not really, as some thought, new—But they received
new emphasis in this lecture—His letter to myself on the lecture—
His lecture at Baltimore—American reporters—A meeting with
Carlyle—Dean Stanley sceptical as to the biblical account of Creation,

PAGE

but conservative on the Pentateuch—" This was because he had seen Palestine, but he wasn't present at the Creation "—A dinner with Cardinal Manning—The education question—Manning charges Huxley with being false to Liberal principles—Huxley's retort: " My attachment to Liberal principles is nothing to my desire for your extermination "—An eminent person who was "not clear-headed enough to tell a lie "—John Bright—Tennyson as a master of melody—The music in Browning, for instance in the " Thrush "— Switzerland—Love of scenery and music could not have helped in the struggle for existence—Royal Commission on Vivisection—A German doctor said, " I chloroform a cat because it scratches, but not a dog "—*Gigadibsius optimus maximus*—Discrepancies in accounts of the Metaphysical Society—" The German critics will prove that it never existed "—Butler's " Analogy "—Meeting of the British Association at Oxford—Evolution theory accepted by all present—Huxley's pleasure at an article, in the *Quarterly*, on his religious position 244

Talk with Huxley after the appearance of Balfour's " Foundations of Belief "—Erasmus (he observed) was persecuted for opinions he did not hold—His views were identified with those of Luther—R. C. Jebb's account of Erasmus—Huxley's preference for Erasmus over Luther—Huxley's annoyance at Balfour's attack—" He has gone to war without ordnance maps, like the French in 1870—He does not know the position of his enemy, and attacks me, as Erasmus was attacked, for what I don't hold—No one holds what Balfour describes as Naturalism—He has drawn out a catechism for ' us wicked people,' to teach us what we *must* hold " 252

Huxley hints that his own answer to Balfour is soon coming— Speaks with admiration of Francis Balfour—A priest in the room— Huxley's parting shot : " I trust he had plenty of holy water with him "—Every one present remarked on his vigour and brilliancy on this day—He was like a man whom the Scotch speak of as " fey "—His last letter to myself—Taken ill the following day—The contrast between his theoretical methods and his practical attitude —His power of sympathetic intercourse with persons at the opposite pole of religious conviction 255

VIII.

TWO MOTTOES OF CARDINAL NEWMAN.

PAGE

It was Cardinal Newman's fate to be an occasional writer—The controversial element in his writings was the result of circumstances —His preference was for philosophical or historical writing—In no work of his mature life was this preference fully satisfied—But some occasional works, controversial in form, are really philosophical—For example the " Essay on Development " and " Tract 85 "—The " University Sermons," though a collection of occasional discourses, afford the best indication of his philosophy of religion —His historical research, too, is best exhibited in occasional writings —His remarkable unity of thought in history and philosophy, in spite of the absence of a formal treatise in which it is fully exhibited . . 260

What is Newman's distinctive contribution to philosophy?— The two mottoes (one chosen on receiving the Cardinal's hat, the other, as an epitaph) point the way to the fundamental elements in his philosophy—These are " Cor ad cor loquitur " and " Ex umbris et imaginibus in veritatem "—His analysis of our knowledge of the existence of our fellow-men, and of their thoughts and character, shows, in the first place, that all we directly know is the *umbra et imago*—voice and face, words and expression—We infer from these the meaning, feelings, character—These are the Reality, the *Veritas* —Yet the inference is so rapid, and the intercourse of spirit with spirit so apparently direct, that the process also illustrates the other motto " Cor ad cor loquitur " 263

A similar combination is found in his philosophy of our knowledge of God—Conscience is the *umbra et imago* of God—Yet he speaks of the self and the Creator as the only two "luminously self-evident beings "—The intercourse between God and the soul in prayer is an instance of "Cor ad cor loquitur "—So, too, with the living Church—Dogmatic truths and liturgical rites are the *umbra et imago* of the Divine nature and revelation, preserved and developed by the Church—Yet the human soul is moulded by their apprehension and use—They become the language whereby the Spirit of God speaks to the spirit of man—Once again, " Cor ad cor loquitur "—This thought underlies the whole " Essay on Development," which traces the organic growth of the Church—When friends

PAGE

converse at long intervals the intercourse is not the less that of the same persons because their bodies have changed or grown, for the soul abides—Similarly the *ethos*, or soul, of Catholicism is conceived by him as abiding behind the development of dogma and liturgy— That *ethos* is a partial reflection of the mind of God, who thus declares the same truth in different language to different ages—Thus does the unchanging God speak to changeful man—Thus we explain the similar ethical character of the holy men of different epochs in spite of the difference in their culture 266

His early controversies hinged on this question : Can we regard the Anglican Church, as an institution, as part of the *umbra et imago* of Divine truth so conceived ?—Has it organic growth similar to that which makes a man's changing body the symbol and expression of an identical personality ?—His final answer was in the negative—The distinctive changes of Anglicanism were not a growth due to the inner life of Christianity, but a corruption due to external causes and making for death—He applies similar principles to his work in founding a university at Dublin—He desired to infuse into it the inner spirit of the nineteenth-century culture—A university, like a Church, should be a body with an informing genius or *ethos* behind it, which should be the principle of its development—His failure at Dublin was somewhat like his failure as an Anglican leader—Dublin *plus* Newman's genius could no more become an Oxford, than Anglicanism *plus* his genius could become Catholicism 268

All such instances are resolvable into a combination of the action of one personality on another—including the action of the Divine Personality, and that of men of genius in dominating and influencing lesser personalities—This holds true in the Church, in a university, in the religious orders—The resulting conception of a quasi-personality, *i.e.* the distinctive genius of Church, university, or order —How is this preserved ?—Partly by personal transmission to disciples—The burning torch kindles its fellow—partly by external rules and rites—Essential innovation is prevented by such external means 272

Newman's deep sense, as part of his philosophy, of reverence for personal genius, and his appreciation of the power of personality for

PAGE

good or evil—His feeling for Keble—His ideal sketch of the Greek
student who sees Plato—His account of Abelard—His sermon on
Personal Influence—"Credo in Newmanum"—Bearing of this element
in his philosophy on his view of religion—" My sheep hear My voice "
—His sense of a quasi-personal Reality behind all great corporate
organisations—The genius of an order, an age, a race, a language—
In history he sees living forces bringing about an orderly result out of
apparent chance and waste—as the type is preserved in nature, by
means of one grain of pollen while a thousand are wasted—National
institutions represent the national spirit—His affinity here to Hegel
—His view of *phronesis* and faith as a personal grasp, defying
analysis—Kinship of this idea with that of the quasi-personal
intercourse between the individual and the Reality he is seeking to
know—" Cor ad cor loquitur "   275

    The consequence of this general view is an overwhelming precon-
ception on the side of faith—The mass of our irresistible and
indispensable certainty depends, according to this theory, on what
may be called faith—If " knowledge is of things we see," we have no
"knowledge " of much that is most important and most confidently
believed by all, but only faith in it—If the visible world is primarily
the *medium* whereby invisible forces and personalities communi-
cate with each other—if voice and gesture are only the media
whereby persons hold intercourse—if colour, sound, and shape are
of use mainly in conveying to us some practical idea of the
Reality behind them—if social institutions are mainly the media for
the interaction of personalities—if religions and schools of thought
are the machinery whereby great minds act on inferior ones,—then
the invisible forces and factors are, on any view of life, all in all—And
if all these processes are too subtle for complete logical analysis, then
the conception of intercourse with a Highest Personality detected by
the truest insight as existing behind the visible world and known to
us by faith, is in accord with the nature of things—The presumption is in its favour, and is against those who would confine our
knowledge to what we can logically justify, a view which would exclude all knowledge worth having—This is substantially in harmony
with the doctrine of the " illative sense "—If the most perfect
spiritual minds detect, behind the vast *umbra et imago* of this world
and of human nature, the voice of God, they are only carrying to
a higher point than others the power which all possess in some
degree of recognising Personality behind phenomena—The religious
insight of all the sages points to Theism—And Christianity is
accepted as its normal development, just as Augustine accepted it—
This is the outcome of Newman's position as indicated in his two
mottoes   278

IX.

NEWMAN AND RENAN.

PAGE

Renan quitted St. Sulpice Seminary and left the Catholic Church
on October 6, 1845—John Henry Newman, two days later, asked
Father Dominic to receive him into that Church—Both men were
products of nineteenth-century culture—How did ideas characteristic
of the century lead them in opposite directions ? 283

Both men were rarely gifted—Both were students of history and
marked by the historical mind—Both were philosophers of history—
Both world-philosophers—Both wrote books analysing the motives
of their great religious change—Both supplemented them, later on,
by autobiographies which every one has read—The idea of "development" is responsible for both these opposite movements of
mind—To Renan the science of everything is the history of its
development—Catholic theology (he argues) professes to be unchangeable, therefore its science must prove it false—Newman finds
the law of development first of all in theology itself—He regards the
semper eadem of dogma as something quite distinct from any denial
of development in theology 283

Whence was this difference in their respective conceptions of
theology ?—The answer will be found in the autobiographies—
Renan describes how the holy M. Gottofrey, long before the period
of Renan's avowed doubts, said to him, " You are not a Christian "
—Renan had none of the deep convictions and principles which were
at the root of Newman's philosophy of faith—To Newman Christian
dogma was the gradual part-analysis of revelation, and of the relations
indicated by revelation between sinful man and God—The sense
of sin and of the presence of God were in his mind fundamental
to the apprehension of dogma—Dogmatic history in the early
centuries is the story of the protection of the primary beliefs that
God is one ; that Christ is God and man ; that man is sinful
and dependent on God ; against Arians, Nestorians, Eutychians,
Pelagians—The defined dogmas were, however, but imperfect
and partial representations of the truths they shadowed—The
" Divine fact " behind theology is, in Newman's eyes, what abides—
The realities *behind* theology are to him the *semper eadem*—
These realities are beyond Renan's speculations, owing to the
absence in him of the Christian temper—Current theology is for
Renan self-sufficient, whether true or false—To regard theology as

PAGE

the growing body with a soul of Divine truth behind it, is repugnant
to him 286

For Newman, at all stages of doctrinal and liturgical development, there is in the typical Christian of every age an identity of
resulting ethical character—One identical Christian revelation, conveyed through the intellectual forms belonging to each age, produces
an identical result—For Renan the deeper ethical results in the soul,
and the Divine truth *behind* theological and liturgical development,
are absent—The liturgy and the existing theology are keenly appreciated by him, but not the two realities, God and the soul, between
which they are, in Newman's eyes, a link—Therefore he looks for the
semper eadem only in that existing liturgy and ritual, and those Scholastic treatises which from his youth he has known familiarly—Finding portions of the latter not consistent with the conclusions of his
reason, he rejects Catholicism—The "neo-Catholics" like Montalembert, Gratry, and Lacordaire, who would develop theology in place of
fossilising it, arouse his wrath—They are to him apostles of "the
vague"—This is because what to them, as to Newman, was most
definite and a beacon-light, namely, the Divine truth of which theological propositions are the shadow, is to Renan an uncertain *ignis
fatuus*—The contrast is here most interesting between Renan and
Lacordaire—The antecedents of both were very similar—Both were
educated at Issy and St. Sulpice—Both were alive to modern critical
problems—Both were regarded by those in authority as intellectual
"innovators"—Yet Lacordaire, whose austerity and deep spiritual life
were the lasting basis of his faith, speaks, near his death, of a faith
which rests on the Gospel as almost passing into sight—To Renan
the realities contemplated in this view as so distinct had practically
no existence—Thus Lacordaire and Newman were, in Renan's eyes,
beating the air—Their religious philosophy was like the Barmecide
feast in the Eastern story, where the gestures of mastication are gone
through with nothing to eat—Renan calls Lacordaire's conferences
"theological buffooneries"—Dupanloup's religion is described by
him as "without frame or bone"—Montalembert's shows "dogmatic ignorance and weak reasoning powers" 290

Newman, as early as 1826, had realised that theology must
adapt itself to advancing science and criticism—He preached in
the mean while the lesson of patience under apparent contradictions
—And he pointed out that this was a lesson which modern science
had brought home as necessary for the whole field of knowledge—

PAGE

The over-positive theologian who treats all his present conclusions as final, is doing what the old Greek philosophers did who made the theories of their own limited minds the measure of the far greater mind of Nature—As the mind of Nature is above that of the natural philosopher, so is the mind of God above that of the theologian—In each case careful study of the relevant phenomena brings us gradually nearer to a true analysis—This is the truth which induction recognises in scientific inquiry—Rationalism is thus seen to be the foe to true philosophy—This is as true of the rationalistic theologian as of the rationalist in physical science—But the truly philosophical attitude of patience and humility is only possible when we believe in the reality of the subject-matter of the science and the possibility of further knowledge gradually emerging —Thus one whose belief in revelation is very deep may attain to this attitude in its regard, and bear with the constant revision of theological speculation in its relations with science—But if faith in revelation is very weak, to find error in those theological forms which have in the past made revelation appear more concrete and tangible, is easily regarded as disproof of revelation itself—Thus it was the first glimpse of the possibilities of inductive science which substituted Baconian patience for Greek impatience 294

Thus, too, Huxley was patient in physical science in which he believed, impatient in theological discussion—Renan, also, showed no patience or humility in theological inquiries, because he did not deeply believe in their subject-matter—Patience with contradictions implies that we believe that time will solve many apparent antinomies, and that truth is objectively consistent—Renan sees only the contradictions on the surface, having no deep belief in what is below the surface—He identified Catholicism with the most rigid expressions of theologians who were repeating phrases of the pre-scientific period—The alternative was to him rationalism—The deeper principles of theology itself are outside his ken, namely, that the Church is guarding a " deposit " not at first fully defined, while science is gaining new secular truth ; that the instruments of theologians are human language and reason ; that in using these instruments they are likely at times to betray human infirmity, and to go beyond the warrant of their science ; but that time is likely to show more clearly the limits of each department—Copernicus disproved what Dante had regarded as part of the teaching of the Church, yet he did not disprove Christianity—The same thing may happen again—Renan never contemplates this general view as possible—Had he done so, and had he possessed the patience which comes of deep faith, he would have lived to see it justified—

PAGE

For since 1845 we have seen the aggressive views of Baur and Volkmar rejected by the best critics (a victory for Catholic tradition), and we have seen Catholic theologians modifying positions which Renan regarded as at once incredible and yet necessary to the faith of a Catholic—This last fact is vividly illustrated by a passage in the " Souvenirs de ma Jeunesse " 296

X.

THE LIFE-WORK OF CARDINAL WISEMAN.

Macaulay, sixty years ago, surprised Englishmen by telling them of the growing victories of the Church of Rome—The Catholic revival of the nineteenth century has affected many, but has only brought *some* of them to the Roman Catholic Church—Its practical outcome still remains undetermined—But it has restored to honour ideals which had been derided and expelled by the Reformation ; *e.g.* the value of authority, and of ceremonial forms as symbols of great truths—the fact that the philosophy underlying the Mass is not an absurdity—We see a new reverence for the saintly characters formed by the Catholic system—The character of St. Francis of Assisi has appealed to persons as different from each other as Sabatier, Castelar, Hase, Carducci, Renan 301

When Wiseman came to England, in 1835, the historical feeling against the "papists " was still very strong—Genesis of this feeling —The idea that they were conspirators—Macaulay speaks of " hatred" for Catholics in Charles II.'s reign as a " ruling passion among Englishmen "—Typical speech in the House of Lords— Englishmen would not have " so much as a Popish cat to mew or purr about their King "—Diminution of the number of Catholics in the eighteenth century—Their isolation from Continental Catholics and opposition to the Holy See—The arrival of the *emigrés* from France—Milner and O'Connell did the work of Wellington's squares at Waterloo : they rallied the remnant of English Catholics until powerful allies arrived—Wiseman from Rome and Newman from Oxford 304

Memories of persecution still green on Wiseman's arrival—Dr. Archer (who was then living) had been present at Challoner's

sermons at the " Windmill Inn," when the company used to order
beer, and to smoke clay pipes to disguise their object in meeting—
Catholic chapels only made legal in 1791—Penalties for importing
crosses, rosaries, missals—Catholics still paid the double land tax
—"Priest-hunting" still remembered—Disunion among English
Catholics themselves 307

Wiseman's design was to restore the old glory to the Catholic party,
both by infusing zeal and *esprit de corps* into the English Catholics,
and by making them reunite with the Catholic movement abroad
and at Oxford—Wiseman's *prestige*—His Continental reputation—
His acquaintance with the learned world in England—His cosmopolitan character—Described by a German writer as an "in-Spain-
born,-from-an-Irish-family-descended,-in-England-educated,-in-
Italy-residing Syriac scholar"—The time of his arrival in England
propitious for a religious movement—Both the disposition of the
Liberals to give Catholics fair play and the Catholic sympathies
of the Oxford school were in his favour—On the other hand, the old
Catholics were not fitted to take advantage of the situation—
Wiseman's desire was to strengthen the alliances of Catholics while
preserving their independence 311

His arrival in 1835, after a visit to Döllinger and Möhler at
Munich—His lectures at the Sardinian chapel—The impression they
produced—Lord Brougham a constant attendant—Wiseman joins
O'Connell in founding the *Dublin Review*—Effect of his writings on
Newman—Wiseman resides at Oscott as President—His letter to
Lord Shrewsbury on Reunion—His argument was, " If Newman
represents the genius of the Oxford Movement (as all say), and
the movement represents the future of the Church of England, then
Reunion should be probable "—Intense excitement in England at
Newman's conversion—It found vent in the excesses at the time of
the papal aggression—Violent speeches and riots of 1850—Yet the
impotent issue (the inoperative Ecclesiastical Titles Act) showed
that really the public exasperation was far less deep than it had
been at the Gordon riots—Anglican Bishops on the situation—
" The Slough of Romanism "—" Rome's abominations "—Her " pollutions "—Döllinger on the new Bill—Cartoons in *Punch*—Wiseman figures as St. Nicholas in *Punch's* "Decline and Fall of the
British Empire" 314

Wiseman, in his subsequent work, aimed at the calming of
English prejudice, and the organising of Catholicism in England—

PAGE

No such things as monasteries, or Catholic hospitals or orphanages existed when he arrived—Before his death he saw established fifteen monasteries, twenty-five convents, and thirty-four hospitals and orphanages—How he succeeded in living down popular prejudice is seen in the *Times'* account of his funeral—His constant lectures on art, science, and history—Appreciation of him by the English press when he died   319

His remarkable personality—infectious energy and enthusiasm— Love of symbolism—Always a school-boy—His love of children— His love of a "progress" in mediæval state—Magnificent progress to Douay College—Once arrived there his one desire was to amuse the boys—An impulsive sermon—High spiritual ideal—Hatred of pretension in doing good—His "lobster salad" side—Newman's account of Wiseman as a linguist—Wiseman's great plans— Frequent failure to carry them through—Evanescence of impulse— Could rise to a great occasion—Failed in long-sustained labour— " Thou couldst a people raise, but couldst not rule "   321

Newman on Wiseman's visit to Ireland—" No other public man in England " could have equalled his performance—Popular impression of Wiseman as something of the *dilettante*—Manifold activity without a definite drift—Browning's sketch of him as Bishop Blougram—The antiquarian student, fond of literary society—His diplomatic missions—His Syriac studies—" Fabiola "—His correspondence with Sir Rowland Hill on the penny post—The Arctic Expedition—His scientific studies—His guests of all sorts—Lord Acton's account of him as "an all-round man "—" We did not clearly see his drift "—Yet his friends detected a unity of purpose in his life— Key to this contradiction given in a letter from Father Whitty— Wiseman (according to Father Whitty) represented the Church as a national poet represents the all-round genius of his country—He represented his own ideal of the Church in contact with human activity—The Church, in his eyes, alien to no branch of human activity—Should assimilate all—He differed from Manning, who desired to rule and control those who worked under him— Wiseman, on the contrary, desired to liberate the activities of others, and thus enable Catholics to take part in all intellectual movements of the time—Manning loved the military discipline of the Church at war, Wiseman the many-sided life of the Church at peace   324

Wiseman was true to the ideals of his early life—" Freedom " and "The Papacy" were the watchwords of the Ultramontane revival of his youth—The Church was to fuse with and purify modern civilisation —Another idea came athwart this one—Modern civilisation was found intractable—It would not fuse with Catholicism—Pius IX. at first tried to effect this fusion in one department—Lamennais in another—Both failed—Lacordaire found by experience that a priest could not continue to sit on the left of the French Assembly—The conception of freedom under the Ultramontane banner gave place to the antithesis between Ultramontanism and Liberalism— Ultramontanism perforce became militant and repressive—" Liberal Catholicism " became a term of reproach—The opposition was accentuated by Victor Emmanuel's attack on the Papal States— Pius IX. took up the position that Christendom had rebelled and apostatised—The appropriate attitude of Catholics became one of close union among themselves and intense loyalty—of separation from the outside world—This attitude could never have been con- genial to Wiseman—It was authoritatively marked out by the Encyclical and Syllabus of 1864—*Felix opportunitate mortis*, Wise- man died a few months later—Wiseman's conception may prove impracticable, but it is the only conception which can realise the early promise of the Catholic revival, namely, that the new life of Catholic ideals should be a means of extending the influence of the Church 331

XI.

THE LIFE OF MRS. AUGUSTUS CRAVEN.

Dulness of many biographies of eminent persons—Johnson's saying as to the absence of "superiority of mind" in many eminent public men—Powers of observation and expression in the subject of a biography the best security for its interest—Mrs. Craven's great gifts in this respect—Her exceptional opportunities—Her contact with the best life in Italy, France, and England—Her mind stamped by the national character of these three nations—Taine's description of her as " la femme la plus spirituelle que j'ai jamais vu." 334

Her deeper and more religious side—Her great reality of feeling and absence of the faults associated with " clericalism "—Pages in her memoirs have the naturalness and freedom from theological bias of a Greville—Other pages recall Fénelon—Passages illustrative

PAGE

of the former aspect—Her account of Palmerston—of Morley—of Gladstone—Her opposition to the Home Rule Policy of 1886—Her criticisms of the Irish clergy—Her sobriety of judgment and insight 337

Her inner life and intense personality—Her undying memory of the past story of those whom she loved—The religious history of France in her time—Her share in the Catholic revival—Total absence in her religion of anything artificial—Account of her spiritual conversion—Influence of Madame Swetchine—Life of religious peace at Castagneto—Death of Madame Swetchine 352

Candour of the self-revelations in her private diary—Unlike anything which a typical Englishwoman could write—Sense of the drama of her own life which is wanting in an Englishwoman—What would be self-conscious in an Englishwoman is not so in a Frenchwoman 362

Her life uneventful—Her literary power of a very high order, but not creative—The " Récit d'une Sœur " (which was a true narrative) remains her one great book—But if her life was not distinguished in the pages of history, history is written in her life—Her contact with the momentous development of the Catholic revival—The best type of character it produced is to be found nowhere better depicted than in the "Récit d'une Sœur"—The *ethos* visible in its pages reveals a unity of ethical character amid theological divergences—The movement in which she took part brought out the identity of the cause of religion with that of authority and of a rational Conservatism—Like Tennyson, she began with sympathy with the cause of freedom—she ended by deploring its excesses—United Italy was the dream of her youth —Anti-Radicalism was the ruling idea of her old age—" Freedom free to slay herself, and dying while they shout her name ". . . . 365

I.

THE TIME-SPIRIT OF THE NINE-TEENTH CENTURY.

THE coincidence of the termination of the nineteenth century with the end of the Victorian era has made a very conspicuous landmark in our history. And the characteristic genius and special achievements of the century are a natural and fruitful subject of meditation.

The century has indeed been very rich in achievement and in possession. But its achievement has not been quite co-extensive with the riches it has been able to display. These have been largely the realisation of potential wealth accumulated by its predecessors. Like money which cannot be touched or put to practical use during a long minority, and which accrues in startling abundance to its owner when he comes of age, so the methods inaccurately dreamed of by Bacon, and reduced so successfully to actual operation by Newton and his successors, have accumulated a wealth of knowledge in observatories and laboratories, which was long tied up before it could be used by the many. The nineteenth-century surgeon, whose art is so perfect, must not forget that Harvey lived in the seventeenth. The substitution of the railway train for the stage-coach has revolutionised one aspect of social life in the

course of the past century, yet the great discovery
of Watt belongs rather to its predecessor.

Mr. Balfour has dealt with the subject before us
in an interesting address, delivered at Cambridge in
March, 1900.[1] " No century," he writes, "has seen
so great a change in our intellectual apprehension of
the world in which we live." And he derives this
change mainly from the "cumulative products of
scientific research."

But the question I would ask is this—Is there any
one great *addition* to or fresh key to knowledge which
belongs to the time-spirit of the century which has
recently expired, which really characterises its genius,
and is something beyond the more or less mechanical
development of past discoveries, or even their im-
provement in the hands of men of special insight?
Is there anything which stands to the nineteenth
century at all in the same relation in which the
conceptions of Copernicus and of Bacon stood to
the sixteenth and seventeenth centuries—conceptions
which, with all their grave defects in elaboration or
in proof, were destined to effect a profound and far-
reaching change in our way of regarding the universe?

Mr. Balfour gives several characteristic notes of
the transformation the century has witnessed. The
first is "a close connexion between theoretic knowledge and its utilitarian application, which in its
degree is altgether unexampled in the history of
mankind." This does not fulfil the conditions I have
laid down, for the reasons already indicated. It is,
indeed, a startling verification of the soundness of

---

[1] " The Nineteenth Century." Inaugural Address : Cambridge University Local Lectures. By the Right Hon. A. J. Balfour, M.P.
Cambridge University Press. 1900.

scientific methods and of their capacity for indefinite perfectibility. And it enriches us with priceless boons for human comfort and happiness. Practical applications of science become multiplied in the end with rapidity, and give the student a satisfaction similar to that which a child feels when he has reached the final stage of putting together a puzzle-map, a process of which the first steps were tentative and slow. Everything at last falls quickly into its place; he finds nothing missing, and the map is complete and fit for use. Yet accuracy—or even approximate accuracy—in the earlier stages, was a more important and difficult step towards ultimate success, though it might leave him for a time anxious and dissatisfied.

Mr. Balfour appeals, again, to the new conception of the inner nature of matter which chemists and physicists are gradually working out. "Differences of quality once thought ultimate are constantly being resolved into differences of motion or configuration . . . even the chemical elements themselves may be no more than varying arrangements of a common substance." These speculations are, I agree, of very high value; but the general view underlying them was at least guessed at in the old metaphysico-physical speculations of the Schoolmen, who regarded all matter as intrinsically homogeneous apart from the super-imposed "form." Matter was the *determinabile*, form the *determinans*. The *materia prima* was "nec quid nec quale nec quantum" apart from the "forma substantialis." However fancifully expressed, we have in these ideas an anticipation of the direction which modern investigation seems to be pursuing seriously.

But Mr. Balfour regards this line of speculation as part of a vast change in "the mental framework in

which we arrange the separate facts in the world of
men and things." And in this conception of a new
"mental framework" in which we place the facts of
the world and of life, I believe that he touches the
really characteristic feature of the century. It is, as
he truly says, not merely an immense increase in our
"stock of knowledge," but a fundamental change in
our "point of view." Mr. Balfour seems in one
passage to regard that change as due primarily to
the development of physical science, but I should
rather ascribe it to the application of scientific
methods to a sphere far wider than the physical.
It is true that we speak of the nineteenth century
as the age of physical science. Geology, physiology,
chemistry, astronomy, biology, all supply a remarkable
justification of such a claim—as Professor Wallace
has reminded us.[1] But we also speak of the century
as the age of biblical criticism and of archæological
investigation. It is the age of the evolution theory
n biology; it is also the age of historical research.
It is the age of specialism in every department. It is
also the age—in some departments—of that necessary
complement to the researches of the specialist, great
hypotheses and generalisations. Darwin stamped the
evolution theory ineffaceably on the popular mind
by his hypothesis of the "struggle for existence
and survival of the fittest." The same hypothesis
shed a new light on, and was in turn confirmed by,
the researches of geologists. The plains of Patagonia
and La Plata, which Darwin beheld in the course of
his five-years' voyage, constantly recurred, as he
himself has told us, to his memory. They set aglow

[1] See Wallace's " The Wonderful Century " (Swan and Sonnenschein),
p. 150.

his faculty of imaginative generalisation. And they yielded facts to the explorer. For the fossil remains found among them by the geologists, supplied, as we know, an important verification of details in the vivid pictures which Darwin's imagination had painted. But so also the hypothesis of the Elohist and Jahvist authors of Genesis, and the document theory of the Pentateuch, have been the life of and the key to industrious and minute research in another department I have named. Kuenen and Wellhausen are as truly typical products of the nineteenth-century "time-spirit" as Pasteur, Tyndall, or Weissmann.

And the same remark applies equally to historical research in other departments. The ideal of Hegel in his "Philosophy of History"—only partially realised by himself—has had many exponents in both its aspects. That ideal was first to scrutinise the facts of history without prejudice, or preformed theory,[1] and then to rise to the ascertainment of underlying forces and tendencies—of the direction in which ideas have been moving towards realisation. The self-realisation of the different national spirits, the development of national institutions, their relation to the forces social, intellectual, moral, of different times and places, the growth of religions, the onward movement of the world-spirit, are subjects for the philosopher of history. Reject the specialist, with his candour and his accurate observation, and your view of history becomes *à priori* and mythical. Banish the philosopher, and you have mere facts without forces, succession without causation, dissolving views instead of the progress—however irregular—of energies and ideas.

---

[1] "The Idea is the expositor of the facts, not their perverter" ("Philosophy of History," Preface).

Can we regard these diverse characteristic activities of the century in specialism and hypothesis, in science and criticism, as parts of one process—just as the discovery of Columbus, the picture of the universe fancifully sketched by Copernicus in the " De Revolutionibus Orbium," the minute astronomical observations of Galileo and his successors, were all ultimately seen to be parts or consequences of one and the same great conception of the universe to which they led ?

I believe that the past century has gradually come to see in them the application to the physical universe and to our earth and its inhabitants regarded as developing in *time*, of the scientific method inaccurately dreamed of by Bacon, revised and applied by Newton to the universe regarded as existing in *space*. Persisting or recurrent phenomena—from the falling of a stone to the movements of the planets—were explained two centuries ago by a great hypothesis, as due to common laws which govern phenomena indefinitely distant. And now we are applying our newly acquired powers of observation and our physical or mental microscopes and telescopes, to the examination of all that throws light upon the movement of the universe in time ;—to the records of the past, to the mutual relations of the facts they disclose, and to their function in begetting the phenomena of the present; to geological strata, to embryology and the evolution of species ; to documentary history. The one process is concerned with facts and laws which remain the same, and phenomena which recur ; the other with an onward movement, which involves the development of fresh conditions and (apparently at least) fresh forces—the organic, the sentient, the rational, the social—and consequently fresh laws. The analysis of this complex development has not indeed been accomplished in the nineteenth century; but it has been first systematically attempted in its course. It contemplates as one whole the nebular theory of Kant, which traces our planetary system and the "million million of suns" to the primitive undifferentiated nebula; the whole process of inorganic and organic evolution on our earth culminating in rational man; the development of man himself, individual and social, religious, artistic, political, philosophical, scientific. It applies to each department the complete scientific method of observation, induction, hypothesis, deduction, verification.

Ernest Renan, writing in the midst of a movement in which he took so important a share, expressed its character fifty years ago. This gradual sifting by science and history of the successive stages in the moving panorama of the world-story, this ascertaining of the true sequence of facts and the underlying forces, has been in his eyes " the substitution of the category of *evolution* for the category of *being;* of the conception of the relative for the conception of the absolute; of movement for immobility. Formerly everything was considered as ' being;' people spoke of law, of religion, of politics, of poetry, in an absolute fashion. Now everything is considered as in process of formation:—not that formerly evolution and development were not, as they are to-day, general laws. But people had no perception of them." [1]

The culminating conception (to which Renan especially refers) of social evolution in humanity itself, is, perhaps, even more characteristic of the century

[1] " The Future of Science " (English translation), p. 169.

than that of the inorganic and organic evolution which preceded it in time. It at all events fulfils the crucial test which has been given for ascertaining whether an idea is truly the product of the "time-spirit." That test is that it is discoverable in thinkers whose training, antecedents, modes of thinking and circumstances are widely different. The conception of humanity as a developing organism was clearly formulated by Comte in the "Positive Polity." Pro- .ssor Caird has pointed out that this idea, which has pervaded the thought of the nineteenth century, had already been glimpsed before its dawn by Condorcet, by Kant, and by Edmund Burke—"three writers of very different temper and tendency, but in all of them we find this consciousness of the organic unity and evolution of the life of men and nations."

Nor have those who arrived at a similar view at about the same time as Comte, but independently of him, been less different from one another, either in their intellectual antecedents or in the accidental forces which impelled them towards the same goal. It is curious to see such diverse influences as the French Revolution and the progress of physical science issuing in a similar result. And yet we have, in the Catholic reaction from the Revolution and from the philosophy of the encyclopædists, —represented on its theoretical side by Bonald and Lamennais in the "Connoissances Morales" and the "Essai sur l'Indifférence,"—precisely that conception of humanity as an organism, of the organic life of the whole as distinct from the individual life, which Herbert Spencer has developed so elaborately, as correlative to the biological views of Darwin. One is not apt to associate Hegel either with the discoveries

of biological science or with the Catholic reaction ; nor
does one look at first sight for agreement between the
French denouncer of metaphysics and the German
transcendentalist. Yet Hegel's metaphysical speculation, not uninfluenced by the Revolution, included a
social philosophy which was based upon the idea of
the evolution of humanity as an organism. This conception underlies his whole work on the "Philosophy
of History."

It is to be found, too, in the Schlegels and other
members of the Romantic school, although in a less
scientific form. The relations of De Maistre to
Bonald and Lamennais on the one hand, and to
Comte on the other, mark out his share in the
common movement of minds, although his purview
was more or less limited by his special attention to
the quasi-political functions of the Catholic Church.
Möhler's analysis of development in doctrine, but far
more clearly Newman's work on the same subject,
written more than ten years later than the "Sym-
bolik," contain the same ideas. And here they are
traceable to yet other antecedents. In Newman the
affinity to Hegel and to Spencer is very noteworthy.
The actual tests of true development in ideas towards
self-realisation (Newman's phraseology is here almost
identical with Hegel's) are in Newman's celebrated
essay couched in the very language of biology. It is
indeed, as the late Mr. R. H. Hutton pointed out, a
remarkable fact that "the doctrine of development,
treated many years afterwards in the physiological
order by Darwin, was anticipated in a theological
treatise." [1] The moving impulse was here solely
the stress of theological controversy in the Church

[1] "Cardinal Newman," by R. H. Hutton (Methuen), p. 185.

of England. Newman was driven back by this
motive power on to history, and his genius found
in it the law of organic evolution. Thus does the
time-spirit, in one who naturally belongs to it—who
is in his degree what Hegel calls a "world-spirit"
—prevail over the strongest influences of surroundings and education. With yet other antecedents
Renan attained to the same view in his brilliant though
somewhat immature work, "The Future of Science."

It can scarcely be fanciful to regard an idea
arrived at *in terms* by so many different thinkers, in
essence by so many more, as the genuine offspring
of the Zeitgeist.

But not only is this diversity of origin a sign that
the idea is characteristic of the age. It is also a *prima
facie* testimony to its value. A conception which has
supplied the key to problems in metaphysics, social
speculation, physical science, politics and religious
controversy, bears on it signs of that important quality,
power of unification. It comprehends as parts of an
organic whole the various lines of thought which have
given it birth.

To the unspeculative and unimaginative mind
such *rapprochements* appear almost irritating. To
point to them seems to be playing with words, or
using words so elastic that they stretch endlessly and
measure nothing. Yet a little patience will show that
we have in this common conclusion, reached from
standpoints so diverse, the outline of the "new framework," through which the nineteenth century has
looked at the world and its story.

The "new framework" involved, we must remember, not merely a new unification of knowledge to

replace a principle of unification already in existence in the eighteenth century. On the contrary. The old synthesis, based upon theology as the *scientia scientiarum*, and supported by the corporate faith of mediæval Christendom, had long ceased to prevail. A period had followed of specialism, involving fruitful labour in isolated departments, but without any unifying framework for the whole of knowledge. Professor Caird echoes the complaint of Comte in this respect. " The decay of the old faiths," he writes, "and of the objective synthesis based upon them, has emancipated us from many illusions, but it has, as it were, taken the inspiration out of our lives. It has made knowledge a thing for specialists who have lost the sense of totality, the sense of the value of their particular studies in relation to the whole."[1] The "new framework" of the nineteenth century is, if I am right, the first sketch which that century has seen traced in ever-deepening lines, of the comprehensive philosophy to which we must look for the restoration of unity to our knowledge, and, in some degree, for the replacing of our lost enthusiasms.

Let us first consider the old framework—the mediæval synthesis of knowledge—and then remind ourselves of some of the features of the individualism which succeeded it.

The old framework was most clearly defined in the " Summa Theologica " of St. Thomas Aquinas, and best illustrated in Dante's " Divina Commedia." If we take a period earlier than Aquinas the element of explicit intellectual synthesis is absent. It was the outburst of speculative thought in the West during the twelfth century, reinforced by the introduction, in

[1] " Social Philosophy of Comte " (Maclehose ; Glasgow), p. 153.

the reign of Frederick II., of the works of the Arabian Aristotelians, which made an explicit and comprehensive synthesis necessary. A century before the time of Aquinas, St. Bernard was resisting the beginnings of the scholastic synthesis as in its essence rationalistic. The mysticism of the Fathers, which " tasted but did not solve," was the alternative ; and the very method of Abelard's *Sic et non* was regarded as the substitution of human reason for divine faith. St. Thomas Aquinas grappled with the problem of the rational unification of knowledge instead of banishing it from the field of theology. He made theology a principle of universal intellectual synthesis, just as the Holy Roman Empire and the Holy Roman Church were already the principles of order and union in the practical domain—guarding for the many that faith on which the intellectual synthesis was based. On the other hand, if we go to a period later than that of Dante, this principle of practical union was showing signs of decay. When the " De Monarchia " was written the Empire was still regarded as universal and Roman. A few years later it ceased finally to have a footing on Italian soil.

Two great facts of history gave to Western Christendom the intense keenness of fundamental belief which threw around the old synthesis such a glory, and imparted to it such force as a motive of action. The first was the rapid spread of Christianity, the outcome of the faith and constancy of the martyrs, culminating in its triumph under Constantine and Theodosius. To this Fathers and Schoolmen alike appeal. The heir to the fisherman triumphed over the heir to the Cæsars. The emblem of Him who was born in a stable and died a felon's death on the

cross became the design which the successor of the
Roman persecutors blazoned on his banners to secure
victory for his legions. Christian basilicas were raised
in Rome over the catacombs and displaced the temples.
The "gens lucifuga" crawled up from their subter-
ranean hiding-places and ruled from the Capitol. And
they repeated the words of their peasant King:
"Blessed are the meek: for they shall inherit the
earth." It is only sheer absence of imagination,
or the dulness of senses jaded by the repetition of
familiar facts, which can prevent any of us from
realising that as long as this victory remained in
possession, it appeared to be a miracle. The spread
of Christianity was, indeed, itself ascribed to miracles,
but it also helped to make those miracles credible. If
you disbelieve the Christian miracles, argued Dante,
there remains this greater marvel, that Christianity
triumphed *without* miracles.[1] To the same effect
Augustine and Aquinas had also written. Look at
it as you may, this triumph appeared to be encompassed with miracle—an object-lesson in the Divine
power working through the Church.

The other inspiring fact was the existing mediæval
Christendom, the ecclesiastical polity which had arisen
from the victory of the Cross among the Western
nations—an adumbration of the Civitas Dei. In spite
of all its incidental failures, the existence of this
great polity seemed to be in no small degree the
realisation of the promise of the first triumph of
Christianity. Western Christendom was the whole
world for the imagination of the bulk of its inhabitants.

---

[1] " Se il mondo si rivolse al Christianesmo
　　　diss' io senza miracoli, quest' uno
　　　è tal che gli altri non sono il centesmo."
　　　　　　　　　　" Paradiso," xxiv.

And the Church was to the eyes of faith the beacon light visible to all, guiding every soul in its struggle against the powers of darkness. The Monk Radulphus Glaber, speaking of the rich sanctuaries which covered the land in the eleventh century, wrote : " It was as if the world had cast aside its old garment and clothed itself in a white robe." [1] Of the thirteenth century, Harnack writes : " If ever ideals were carried out in the world and gained dominion over souls, it happened then. . . . What a spirit of romance filled those souls which, at a single view, could see in nature and all sensuous life an enchantment of the devil, and could behold it, at the same time, as illumined by the Church, the reflection of the world beyond ! " [2] The Church, the oracle of the Divine revelation, was then, indeed, like the "sun in the heavens." If minor facts did not at once seem to square with the broad outlines of God's visible rule, such facts were naturally treated with impatience, as we should treat objections to the Copernican astronomy. In an uncritical and highly imaginative age, unwelcome facts, inconsistent with overwhelming presumptions, were got rid of. They were rebellious, and were put out of existence. They contradicted what was intensely believed as Divine ; and, even though visible, they were incredible—suggestions of the Evil One. They were crowded out by traditions, suppositions, or even inventions which bore out the Divine presumptions. If men forged documents to justify from history the instruments whereby the visible rule of God was carried on before their eyes, it was done largely in that spirit in which an imaginative child tells a

[1] *Vide* Radulphus Glaber, " Hist.," lib. iii. 4.
[2] " History of Dogma," vol. vi. p. 7. (Theological Translation Library.)

fairy tale and then half believes it. The visible fact of the Papacy seated in Rome, and thence dominating Christendom, produced in the early Middle Ages the invention of the Donation of Constantine and the "Forged Decretals." And their acceptance as genuine helped in the further realisation of the ideals they represented. The Holy Roman Empire is in Dante's "De Monarchia" the normal and providential basis of Christendom. It is to Dante the coalescence of the great providential fact of the Christian Church with the great providential fact of the Roman Empire founded by Augustus, of which the Italian poet has an entirely Utopian conception, based in turn on the conception of what must have been. *À priori* reasoning moved forwards easily and naturally from the belief in God's ever-active providence. It was met halfway by reasoning *à posteriori* from the triumph of Christianity and from the dominion of the mediæval Church in Western Christendom. The process was thus on rough lines, and with a total lack of scientific precision, an application of the method of induction, hypothesis, and verification. The existing mediæval Church was the verification of the Christian view of the world. Her triumph and her universal rule were palpable evidences of Divine power.

In an uncritical age these overwhelming considerations from faith and from sight swept out of view the lesser evidences and smaller facts apparently inconsistent with the general trend of events. Historical and physical science were tried at the bar of theology, which was, according to Aquinas, the most certain of sciences, because its principles were revealed by the All-knowing God. The intellectual genius of those ages was strongest where a child's intellect is strong—in logical consistency. It was weakest in the sense of fact and of history. And theology which deals with the Eternal God, to whom time is a stranger, did little to correct this defect. Types running through history seemed but illustrations in the concrete of the ever-living principles of God's Church. Events, however distant in time, all stood side by side on the same Divine canvas. Even foreshortening was unknown. Constantine and Sylvester in the fourth century, Charles and Leo in the ninth, conferring or receiving gifts spiritual and temporal, were but incidental illustrations and realisations of the divinely appointed order of things. And we still see them depicted together in mystic parallelism on the Lateran façade. The Papacy and the Empire were the two lights placed by God in the firmament. The temporal rule of the Emperor was described by Hildebrand as the moon deriving its light from the Papacy, which was the sun. The deposing power was but a corollary gradually worked out from principles already in operation when Leo crowned Charlemagne. What the Pope could give he could take away.

The spirit which made Fra Angelico paint St. Laurence in a mediæval dalmatic and Pope Sixtus in a tiara runs, indeed, through the whole mediæval polity. As the tiara was reflected back on to the picture of Sixtus, so was the proud sovereignty of Leo III. upon the picture of Sylvester ; so were the dogmatic symbols inscribed in mediæval manuscripts regarded as the precise *depositum fidei* committed by Christ to the Apostles.[1] The great power of the

---

[1] The third essay in the present volume deals with the difference between the mediæval conception and our own on this subject.

Church in Christendom, and her vast dogmatic system,—both were sealed by the Divine stamp. What was Divine was unchangeable. Thus the dogmatic system and the prerogatives of the Papacy must ever have been the same from the time of St. Peter. And the temporal possessions of the Holy See must be traced to the first days of the Christian Empire. Consistency of view was essential. Facts in an uncritical and unscientific age were apt to yield sheer useless chaos. Science had not yet awarded her prizes to accurate observation. Patience in presence of temporary inconsistency, faith alike in observed phenomena and in the future unification of what appeared disparate and perplexing, was unknown. Lesser facts of past, present, or future must be worked into a scheme, which was determined by revelation and confirmed by greater facts so full of significance, so illuminating in the twilight of life. Thus the past was treated in the spirit of Lactantius, in whose eyes all persecutors of the Christians incurred God's visible chastisement. The practical problems of the present must be met by the attitude of the Popes from Gregory VII. to Boniface VIII., who strove ever further to realise what they held to be the providential ideal, "to give effect," in Harnack's words, "to the supremacy of the Church on earth." For that ideal was already largely realised. The monk who had vowed poverty was invested with the power of a noble. The meek had inherited the earth. "The servant of the servants of God" wore the imperial crown,[1] and ratified or abrogated the claims of kings.

---

[1] The triple crown was not worn until the middle of the fourteenth century.

The Crusades were an outcome and illustration of these ruling ideas. Such an anomaly as the possession by the infidel of the very central shrine of Christian devotion, the Holy Land—the rule of the crescent in the very stronghold of the Crucified—must summarily be got rid of. " It was," writes Harnack, " the ideas of the world-ruling Monk of Cluny that guided the Crusaders on their path. The Holy Land and Jerusalem were parts of heaven on earth. They must be conquered." God, who was realising visibly the Civitas Dei, would be with the soldiers of the Cross. Peter the Hermit and those to whom he preached were but instruments in the completion of what had been already so wonderfully begun. The Crusades were an obvious duty, and promised an assured triumph. " God wills it."

Such was the tower which men confidently hoped would reach the heavens. But it tottered and fell. And the builders of Christendom came to speak different tongues. The Crusades were accompanied by immorality, and ended in disaster. The Empire failed utterly to realise its ideal. Indeed, in some respects, it never afterwards so nearly approached that ideal as under Charlemagne himself. After four centuries of vicissitude it ceased effectively to claim more than local authority. Dante, who celebrated its glories, was really, in Mr. Bryce's phrase, " writing its epitaph." After Boniface VIII. the papal power gradually declined. Physical science had already begun to assert itself under Roger Bacon. The Christian ideal—"the white robe" of the Church— was rudely torn by the Renaissance. The robe remained indeed, but no longer invested the countries of Christendom with one uniform supernatural glory.

Wide spaces became visible in which unclothed pagan nature was apparent. The spirit of doubt had already appeared, now and again, even in the ages of faith, notably in the days of Frederick II. The extraordinary activity and zeal of the thirteenth-century Schoolmen subdued the movement of free-thought for a time. But the subjection was partly artificial. The seeds of rationalism remained in the scholastic method. The Renaissance brought before the imagination of Christendom the beauty and poetry of the old Greek civilisation. The pagan ideal was exhibited by the side of the Christian altars in the Rome of Julius II. and Leo X. The confidence, intensity, and volume of Christian energy were lessened. Cross-currents dissipated its strength.

And to these blows at the old prestige of the Church succeeded the far heavier blow of Luther's reformation, the confounding of the old common speech. The Reformers had, indeed, little of the critical or scientific spirit, little in common with cultivated and sceptical humanism ; but they claimed and exercised, crudely it may be, a right of private judgment which refused to be carried away by the large presumptions ratified by Church authority. They exercised, at first clumsily, and in a limited field of the interpretation of Scripture, the weapon of independent criticism, which was later on to be melted down and forged afresh, and then skilfully wielded by free-thinkers against the inspiration of Scripture, and against Christianity itself. The visible standing facts, which long seemed to be almost a miraculous justification of the mediæval synthesis, had been one after another partly or wholly dissolved. Palpable corruptions, added to promises apparently not fulfilled on the part of the infallible Church, gave the protesting individual his foothold. He took it, roughly, largely on false issues, on grounds deprecated by the culture of Erasmus, Colet, and More. But for the movement of disintegration, which was to break up the old polity, a strenuous, bigoted, one-sided protest was exactly what was needed. The remaining "fact" which had been the chief stay of the mediæval synthesis in the West, the visible unity of Christendom, had in the course of thirty years utterly disappeared. The theoretic claim of theology to judge the pretensions of physical science expired in the following century, when the Copernican theory was first condemned by the Inquisition as heretical and then reluctantly accepted by the theologians.

Then came the individualist movement with which we are familiar. Descartes formulated the methodic doubt and initiated that analysis of the individual consciousness as the test of certainty which has lasted with such unsatisfactory results to a period within our own memory. "Dubito ergo sum" or "cogito ergo sum" was a point of departure for speculations which had great value ; but the individualistic analysis it began proved barren. It was, in truth, strictly adhered to by no one. It was deserted really by Descartes himself, to whom God was a veritable *Deus ex machina* invoked to save his method from a purely sceptical issue. It was deserted more patently by Malebranche and Spinoza. But the rejection of preconceptions, the critical scrutiny of phenomena which the method involved in its examination of the facts of consciousness, took shape with remarkable results in the Baconian view of physical science.

The method of the "Novum Organum" was, like
Luther's assertion of private judgment, one-sided,
and not strictly scientific. But it was effective as
a protest against the "intellectus sibi permissus,"
against theorising irrespective of fact, and as clearing the ground for the great movement which was
to follow. It undervalued hypothesis. And Bacon
even failed to recognise the truth of Copernicanism.
His method was unsuccessful at first in its practical
application. But it had the influence on thought
which one true idea, urged in exaggerated form and
with exclusive importunity, at the right moment,
seldom fails to have. It established once for all
accurate and systematic observation as the basis of
science. In the hands of Newton, observation,
hypothesis, experiment, verification—the method subsequently analysed by Mill—conquered so vast a field
of knowledge that the beginning of the scientific period
was attained. A new faith and hope dawned, though
not looking beyond this world, or beyond a limited
department in it. The faith of the mediæval Christian
had, we have seen, been borne in upon the popular
mind by the visible triumph of the powers he trusted,
by the approximate realisation, from such small beginnings, of the City of God. And so, too, physical
science justified its methods by its conquests, and thus
began to inspire the many. Faith in a coming realisation, in the domain of physical science, of Bacon's
dream of victory by obedience, dawned and spread.

In that domain individualism involved an exact
scrutiny by every mind, which issued in common conclusions acknowledged by all. It proved constructive,
and the synthesis between individual effort and general
knowledge was attained.

But it was not so in other fields of research.   Elsewhere individualism either proved largely barren as
in metaphysics, or occupied itself in destruction and
negation as in history and theology.   Locke began as
confidently as Bacon.   The treatment of the human
mind as a *tabula rasa*, the banishment of preconceptions, was to issue in a systematic recognition of the
laws of the mind based on observation of its phenomena.   But instead of a law of gravitation unifying
phenomena which had hitherto appeared totally
unconnected, an unfertile speculative chaos supervened
in Hume's negations.

Theology dethroned stood apart, grey-headed,
solitary, not holding converse with her neighbours—
deserted like Lear by those who had formerly paid
her allegiance.   The one surviving organisation which
witnessed to the old synthesis—the Papal Church—
remained isolated, while passers-by smiled at Giant
Pope and reported him to be mumbling and toothless.
No longer understanding the "time-spirit" (it seemed),
no longer assimilating and subduing it as Origen took
in the new Platonism or Aquinas the new Aristotelianism, the Church appeared only to cling to the
relics of her lost dominion.   The picture was the more
pathetic because she would part with nothing which
recalled happier days.   Even the assertion of the
deposing power, even the condemnation of Galileo,
were long persisted in.   The *Regnans in excelsis* which
Pius thundered so impotently against Elizabeth had
all the masterful tone of Boniface's *Unam Sanctam*
two centuries and a half earlier; and the claim it
advanced was maintained up to the eighteenth
century.   The old proud intolerance was stereotyped
in the establishment of the Congregation of the Holy

Office of the Inquisition in 1542, which continued thenceforth to use the language and method of the days of papal power. In her old age the Church appeared to be unable to put off the masterful habits of speech acquired during so long a period of active dominion. The antithesis between the old standpoint and the new seemed almost complete by the time the eighteenth century was reached, and it only deepened as the century advanced. A reconciliation appeared beyond hope. The dogmas, the "donation of Constantine," the claim to depose kings, the claim to correct science, had all been found out. They were an imposition on mankind. They had been the "frauds of the priests" designed by them to gain power for their caste. Such was the view of Protestant England and of the intellectual pioneers of the French Revolution.

The Church had in reality been active behind her own entrenchments, both intellectually and morally. She had gone through a period of penance and purification after the rebellion of Luther. Ignatius Loyola, Charles Borromeo, Philip Neri had inaugurated a far-reaching moral reform within the territories that remained to her. She could hold up her head once again, and to the faithful remnant she was still more venerable in her age and isolation than in the days of her lost dominion. The world had for them simply gone astray. They served their mistress patiently and waited for happier days. But active commerce grew less and less between the Church and the intellectual world. To the more advanced representatives of the time-spirit she gradually came to be an object of hate, or of derision, or of often impertinent curiosity. The eighteenth-century Deists attacked the Christian

dogmas openly. In the Church of England lati-
tudinarians—more effectively—banished them from
the intellectual arena, and relegated them to the
position of *rois fainéants* of religion. The old
theology, but above all the Catholic theology, represented, for those minds which were most typical of
the age, a civilisation for ever bygone. " The period
of conquests," wrote Goethe, "seems to me to have
for ever departed from the Catholic Church."

But when her assailants turned to their own
sciences they found them indeed friends with the
friendship of Pilate and Herod, but with little unity
beyond common opposition to their discrowned ruler.
History retained in Bossuet a coherence which it
lost in Hume. In its new exponents it no longer
subserved the great providential conception of the
Church, to which that was true which supported or
illustrated her claims. Its genius, so far as it was
scientific, was negative rather than constructive. It
affected to discard and despise mythical tradition, but
it had not analysed or mastered its own sources of
positive knowledge, nor its relations to other sciences.
And it often ministered (in fact) to prejudices scarcely
less strong than the preconceptions of those ages
when beautiful legends were no sooner imagined than
believed, no sooner believed than they were illumi-
nated with strange and inspiring beauty on the scroll
of Church history. The individualist metaphysics
which had broken up into different schools—into
the different varieties of empiricism, intuitionism, and
idealism — eventually tainted with its characteristic
vice social and political speculation. An individualistic theory of the rights of man and the doctrine of
an ideal state of nature as untrue to fact as Locke's

tabula rasa, obscured in different ways the perception of the organic unity and development of the race.

Scientific history and sociology had, it may be truly said, no existence in the first half of the eighteenth century. Physical science alone was orderly and fruitful, and it stood almost as much out of relation to the rest of knowledge as theology itself.

Theology, indeed, the basis of the old synthesis, was in an anomalous position—not really accepted by the genius of the time-spirit, and making no organised attempt to trace its relations to knowledge in general. Yet it retained a hold on the masses, and its old unifying function was not replaced by any rival power. The universe as a whole, considered as existing in time and culminating in man, fell under no unity of conception. No world-philosophy or life-philosophy could be satisfactorily attempted. The age shrank from avowed scepticism, and yet had lost the sources of enthusiasm. In the sixteenth and seventeenth centuries there still lingered among master minds much of the faith associated with the mediæval synthesis. Bunyan and Milton regard the unseen universe and the drama of the Christian life with a vivid and imaginative faith, not far inferior to that of Dante. From Shakespeare to Jeremy Taylor there still survives the clear recognition of the relations of man with infinite spiritual forces. But with the dawn of the eighteenth century this gradually fades away. To the seventeenth-century writers, in Sir Leslie Stephen's words, "man is in the presence of infinity and eternity; life is a brief dream; . . . heaven and hell are behind the veil of phenomena, which at every step one finds vanish into the vast abyss of ever-present mystery. To all such thoughts the writers of the eighteenth century seem to close their eyes as absolutely as possible." [1]

The phenomena of life and of history thus tended to become meaningless and disconnected. The old canvas on which the history of the world had been depicted as an ever-present scene before a God external to time, justifying His ways, exhibiting His providence and His judgments, was by some set aside as an interesting but unscientific relic, in part venerable; by others it was rent and put away with contempt. But what existed in its place? No coherent view of history at all. Authority and tradition were rejected. They belonged to the superstitious past and were done with. In their place we have the thin optimism of Shaftesbury or Bolingbroke—the satisfaction at having outgrown superstition, the pleasures of contempt. Sir Leslie Stephen's account of Hume's attitude towards history is, as he himself intimates, substantially applicable to most of the typical historians of the period:

"Hume, having abandoned the old theological and metaphysical synthesis, has reduced the race to a mere chaos of unconnected individuals. He cannot recognise, even when they are brought before him, the great forces which bind men together. A nation is not a living organism, but a temporary combination in various conformations of colourless units. National character results from forms of government; forms of government are the work of chance. . . . Even the great movements of thought present themselves to him as accidents. Religious wars are simple follies, for a controversy about an article of faith which is utterly absurd and unintelligible is not a difference in sentiment, but in a few phrases and expressions which one party accepts of without understanding, and the other refuses in the same manner.

[1] "English Thought in the Eighteenth Century," ii. 370.

. . . It is no wonder if history presented itself as a mere undecipherable maze to the eighteenth-century thinkers, of whom Hume is the most complete representative." (*Loc. cit.*, ii. 184.)

And to live in an unexplorable maze, like living in a land of darkness, deadens certain faculties. When there is no clue or no light, speculation seems vain, and tends to cease. Enthusiasm is killed. Enterprise is without motive. A desire to make the best of things, and to learn to feel your way about without troubling as to the unexplorable and unknowable, is the appropriate temper. It is an utilitarian temper, and keeps to the work ready to hand—*cultivez votre jardin*. In the complacent it refuses to grumble, and makes the most of work done under inevitable limitations. Hence the optimism of Shaftesbury or Tindal. In profounder and more restless spirits a natural vein of melancholy is deepened by the darkness. And so we see it in Swift. Cynicism and absence of enthusiasm are inevitable—and they are visible in various forms in Shaftesbury, Mandeville, Voltaire, Gibbon, and Swift himself. Such thinkers as Butler and Johnson upheld a religious philosophy—but it was a philosophy of patience under untoward appearances which were unknown to the buoyant and triumphant faith of the mediæval world. This darkness as to the great world-problems lasted after the old light of the philosophy, which explicitly connected men and their thought with God and a Divine revelation, was extinguished, until the new philosophy dawned of their relation to one another, to the environment, to the time-spirit, to the deep spiritual forces underlying history, and to the evolution of the universe of mind and matter, — until the view apparent in Hegel's

"Philosophy of History" prevailed—a view first glimpsed by such writers as Montesquieu and Herder.

Moreover, not only had the old faiths ceased to inspire, but their former power of inspiration was largely overlooked or disbelieved. The historians of no period have more needed Disraeli's rebuke that "great movements are due not to intrigue but to faith." Thus even Gibbon fails to appreciate the intense force in history as *motives*, of beliefs and inspiring enthusiasms which he does not share. With all his power of reproducing the outer facts of the past, the inner forces are often inadequately realised in his "Decline and Fall." His own cynicism or scepticism touches and blurs his best pictures, and it is only an exaggeration of the truth to say what an acute critic has said— that his stately array of *dramatis personæ* of history passes at times before the reader like a funeral procession. Hence also the astonishing want of perception visible in Bolingbroke's verdict on great men, landmarks in the evolution of thought—on Descartes, on Malebranche, on Leibnitz, on Plato himself. They are all victims, in his language, of "metaphysical delirium." And Plato alternates between the "false sublime" and moods in which he "sinks down, and lower no writer can sink, into a tedious socratical irony, into certain flimsy hypothetical reasonings that prove nothing, and into allusions that are mere vulgarisms, and that neither enforce nor explain anything that ought to be explained or enforced."[1]

Such verdicts could only be possible in the peculiar darkness of a period which in relation to these subjects was passing through the night between two days. Plato was no longer the man God-inspired

[1] Bolingbroke's "Works," iv. 141.

who had beheld the *Logos* before He came. He was not yet viewed in relation to those to whom he spoke, and to his predecessors and successors. Platonism was not understood in its extraordinary fruitfulness for the ages which succeeded it. It was regarded as a group of dead formulæ vivified provisionally by an eighteenth-century spirit and then measured by an eighteenth-century standard as by an absolute norm of truth. Such is the marvellous courage of conviction, worthy of " Athanasius against the world," which a strong individualist temper may give. The old *securus judicat* of the Church was gone. The new *securus judicat* of historical science had not come. The individual could think as he pleased.

But while science and negation were working hand in hand and triumphing over tradition, authority, and the Church, there came a very curious reshuffling of the cards with unexpected consequences. While individualism was claiming to share the triumphs of science, proofs sprang up in opposite and unexpected quarters, to show that the claim was false and even absurd. Individual effort, intent on ascertaining the objective law and framing a synthesis, had triumphed in physical science—because, as we have already seen, it was not in the last resort individualism. It obeyed the law which bound together individual effort and made it organic and corporate. It had little temptation to disobey it, for the terrain of physical science was removed from the angry passions which agitate and divide. The observatory shared the atmosphere of serenity, in the light of eternity, of the starry heavens themselves. But individualism in an atmosphere of conflict was widely different. Defiance of law and indifference to synthesis failed, for the reasons

which made obedience to the law and the attempt at
synthesis succeed. And thus a few critical years so
completely wrecked the eighteenth-century individualism that sanguine spirits among the adherents of the
older order thought that the Church was to regain
her ancient sovereignty, and that the main lines of
the mediæval synthesis were to be restored.

Had individualism, then, been simply a failure?
Far otherwise. But the shock of the Revolution
brought out with intense force the fact that its work
was not an end but a means; that individualism when
self-willed was a curse; that the true function of that
liberation of the individual mind in which the reformers had gloried was to give it liberty to attain
the *best*, unfettered by a premature synthesis, which,
though it might be unifying, was clearly seen to be
not commensurate with the facts. Such freedom
tended not to the denial of authority, but to the free
acceptance of that highest expert authority which it
helped to create. It may be said that the lesson of
the Revolution, coming as it did with the lesson of
scientific achievement, revealed with startling clearness this discrepancy between the two views of liberty
which had been marching together under one banner.

Two paths were then open, the " Romantic " and
the scientific—to reject individualism and return to the
old synthesis, or to correct it and attempt to make it
subservient in sociology, politics, history, as it had
been already in physical science, to a higher synthesis.
De Maistre and the German Romanticists took the
one path; Niebuhr, Ranke, and the scientific historians
took the other. The world-philosophy which each
course represented was sketched, in the first instance,

on the one hand by Bonald and Lamennais, on the other by Comte. With a Frenchman's penetrating quickness and exaggeration of statement, uncorrected by any sense of humour, with an utopian divorce from what was practicable in the concrete which repelled slower thinkers, Comte was the first to see clearly the central issues from the purely scientific standpoint. Both lines of thought are now yielding to a view which comprehends the two.

My limits will not allow me to do more than briefly indicate some of the various sources of this new synthesis. And I can only point to main currents in a stream which has had many tributaries.

Bonald and De Maistre set up against individualism and anarchy the banners of tradition, social and family life, and authority. They brought back into the field of speculation the old Church, wonderful still in its vitality and organisation, so long unnoticed and despised by the thinkers. The Church had sullenly refused to acquiesce in rationalism, or, to test by the results of a smart argumentive duel the convictions on which it had lived. And Bonald now pointed to the wise practical instinct which this course displayed. The customs and immemorial beliefs so contemptuously rejected by the individualist philosophers as irrational, were, he said, justified practically as embodying wisdom gained from the experience of generations or tested by it, and as the basis of order in the community. Their rejection had issued in the anarchy of '93. Bonald renewed the old philosophy of Euripides. "We do not reason subtlely about the gods. The traditions of our fathers and those which we possess coeval with time, no argument can overthrow these." [1]

---

[1] "The Bacchæ," 201.

And the distinctively Christian beliefs, too, were justified by their yet higher practical value, and traced to the revelation of God to man. The corporate reason of man is analysed by Bonald to some extent on the lines of the evolutionary philosophy. The family, the nation, the Church treasure up and accumulate wisdom and hand it down from generation to generation. Christianity is the basis of the synthesis. The Church is to Bonald the providential guardian of knowledge, divinely imparted and enlarged by practical experience.

On this basis of philosophic traditionalism was reared a movement which brought back for a brief space many ideals of the Middle Ages. De Maistre's "Du Pape" was the earnest and practical enforcement by a statesman of the value of the Papacy as a factor in international politics. Pius VII. by his high character was able to stand the light which was thus cast upon him. Lamennais emphasised the lessons of De Maistre. Both writers expressed a feeling which, for a few years, was general. We remember its chief manifestations in Chateaubriand, and in the Romantic school. Napoleon himself had for a brief space conceived of himself as a Charlemagne. Men dreamt of the ages of chivalry and faith. Frederick Schlegel elaborated his ideals in a philosophy of history. Augustus Schlegel prophesied the return of thinking men to the old Church.[1] Romance became Christian or mediæval from Chateaubriand's "Atala" to the stories of Tieck and La Motte Fouqué. Cornelius and Overbeck breathed into their pictures the spirit of Fra Angelico. The German Romanticists were the flower of the age. Many of them—though

[1] See his letter cited by Lady Blennerhassett in her "Madame de Staël," vol. iii. p. 345.

by no means all—joined the Church of Rome. Sir
Walter Scott kindled even in Protestant England an
enthusiasm for ideals which he professed to criticise.
And his was one of the influences to which the revival
of Catholic sympathies in the Oxford Movement
was due.

This Catholic revival, preceding in order of time
the scientific and critical movement in history, supplied
materials for it in two ways.

In the first place, Chateaubriand, Bonald, Lamennais, the Schlegels, and the German Romanticists
brought the past to life again and called attention
to it. The light they threw around it by their
enthusiasm made the Middle Ages once again vivid
and conspicuous in the eyes of those who denied
that it came directly from the heavens. The light
was designed as an aureole; it served as the limelight in which the scientific historian could see to do
his work. Men studied the records of history with
new zest and intelligence.

Secondly, the irresistible rehabilitation by the
Romantic school of the nobility and beneficence of
Christian institutions against the exaggerated depre-
ciation of the eighteenth century raised at once the
question of relativity. The only possible reply was,
"These may once have been valuable; they are
now outgrown." This immediately raised problems
essential to the new historical method—the relation
of institutions to their time, and to their place and
environment.

In the Church historian Döllinger the Romantic
tendency and the scientific coalesced. So too in some
degree with Frederick Schlegel. Ranke received his
first impulse towards critical history from reading

"Quentin Durward." Hegel has placed on record his own obligations to the Catholic historical revival, not only to the philosophy of history as represented by F. Schlegel and Lamennais, but to such Catholic students of comparative literature and religion as Abel Rémusat and Saint-Martin.

Influenced on the one hand by De Maistre, on the other by the collectivism of Saint-Simon, Auguste Comte brought to his survey of history elements both of scepticism and of enthusiasm. With romantic attachment to the old stately machinery of the Church, he was yet intellectually an empiricist of the deepest dye. With French logical precision and French superficiality, he reconciled his opposing tendencies by a sharp division between heart and head. For the head science alone was (he held) possible. For the heart a religion might be found in the subjective synthesis. For the head the whole universe, including the history of man, was amenable to the strictest scientific methods. To the intellect the transcendental was utterly inaccessible. Positive facts and their connecting laws were all in all. The contents of physical science are analysed in the " Positive Polity," though without fully adequate knowledge. The laws of human development in history are treated in some respects with a masterly hand. The application of the inductive method to the story of man is attained, though only on broad lines and with an undue predominance of theory over fact. For the heart religious enthusiasm may reign as it did of old in the monk's cell or in the mediæval cathedral. But man knows nothing beyond the visible universe and its story. Humanity —the developing organism—idealised, regarded as gradually working out the salvation of the human race with increasing civilisation, was the object of love and awe. The new Church—the basis of the new synthesis —was to have men of science for its high priests. Symbolism of the great known forces and facts was to replace symbolism of the unknown, in ceremonial pageant and liturgy.

Hegel had already laid down lines on which later on these two views, the Christian and the scientific, have been partially reconciled. Starting from Idealism, and from the conception of spirit, while he deals less elaborately than the French philosopher with the practical field with which Comte concerns himself, he supplies nevertheless the missing link. Comte's presentation of historical development, which fascinated J. S. Mill, took the external point of view to which Hume's philosophy had led. Comte stands without, a spectator of the great procession, whose order and arrangement he analyses. By Hegel historical evolution is regarded from within as the development of spirit. The outer facts are expressions of inner forces. For Comte patriotism gradually gives place to the worship of Humanity. Hegel attains a similar result from his somewhat different standpoint. In his eyes national spirits gradually realise themselves and tend to merge in the world-spirit. The development of institutions, of ideas, of nations, of religions, under the influence of local surroundings, becomes the subject of history. He attains to the comparative method, and the scientific conception, though with insufficient recognition of those canons for testing and weighing evidence which the specialists have since formulated.

But Hegel's world-spirit is, moreover, God realising Himself in the history of man. It precisely fills up the *lacuna* which Comte's philosophy necessarily left void, unable to advance further along an empirical and positivist road.[1] Comte's Humanity was avowedly and necessarily incomplete. Its completion must involve the recognition of a transcendental element. This element Hegel distinctly contemplated. The Divine realising itself in the human, by a process in its outer manifestation amenable to scientific investigation, supplied the missing key to the position. It gave a flat negation to positivism as a final creed. But it may be regarded as really explaining and developing the system of Comte. It justified Comte's admirable historical survey, and stripped his religion of its absurdity. It destroyed the absolute antithesis between heart and head, and substituted the antithesis in the history of man between spirit and its outer manifestations.

Mr. Balfour—once again seizing with quick intuition a vital distinction which affects contemporary thought—has perhaps done more than any thinker to popularise the word " non-rational." And this phrase will help us in tracing clearly the line of cleavage between the characteristic temper of the eighteenth-century thought and the historical and evolutionary standpoint of the nineteenth century. To the individualism of the eighteenth century the conquests of the individual analytic reason were coextensive with the rational. Subjection to Authority and Tradition was irrational. From the standpoint of a social and evolutionary philosophy there was in addition a vast mass of human conviction which belonged to neither

---

[1] This point is admirably developed by Professor E. Caird, Master of Balliol, in his " Social Philosophy of Comte."

category. It was "non-rational." It was the product of human experience, or a legacy from the past,
often recognised as in some degree authoritative from
its practical value, but not yet analysed ; much of it
the conquest of the reason of the race, although not
yet traced to its rational sources by the reason of the
individual. Hence a mass of tradition, religious and
social, at once found a place again in the thought of
the time, not as exact knowledge, but as material ;—
as containing wheat and tares ; to be preserved and
sifted, but on no account to be destroyed.

Hence we have a marked change in our estimate
alike of the material for history, of the standard
whereby it is to be appraised, and of the faculty
whereby it is to be utilised. To the dilemma "true"
or "untrue," Mr. Balfour adds the Scotch verdict of
"not proven." To the optimist of the eighteenth
century his own standpoint was absolute and final.
The characteristic convictions of his time were
therefore true. Discarded tradition was untrue. To
those who recognise that history is still in the making,
human faculty and knowledge still developing, still
falling short of inherent possibilities, it is impossible
to regard their own standpoint as ultimate, or their
own convictions as absolute truth; impossible to
regard those past conditions of thought from which
these convictions have been evolved as simply error.
We see more than our predecessors if we rest on their
shoulders. But we do not yet see all. This view is
essential to the new spirit in history. Hence the
desire of the modern historian to learn from all sources,
and the diminution of the old dogmatic authoritative
tone, which are obvious to the present-day observer.
The thirteenth century was quick to accept. The

eighteenth was quick to reject. The nineteenth
has been slow to do either finally. It has extended
to all fields of knowledge that patient waiting on facts
which was the secret of Bacon's hoped-for "victory
by obedience." It has canonised in the intellectual
sphere an old virtue—patience. It has thrown a
glory, in certain departments, round that which was
to the inquisitor a vice—doubt and suspense of
judgment.

To explore the non-rational sources of knowledge
in the past history of the race is, then, one of the
characteristic labours of the nineteenth-century historian—to collect and sift what the eighteenth century
simply rejected. "L'esprit du XIX. siècle," writes
Vacherot, "est de comprendre et de juger les choses
du. passé. Notre œuvre est d'expliquer ce que le
XVIII. siècle avait mission à nier." For this reason
the sympathy with the past, which is so whole-hearted
in Chateaubriand, in De Maistre, in the German
Romanticists, that they would fain bring it back
again, is of necessity *dramatically* strong, in the best
scientific historians of our time. If we would really
know and judge the facts we must know the relevant
conditions, motives, forces. If we would know them
we must at least have that sympathy with those
who lived in their midst and were affected by them
which Edmund Kean would have with Shylock. His
own judgment may disapprove when Shylock produces his scales; but for the moment the feeling of
the actor is that of the Jew. The historian must be
sympathetic before he can master the very material
for critical examination. Contrast the treatment of
mediæval or Christian ideas by Gibbon and by
Harnack. With Gibbon the truest vision of outer

fact cannot prevent the constant suggestion of an eighteenth-century ethos—of cynicism, with perhaps the alternative of ignorant fanaticism, in the ages when poetry, heroism, and uncritical faith governed so many lives. Harnack, on the contrary, lives in the ages whose thought he depicts. Even Gregorovius, inferior no doubt to Gibbon in critical acumen, is in this respect the child of his century. He gets far nearer to the attitude of sympathetic impartiality and gives at times the truer picture. Contrast Hallam—an eighteenth-century survival—with Ranke ; contrast Voltaire with Renan. Ranke's masterly impartiality, Renan's extraordinary sympathetic insight, often restore to history true perspective, and that inner life of ideas which Hegel in his turn appeared sometimes to see almost stripped of its external clothing.

Contrast, again, Hume's treatment of religious controversies and religious formulæ with their treatment by Auguste Sabatier. To the former the history of dogma is a story of puerile folly ; to the French thinker, as to Harnack himself, it is a drama of surpassing interest in which the deepest passions and convictions and most real interests of humanity, as conceived at each epoch, are concerned. Contrast, again, Bolingbroke's contempt for Plato and Descartes—to which I have already alluded—with Hegel's attitude towards the thinkers of the past. By the former, thoughts which were the germs of great discoveries are judged without any realisation of their potential content or of the limitations imposed on their expression by the conditions of contemporary culture. To Hegel they are precious stones—though at times roughly hewn—in the great edifice which

evolution has been gradually building. Bolingbroke
can only see incidental defects of form which his age
has outgrown. Hegel detects the living spirit within,
the life of further development.

Living in the glow of a Zeitgeist which found
expression in such world-spirits as Comte and Hegel,
the specialists worked with a new faith, while science
supplied them with new methods and weapons. We
have recently been reminded by several able writers
of the nature of their work. No cleavage is absolute
in point of time. Nineteenth-century methods were
here and there apparent before the century began.
Eighteenth-century methods have survived within
our own memory in some departments and some
men. But Hegel's doctrine of the organic unity of
all knowledge and of the movement of Ideas in
history has gradually leavened the thought of the
age. Its influence is often strong even where it is
latent. And the determination to bring the past
under scientific examination, and thus to accumulate
materials for appreciating the function of each department in the evolution of the whole, is unmistakable.
In history Niebuhr stands out as a landmark in his
endeavour to apply the critical method to early
Roman history and to rescue the underlying truth
from mythical accretions by the observation of the
laws of historical evolution. Ranke was perhaps the
real inaugurator of documentary criticism. "He
supplemented the critical method," says an able
writer, "where Niebuhr had left it deficient. Documents were submitted to the same questioning as
traditions." "He is," writes Lord Acton, in his Cambridge address on the "Study of History," "the representative of the age which instituted the modern

study of history. . . . We meet him at every step, and he has done more for us than any other man." [1] His serene and judicial fairness completed the work begun by Voigt in obtaining just treatment for the Papacy, "the key to the Middle Ages." Mignet's study of manuscript sources was an advance in the path traced by Ranke. Sir Henry Maine, in his "Village Communities," marks, perhaps, the organic connection between the new history and the new political economy. The *laissez-faire* method was an individualist survival as much belonging by nature to the eighteenth century as the histories of Hallam and Merivale. The historical and inductive methods of Schmoller and Wagner, and, in another department, of Le Play, have also triumphed.

So too in philosophy. Sir W. Hamilton's standpoint was largely that of the eighteenth century. To him, in Mr. Alexander's words, philosophy was "a number of separate problems falling apart like atoms in the void." Here the landmark is probably Hegel's "Logic," with its unifying power and its wide imaginative sweep, and in some degree Hegel's "History of Philosophy." Historical evolution is to Hegel but one aspect of a wider conception. The Idea realises itself in Space as Nature, in Time as History. His daring imagination brought the unity of human knowledge to the highest conceivable point. The "Logic" "is as aerial a flight as the 'Paradiso' itself." And the history of philosophy is, in his eyes, the key to the unity attempted in his own system. Individualist reactions there will doubtless be, and ought to be, as a check upon exaggerations of the organic conception. We have witnessed such a reaction in the land of

[1] "The Study of History," p. 48. (Macmillan, 1896.)

Hegel himself. But the thought of the individual can never again ignore that wider corporate thought of which it is itself a part, and to which it ministers.

Mr. Balfour terminates the address to which I have more than once referred by a prophecy. He asks whether the immense extension in our time of scientific knowledge, and of the application of scientific methods, will be unfavourable to religion and will tend to materialism? And he prophesies that, on the contrary, the so-called conflict between science and religion will cease. " The very completeness and internal consistency " of the purely scientific view of things "would establish its inadequacy. The very fact that within it there seemed no room for spirit would convince mankind that spirit must be invoked to explain it." [1] He is concerned with physical science —to which he regards all science as ultimately reducible. But the question is equally applicable to the different view of science which has been taken in these pages. Does then, we may ask, the growth of

---

[1] The scope of the present essay does not admit of my discussing Mr. Balfour's position as to the abstract possibility of a complete mechanical explanation of the universe. His argument in the address only postulates a great extension of the mechanical view—in other words, of our knowledge of uniform law. Even he cannot look for more than this in our own century. And it is with this prospect that I deal in the text. With respect to the further view that if science completed its work there would " be only one natural science, namely, physics, and only one kind of explanation, namely, the dynamic," it must suffice to say that I hold with Wallace that the ultimate explanation even of such a force as electricity is to be looked for outside physics ; and that the evolution theory presents " three stages in the development of the organic world where some new cause or power must have come into action "—causes " beyond all possibility of explanation by matter, its laws and forces," and to be referred to the " spiritual world." (" Darwinism,'' pp. 463–476.) *A fortiori* the social and historical sciences would not be reducible to physical explanations.

evolutionary science, which the century has applied in different ways to all knowledge, tend to exclude religion or to dethrone Christianity?

I shall best obviate an almost inevitable confusion if, before answering this question, I glance once again at the mediæval setting of Christianity with which, from long habit, the religion itself is so often largely identified, and from which it is so seldom adequately separated. Let me for a moment attempt to contrast the intellectual habits and methods of the old and the new syntheses—the secret of their respective power over the human mind, their limitations and tendencies.

The mediæval synthesis was, as we have seen, impressed on the imagination of Western Christendom by the pervading power of the visible Church. Regarded intellectually, it comprised a philosophical method, a resultant philosophy, and a religious faith.

The method was logical and dialectical—partly suggested by the Greek subtlety which, under the auspices of a diluted Aristotelianism, came into fashion in the twelfth and thirteenth centuries. " Partly," I say, because it also exhibits the peculiar childlike acuteness and teachableness of the youth of the new semi-barbaric Christendom. It combines the most critical logic with the utmost credulity as to facts. It is interminable in its questions, docile in accepting an answer, provided the answer be coherent. Lord Westbury's advice to the young barrister applies closely to its method—" Never make a mistake in logic. The facts remain at your disposal." Induction and the unfolding of Nature's objective laws were not yet glimpsed. Yet the keen deductive and synthetical tendency in the thinkers of the time made them long for system.

They could not rest satisfied with Bernard's "taste, for you cannot solve," or even with Anselm's "crede ut intelligas." The human mind could, at all events, supply a subjective unity for those who had no hope of finding objective law. Nature was largely outside the orderly scheme. It was a series of vivid dramatic scenes enacted by unseen agencies; not reliable or necessarily coherent, for the cheating devil was at work as well as the God of truth. Its more obvious and constant phenomena were worked into the intellectual system. But the idea of pervading rational law—the idea underlying the scientific unification of the seventeenth and eighteenth centuries—was not attained. Still less was the further conception of law underlying the onward course of the universe entertained. On the larger forces of Nature men looked with admiration, awe, and terror. These forces fell outside the rational synthesis, and were the shadow of the inscrutable Divine action on the world. And the designs of God were sometimes for the moment thwarted by those powers of darkness, over which, however, they finally prevailed.

But knowledge had its principle of order. Men looked for a clue to the intellectual maze, and they found it, in the Aristotelian Philosophy. The Logic of the Stagirite was already known to Abelard. The Metaphysic came over half a century later—at first in Arabian translations. In the pages of St. Thomas Aquinas its authority is absolute. "The Philosopher" is as final an authority as the Bible. Under the guidance of Aquinas the dialectical method attained to a complete synthetic philosophy. Holy Scripture, the Fathers, Aristotle, are the sources. Every conceivable question which the imagination can suggest is found in the problems which the philosopher-theologian is called upon to solve. Dialectic between *pros* and *cons* is the method of inquiry. Complete logical reconciliation is the object to be attained. Such is throughout, as we know, the form of the "Summa Theologica." Each section—or "article"—is introduced by a question—sometimes at first sight as fanciful and beyond human ken as a child's. Then follows the "Videtur"—a plausible answer opposed to the final solution, and worked up ingeniously : then the "Sed contra est"—a weighty consideration on the other side : and finally the "Respondeo dicendum" —the ultimate solution.

But while the synthesis proposed to unify—to show the consistency of Theism, Christianity, and Reason— it also left an important place for "Faith" in the individual. Here the later scholastics did not quite faithfully follow out the deeper suggestions of Aquinas. The Angelic Doctor holds that even Theism, though proveable by the highest *philosophical* reason, must for the multitude—and even for the average non-philosophical mind—be imparted "after the manner of faith." This is necessary not only from the insufficient philosophical endowment of the many, but still more because among those reputed wise (*qui sapientes dicuntur*) different conclusions are reached.[1] He had before his eyes the Pantheism of the great Arabian philosophers. Theism and Christianity are, then, regarded as consistent with the very highest knowledge attainable. They are provable by the truest process of reasoning coupled with revelation. But the educational force of the great mediæval Church imparts them to the multitude as a faith. This point is

[1] See "Summa contra Gentiles," c. 4.

of interest and importance in estimating the synthesis
of our own day.

The new synthesis began on very different lines
from the old. The chastening process of scientific
training and the eighteenth-century negations had
humbled the intellect and taught it its place. The
questioning which has led to the elaboration of the
new synthesis—unceasing as the mediæval—was no
longer the universal questioning of the child, but that
of the intelligent student who sees where real knowledge is attainable and valuable replies are really to
be looked for. The child interrogates his parent as
though he were omniscient. The youth asks his tutor
to complete a half-understood process. Mediævalism
inquired "de omni scibili et quibusdam aliis;" Science
"interrogates Nature," of whose ways it already knows
something.

This recognition of the limitations of possible
knowledge was the starting-point of the inductive
method.

It began, as we have seen, in the limited field of
physical science. Its very life has consisted in patient
recognition of fact—where mediævalism was weakest.
It is most tolerant of temporary logical incoherence,
of which mediævalism was most impatient. The intellectual qualities it calls for have in them a moral
element—candour, patience, love of truth, confidence
in its ultimate attainment—akin indeed (as has been
pointed out by Cardinal Newman[1]) to elements in
that Christian Faith which trusts to the future to solve
the enigma of the present, and to justify the perplexing
ways of God, but most dissimilar to the qualities called
for in the purely logical and dialectical tournaments of

---

[1] See the first of his Oxford University Sermons.

the Scholastics. And when the scientific method with new boldness advanced to the consideration not merely of existing nature, but of its genesis; not only of the physical world, but of human life and of history; when laws of progress and evolution in these departments were generalised by the inductive method, such moral qualities were the more necessary. Uniformity was less. Verification was far harder, often impossible. The conviction that patient research, absolute candour as to facts, the scrupulous and judicial estimate of evidence, would in the long run yield the nearest approach to truth of which man is capable, became a deep and inspiring faith and trust. This trust was of the essence of the synthetic process, which was not, like the mediæval, already logically complete for the individual mind, but has been and is a gradual attempt to find the objective law or unity in things; an attempt based on a belief in the ultimate consistency of knowledge, which, though it constantly receives a measure of verification, yet is still indefinitely distant in point of realisation.

We have then to consider, in each synthesis, first the great imaginative force which has given it power over the many; then its method and philosophy; and finally the religious faith which this allows and justifies.

Now, it seems evident, in the first place, that the great overmastering imaginative impulse which dominates the new synthesis is no longer theological, but scientific. In this respect there is a vast change in the position of religion. The mediæval Church, which seemed almost a tardy realisation of the material glory once associated with Messianic prophecy, has ceased to rule. But the question is asked—Is Christianity justifiable as a faith, though no longer as the dominating teacher of all knowledge? Is it consistent with the new philosophical synthesis? Can Christ Himself rule, though, once again, as a Child in the manger? Can He rule as He ruled over the Greek Apologists, to whom faith was imparted, not by a world-wide Church subduing the imagination, but by the intrinsic nature of the Christian message?

Scientific knowledge is no longer sought by the many amid the rays of light which surrounded the chair of the mediæval doctor of the Church of whom the Liturgy proudly sings : " In medio ecclesiæ aperuit os ejus et implevit eum dominus spiritu sapientiæ." Science now rules in her own Ecclesia. And she has expelled certain visions very dear to our ancestors, and closely entwined round their religion. Her researches have widely extended our realisation of the reign of law. The visible interferences of the supernatural, which appeared in pre-scientific times to be constant, and seemed evident to the mass of men, are now regarded by very few in the same light as of old.

Apart from this, however, the trend of thought appears to be moving already in the direction indicated by Mr. Balfour's prophecy. We can only speak of tendencies, because the new synthesis is, unlike the old, not a final mechanical system, but a gradual organic growth ; and we have no specimen of the full-grown organism. The philosophical method of the new movement is a complete synthesis of all knowledge *in the making ;* and religion is not excluded. Very much which in the controversies of the eighteenth century seemed threatened with destruction is now asserting itself. The sayings of Plato were laughed at by the eighteenth-century critic. Yet his words, ὁ θεὸς γεωμέτρει, come to us through two thousand years richly laden with the verifications supplied by modern science. The mathematician finds his own science at work in the laws of motion, in the phenomena of the planetary systems, in the laws of chemical combination.

The "Divine Child" seems, indeed, to many eager but very different onlookers, to be once more sitting in the temple among the doctors of science, hearing them and asking them questions, touching their answers with light from a world they had forgotten. Thus we have Catholics who find in the scientific view of evolution a new interpretation and justification of the actual past developments in their theology, and of the organic unity of the Church which the Reformation destroyed ; Protestants who see in modern science the fruits of the liberation of the intellect at the Reformation, which can be combined now as then with those personal relations with God to which Science can say neither "Aye" nor "No ; " deep thinkers who believe that the scientific study of the history of religion should issue in a Catholic theology which would allot its true function to that individualism of which Protestantism was a travesty—whose dream is of a Catholic Church uniting the deep spirituality which the saints have ever maintained with a comprehensive intellectual outlook, combining the fulness of personal and intellectual, with the fulness of organic life. To all of these Christianity appears to be necessary to the completion of the new as of the old synthesis.

The new mode of controversy differs from the old. "We will not attack you," Mr. Morley has said to the orthodox Christianity; "we shall explain you." Absorption by a higher explanation, and not acute argumentative opposition, is the victory known to the

new method—which sees a measure of truth everywhere, and victory only as the greater comprehensiveness of the higher. Thesis and antithesis are giving
place to synthesis. And it may well be maintained
that the last word by way of explanation can never
rest with science, but must appeal beyond it. The
agnostic, indeed, will say now as ever that the appeal
meets with no reply : that the apparent answer is but
the echo of our own voices. But if answered at all, it
can only be by religion. Details in once-accepted
theological speculation may be outgrown, but not the
essence of religion. Phœnix-like it will rise from its
funeral pyre. And this is, as we have said, what has
actually happened and is still happening. The pre-
posterous enterprise of Rabaud de St. Etienne, "Tout
détruire, puisque tout est à recréer," has proved utopian
in religion as in politics. The reactionary Conservatives
and the materialists, who feared and hoped that the
development of science would finally banish the conception of mind as the source of all, have both proved
wrong. The Darwinians seemed to begin by denying
teleology. Natural selection was supposed to have taken
the place of rational purpose. But eventually even
the more destructive of them admitted, with Professor
Huxley, a "wider teleology"—a *régime* of rational law
which led from the formless and simple to the more
complicated organisms, and from the inanimate to the
highest intelligence. And such a representative biolo-
gist as Wallace felt constrained to postulate a spiritual
world underlying the whole process. A view akin to
Wallace's, of spirit underlying the evolution of phenomena, is that of the best philosophers of history.

But we find a similar and still more interesting
process of synthetic revival, transcending the older

oppositions, in the dogmatic systems themselves. The old fixed structure of dogmatic theology, regarded statically, was fiercely attacked by Voltaire and by the last-century philosophers as a mass of superstition; by Hume as empty words. The various preachers of Deism, and of the scientific agnosticism which succeeded it—nay, even the liberal exponents of Protestantism exemplified by such thinkers as Whately and Arnold—treated much or even most of it as an arbitrary addition to Christianity. Auguste Sabatier, in his celebrated "Esquisse d'une Philosophie de la Religion," voices the spirit of his time when he regards theology dynamically and almost reverses the eighteenth-century verdict. Dogma is to him the expression of religion in various ages. It is necessary to the life of religion and to its transmission, as language is a natural and necessary vehicle for the expression and communication of thought. Professor Harnack's "Dogmengeschichte" supplies the *pièces justificatives* for Sabatier's view, although Harnack himself fails fully to analyse the philosophy underlying his own facts. And we have been lately reminded that John Henry Newman had already anticipated the deeper suggestions of these writers, supplemented them by a more accurate historical survey, and pointed out their bearing on Catholic theology in a work the full significance of which his contemporaries were not in a position to understand.

And the names of Sabatier and Newman remind us that this reconciling power of the evolution of thought has explained, and, in the small minority of deep thinkers, largely transcended the deadly quarrel between the popular Catholic and Protestant philosophy of religion. The tendency of Protestantism had early become anti-dogmatic. It fell back on the simple forms of Scripture. It rested on religious feeling rather than on complicated definitions. Later developments were in its eyes superstitions and accretions. Catholicism, on the contrary, had been throughout dogmatic, and had stereotyped its dogmas. On the one side it was urged, " These dogmatic formulæ are superstitious additions to Christ's teaching ; " on the other, " They are immutable and eternal truths." The antithesis, apparently fixed and unsurmountable, was solved by history. Both views were inadequate and unhistorical, yet both were based on a partial truth. The *formulæ* did represent the eternal truths taught by Christ, yet to view them as identical in *form* with Christ's teaching, to deny the doctrine of "development," was inaccurate. History supplied to each view that unknown coefficient which was needed to make them both true. History showed that the primitive biblical teaching must, if it lives and energises among men, develop in relation to the philosophies and civilisations amid which Christians lived, reacting upon them, absorbing, rejecting, modifying, and being itself changed in outward form and expression. Hence the gradual multiplication of the dogmatic formulæ. History thus showed that the formulæ, though they may be the lawful heirs and representatives of Christ's teaching, could not be regarded as having been crystallised from the first and for ever into their present form by Christ Himself. A more enlightened Protestantism had to admit the value of the dogmas, deeper Catholic thought came to recognise that it was only in germ that they had existed from the first.

Once again, Sabatier recognises the evolution of dogma. But the living organism which preserved the dogma and effected its development was the Catholic Church. Of this organism Protestantism had got rid. Yet its value—apart from its abuses—is now more and more generally appreciated. Here again a distinguished writer, whose antecedents are those of a Scotch Presbyterian, and an English Jesuit Father, approach each other very nearly. Speaking of Protestantism Professor Caird writes : " To the Protestant it seemed to be simply a return to the original purity of the faith; to the Catholic it seemed to be a fatal revolt against the only organisation by which Christianity could be realised. *Really it partook of both characters.*" And each writer seeks to urge on his co-religionists the necessity of a world-religion at once personal and organic. While the Scotch professor would desire the renewed existence of an organism which should voice the universal religious reason in the development of Christianity, Father Tyrrell in his "External Religion" has ably insisted upon the entire consistency of the Catholic ideal with that personal apprehension of religion by each man for himself which Professor Caird regards as the true aim of Protestantism—although that aim has been in fact combined with an individualism which in itself was "mere anarchy." That an inspiring faith which is based on corporate conviction, which realises and liberates the highest aspirations, is essential to the highest religious life is the persuasion of both writers. The Jesuit might have written the following words, which are actually those of the Scotch professor :—

"To us who have outlived the period when it could be supposed that the destruction of old, evidences in itself the construction of new forms of life and thought, it cannot but be obvious that the principles of private judgment and individual liberty are nothing more than negations. For as the real problem of an intellectual life is how to rise to a judgment which is more than a private judgment, so the real problem of our practical life is how to realise a liberty that is more than individual licence." [1]

Within the Anglican Church itself we have signs of the same *rapprochement* between the synthetic principles of Catholicism and the individualism which is progressive but not disruptive. The reconciliation is visible in the best minds, notwithstanding party antipathies which remain very strong. " Essays and Reviews" represented a survival of the old individualistic liberalism. " Lux Mundi" voices the most intellectual school of Anglican divines. The former was historical mainly in the sense of destroying the old—after the fashion of Colensoism. It was on the whole anti-dogmatic and unconstructive. Its genius was that of the eighteenth century rather than of the nineteenth. Historical reconstruction is very near to the heart of the school represented by " Lux Mundi."

Evolution is, in the view of most of its exponents, essentially optimistic. And it has good reason to be. It regards the wonderful mental equipment of man, sensible and intellectual, as the lineal descendant of the consciousness of the amœba. Reversion it recognises, but as temporary—like the receding wave in a flowing tide. It may be pessimistic with regard to a limited time. For the wave may recede during a generation or a century. But the world-spirit on the whole advances. Hope and Faith are justified and

" Social Philosophy of Comte," 2nd edit., p. 195. (James Maclehose; Glasgow, 1893.)

substantiated by a process which has already achieved so much. And this very quality tends towards the realisation of Mr. Balfour's prophecy. For ethical evolution can only attain its highest conceivable limit in religion.

The Christian Ideal, the relations of the human spirit with God, and Hegel's moral goal — self-realisation through self-denial—may well be regarded as completing the evolutionary scheme rather than as clashing with it. For Comte the highest in man sums up the best that has been achieved in the whole course of evolution. For Herbert Spencer the Unknowable is the underlying Power behind evolution to which this achievement is due. Comte, under the symbol of Humanity, would worship the best we know. Spencer would worship the Unknown Cause. Professor Caird truly says that each has half the truth. The two halves may well be combined in the Christian faith which, in Caird's words, "finds God in man, and man in God; which makes us regard the Absolute Being as finding His best name and definition in what we most revere and love, or, what is the same thing, makes us see in that growing idea of moral perfection—which is the highest result of human development—the interpretation or revelation of the Absolute."

"All criticism of the world," writes Caird, " while it detects evil in particular, implies an ultimate optimism. For if such criticism pretends to be more than the utterance of the tastes and wishes of the individual, it cannot but claim to be the expression of an objective principle—a principle which, in spite of all appearances to the contrary, is realising itself in the world. If, as Hegel said, the ' history of the world is the judgment of the world,' then conversely every true moral judgment is an anticipation of history ; it is a discovery of the hidden forces that are already working out their triumph in the world even by means of that which seems most to oppose them ; it is a prophetic sympathy with the spirit of the years to come which is 'yearning to mix itself with life.' It is this objective character which often makes the words of genius carry with them such weight and power. ' He spake as one having authority, and not as the scribes,' can be truly said only of One whose speech was like some natural force in its independence of merely individual or of temporary influences. . . . The universal spirit of man in the long struggle of development is becoming more and more clearly conscious of itself and of the law of the world. It is only as the organ of this spirit that the individual can claim to judge the world ; nor can we make that claim without taking up the ground of philosophical optimism and acknowledging that the soul of the world is just." [1]

I have attempted to outline a movement characteristic of the time-spirit of the past century—a movement the general nature of which appears to me remarkable and quite unmistakable. Yet there are in the nature of the case certain appearances which do not at first sight tally with what has here been said.

In the first place, there have been many eighteenth-century survivals visible among us in the nineteenth century. We may glance at a few obvious instances in our own country. Hallam, Dean Merivale, and even Macaulay do not entirely fulfil the ideals of Ranke in their historical method. The Mills are at first sight utilitarian survivals of Benthamism. Hamilton is an individualist. The *laissez faire* of Cobden is essentially unhistorical. The Liberalism of John Bright and of Lord Macaulay is also, like

[1] " Social Philosophy of Comte," pp, 130, 131.

J. S. Mill's Liberalism, individualist. Nay, the whole
Liberal movement of the fifties and sixties partook
of the same character.

I believe that such instances are not really at variance with the general movement I have sketched.
They only remind us that the characteristics of a
contemporary movement are unequally exhibited in
individuals according to their special circumstances,
and that the majority only gradually recognise its
exact nature. But they are often the instruments of
a movement whose principles they do not adequately
master. Strenuous individualism is, as we have seen,
an important factor in intellectual developments which
are in their ultimate analysis corporate. Macaulay's
mind was not speculative. His traditions were Whig,
and they acted as prejudices. But he put into his
historical work that indefatigable and conscientious
research which the new historical spirit inspired.
And, in spite of bias, he made a noteworthy contribution to its objects by making the past really live
again. John Mill was eminently characterised by
the splendid impartiality of the new method and its
teachableness, as opposed to eighteenth-century contemptuous dogmatism. Although his inherited standpoint was individualist, he was, on the other hand,
deeply affected by Comte, and had a share in the
intellectual parentage of Spencer. The Kantian
element in Hamilton prepared the way in England
for Hegelianism. The standpoint of Cobden and
Bright has largely given way to the organic principles
of Conservatism or Socialism in politics ; and *laissez
faire* in economics is almost dead. Mr. Morley and
Mr. Balfour both have an affection for the eighteenth
century, but both have made remarkable contributions

—as I have already indicated—to a view of the history of thought which cannot be fully developed without a clear recognition of the organic structure of that society in which the thought of the individual energises.

So much may be said as to the survival of eighteenth-century methods and their value. And I might point to survivals among theological writers of methods belonging to a much earlier date. The organic view explains these symptoms rather than suffers from them. For very unequal development among individuals, who form, nevertheless, units borne onward by the corporate tendency, is just what characterises that view.

But there is another phase now visible which appears to be not a survival but a reaction, and yet embodies an important element of the very time-spirit it opposes. It was pointed out by Lord Acton a few years ago as one of our "rocks ahead." It has recently been emphatically noted by another writer as a growing danger. Of late years in England the tremendous increase of available material and development of specialisation in history—a development in itself due to research under the influence of the new scientific faith—has had the curious result of an apparent return to an eighteenth-century defect— to the defect of *mere* specialism, which has lost all sense of the synthesis to which it should minister. Faith in the value of the new methods has, like other faiths, sometimes forgotten its rational basis and meaning. The specialists have become so attached to critical research exercised over a small area of investigation, and to facts apart from motives or tendencies, as to disparage higher and more comprehensive views of history, and in general to view "ideas" with suspicion. "They assert," says an able writer,[1] "that history ought to deal only with facts. So did Ranke. But Ranke meant that the historian should stand by absolutely impartially, and let the epoch which he was studying develop itself, in all its aspects, without incurring either his moral condemnation or approval. The new school mean that the historian has no business with ideas, or motives, or tendencies; it is his business solely to inquire, Did this happen or not happen? Did it happen this way or that? This intention to limit the historian's view to the concrete fact is naturally joined with an intense specialisation. Nothing could be further from the historian of to-day than the desire to work with the whole field of history constantly before his mind, as Ranke worked. Large views are false; the only genuine work is done in a corner."

As Bacon utterly failed to understand the light cast on observation by hypothesis, based on a wide view of facts and uniformities, so these modern English historians, with British unimaginative practicality and a British contempt for that in which they do not excel, have incurred the risk of turning into very refined and highly developed Dryasdusts and Casaubons. Such writers should remember the late Lord Acton's warning: "The want of an energetic understanding of the sequence and real significance of events . . . is ruin to a student of history. . . . It is playing at study to see nothing but the unmeaning and unsuggestive surface." Historians should learn from men of science "how to secure fulness and soundness

[1] Mr. J. A. Nicklin, in "The Mind of the Century," p. 68. (Fisher Unwin.)

in induction, how to restrain and to employ with safety hypothesis and analogy."

Very different from the ideal of this modern English school is that exhibited by the great German writers Mommsen and Droysen—the historians of Republican Rome and of the Macedonian Empire—or by Döllinger, the historian of the Church. Very different, too, is the model exhibited by more recent German masters. To turn the limelight on facts from every point of view, by imaginative hypothesis as to tendencies and motives, provided only that hypothesis is suggested by objective fact and not by subjective prepossession, is again the way of such writers as Harnack and the great biblical critics of Germany. Facts in the unimaginative are often barren. They cannot by themselves make the past live again, and it must live in order to disclose its vital secrets. True, the historian who speculates must, like Darwin, have a keen eye for opposing facts, and must be ready, in deference to them, to amend his theory. But facts without hypotheses cannot yield a knowledge of the deeper forces of history, any more than physical phenomena can, without hypothesis or experiment, disclose the secret laws of Nature.

That this tendency among English historians to neglect "ideas" is only temporary I cannot doubt. The time-spirit which it opposes is too strong to be checked. And the causes of such a tendency are partly ascertainable.

To some extent they are to be found, it may be, in a reaction against Froude and Macaulay—partly just, perhaps, in Froude's case, unfair in that of Macaulay, as Sir Richard Jebb has, I hope, convinced everybody. The dominion over Froude of ideas which were prejudices, his skilful use (on occasion)—under their influence—of research undertaken with a bias to make something live again which did duty for the past, but was not the past, offended against one of the most fundamental principles of the historical spirit. Froude substituted the insertion of his own ideas into history for the search for the ideas underlying history, and for their organic connexion. This jugglery—the professing to find in the past what he had in reality put there—made people suspicious. Ideas were discredited by their somewhat unscrupulous use.

But, again, the enormous growth of material, and the consequent discovery of evidence which modifies received conclusions, have led some of the best historians to regard all philosophy of history as premature. I would submit, however, that this view—very similar to Bacon's view of physical discovery—admits of a similar answer in both cases. Hypothesis is necessary to test the bearing of each fact. It is not necessarily final, but is more often itself material for further investigation. Copernicus's famous work is an object-lesson in the value of hypothesis, even though its first form be crude and fanciful. The highly trained historical imagination is the key to the laws of historical evolution. Its possessor is the pioneer. For one verdict of historical genius, which fresh discoveries change, they will confirm or partially confirm ten. It is the very fact of Nature's uniformity which justifies the scientific imagination as a clue to realms of fact and not of fancy : and so, too, that ideas and tendencies do develop largely according to law, justifies the wide imaginative sweep of a great historian. But the sure use of this faculty involves constant practice and severe training. If it is not cultivated, it will become unskilful and uncertain. It may conceivably be almost atrophied. And consequent failures and blunders will seem to justify a policy of limitation prompted in some instances by fastidious scrupulousness, in others by mediocrity. The study of forces and causes in history is necessary to keep up to its highest level the very mental instrument for turning facts to good account. Let us here again note Lord Acton's wise advice: " Study problems in preference to periods ; for instance, the derivation of Luther, the scientific influence of Bacon, the predecessors of Adam Smith, the mediæval masters of Rousseau, the consistency of Burke." [1]

That there is some truth in what has recently been affirmed—that " the age has suddenly become bankrupt in ideas," if the remark be applied to England, many of us are uneasily half-conscious. The defect is not confined to English historians. The complaint is made that our philosophers are coming to be mere compilers, or exponents of the system of others rather than thinkers ; perpetuators of the mannerisms and limitations of great philosophers, rather than heirs to their spirit bent on developing their thought ; well equipped for examination, rather than productive disciples ; that ideas are imported ready-made from Germany, and exhibited rather than used. In statecraft we have (it is said) few men of creative genius. Among our younger statesmen especially, for one who is characteristically a "man of ideas," as, for instance, Mr. Wyndham, we have very many whose ability, however considerable, is exclusively practical. With the passing of Tennyson, Browning, and Arnold, ideas

[1] " The Study of History," p. 63.

have diminished among English poets. Newman and Martineau have not left their equals in this respect in our theology. In the intellectual sphere a certain loss of individuality which often leads to the indiscriminate adoption of the conclusions or even the *obiter dicta* of the specialist authority, as so many dogmas, with little regard for context or antecedent reasoning, is apt to create for some the difficulty which David experienced in Saul's armour. One is tempted sometimes to wish for a little rashness, for the scrip and stone and sling, for some exercise of adventurous faith in place of barren correctness.

All this means, no doubt, that we are at times oppressed by the magnitude of the task which the scientific view of the world has opened before us. But it does not mean that at bottom we question that view. The youth of the nineteenth century was sanguine and free. Its mature age seems in some degree to have got into certain grooves, under pressure of work, and to have become overweighted by the actual presence of an accumulation of material which could be dealt with very buoyantly in imagination. But the ideals of its youth have not passed away, and accidental causes will bring them again to the surface in our new century as accidental causes have obscured them. Most disorders tend eventually to work their own cure if they are not fatal.

A somewhat similar paralysis of the thinking powers threatens us in the ordinary daily life of an over-civilised time. As the crowd of material oppresses the student so the dazzling multiplicity of events, places, writings, brought before us by the modern press and modern appliances, confuses the average mind. In both instances the result tells against real thought. It leads in the one case to somewhat mechanical labour, in the other to a life of passive impressions.   But as the boy who, emerging from college, is dazzled by the variety of life into which he may be suddenly thrown, eventually (it is to be hoped) finds his level and chooses his own line, so with society as a whole.   Further specialisation will tend to make the historian bring back a more comprehensive method into his own sphere.   He will not attend to what he cannot deal with quite freely and fully, with the whole sum of his faculties, and not merely with the narrower instruments for estimating evidence.   The impressionableness of English society will, we may well believe, be again replaced by the sturdier qualities of John Bull—who was a very good sound thinker in his own way.   Ideas will return to the intellectual ; sound, active, independent thought to the mass.

But perhaps this complacent prophecy is due to that optimism which Professor Caird holds to be at the heart of the evolutionary view of the world.   Be this as it may, I cling to it as a hope, unwilling to acquiesce in the supposition that the specialists in England will be ultimately false to what Renan has described as the very essence of the historical movement of the century.

"If the immense historical development of the latter end of the eighteenth and the nineteenth centuries has been productive of any result at all," Renan writes, "it is that which proves that there is a life of humanity, just as there is a life of the individual; that history is not a purposeless series of isolated facts. . . . History is the necessary form of the science of everything.   The science of languages means the history of languages; the science of literatures and religions means the history of literatures and religions.   The science of the human intellect means the history of the human intellect. To attempt to seize a given moment only of those successive existences in order to dissect and to fixedly examine it, is simply falsifying their nature. For they are not complete at a given moment, they are merely tending towards completion." [1]

[1] "The Future of Science."

II.

THE RIGIDITY OF ROME.

An acute observer has remarked that a "novel of the time," to be successful, should put into concrete form some phase of the "time-spirit." Men should find in it the definite expression of what had been vaguely dwelling in their own minds. I think it may be said similarly that the somewhat contemptuous comparison instituted a few years ago by Dr. Jessopp, between the Papacy and the Celestial Empire,[1] is effective, as expressing (in an exaggerated form) a thought which is vaguely in the minds of many. It conveys just that conception of the Papacy which makes many Englishmen impatient at the bare phrase "reunion with Rome." Many who have had a personal respect for Pope Leo XIII. and who are not insensible to a certain rigid strength in the papal power, or even to the value of Continental Catholicism as a breakwater against the running flood of Anarchism and Socialism, refuse to consider seriously the claims which the Papacy makes in its own behalf. As a matter of political expediency the Papacy may be utilised. It may even be approached, as China might, in a spirit of conciliation—as a power which might still on occasion prove a valuable ally. But to take seriously

[1] See *Nineteenth Century* for June, 1895.

the claims of the Roman See as a whole is like contemplating the possibility of a reign of pigtails and mandarins in Europe. The Immaculate Conception and Papal Infallibility remain as standing reminders that an acceptance of such claims is not only impossible to realise, but absurd to think of.

That a fusion between English religious thought, with its existing preconceptions, and the Papal Church as it now is, is simply out of the question, few will be found to deny. And if we add that the man of the world in the days of Justin Martyr would have held truly that any fusion of the "pernicious" Oriental "superstition" known as Christianity with the then existing civilisation of Imperial Rome was out of the question, it is not because the cases are quite parallel, but only to remind ourselves that potent spiritual forces may be held very cheap even by highly civilised men of the world. What seems and is out of the question in one generation may, where living and powerful forces are concerned—forces which can work wonderful changes, whether in the sphere of adaptation or of destruction—come eventually into the region of practical politics. Without saying that this is a reason for maintaining seriously that the union of all Christians under the papal obedience is a probability in the future, it is a useful reminder that to arrive at the eventual possibilities of the case, we must go somewhat beyond the so-called common-sense judgment of men of the world. In such men the instinctive sense of the existing state of things is strong and accurate; but their realisation of the nature of the true forces at work, and of their probable effects in the long run, is often proportionally defective.

And Dr. Jessopp's analogy itself brings out

strikingly both the excellence and the defects of such practical judgments.   It would be difficult to express more forcibly (with the additional vividness given by caricature) the existing relation between the average Englishman and the Papacy, than by comparing it to that of a European with the Chinese civilisation.   And yet it would be difficult to give a falser idea of the forces really at work, which must be estimated in forecasting the future.   Both Empires, the Papal and the Celestial, are apparently self-contained and self-sufficient, dealing in their daily life with a different class of ideals and aims from any with which Englishmen are familiar, refusing to acknowledge an inferiority which seems to Englishmen obvious—nay, each in its special sphere incurring the imputation that it is haughty, unbending, uncompromising.   Both Empires are ruled by a supreme authority which strikes outsiders as autocratic and exacting.   Both are in occasional contact with the surrounding civilisations— forces to be reckoned with by them, yet in the opinion of their critics learning little from them and assimilating still less.

So much for the apparent similarity in the present. But how far are these features of present resemblance significant for the future ?   If you point to the marble statue on the Pincian Hill in Rome, which is supposed to be a perfect likeness to Savonarola at the age of thirty,[1] and argue that because the bust is very like him as he then was, and will never change, therefore the rèal Savonarola could never have altered, or grown, or assimilated food and oxygen, or responded to surrounding conditions, your reasoning is obviously defective.   The resemblance between him and the statue

[1] I speak from memory as to the age represented.

was external and temporary. The same living forces which made him the manner of man from which the statue was copied, must later on have made him grow unlike it again. And if we look at the supposed resemblance in type between the Papal Church and the Chinese Empire, we find (even apart from the obvious caricature involved) something of the same sort.

Briefly, the Chinese Empire is, as the writer to whom I refer reminds us, rigid and exclusive for the reasons which have made it so for four thousand years. Self-contained immobility is, as Dr. Jessopp explains, its genius. The Papal Church, on the other hand, would seem in part to owe the rigidity which impresses its critics (paradoxical as it may sound) to its very adaptability. Rigidity and exclusiveness were in their degree the indispensable means of adapting itself to a critical situation—of withstanding the widespread revolt of the sixteenth century against the principles of its constitution.

To appreciate this difference let us read Dr. Jessopp's account of the Chinese civilisation. While enjoying "an unbroken peace and liberty," he writes, " it held itself aloof from all other nations of the world ; " it "engaged in the study of *its own literature*," and was "in all things self-contained and self-supporting." And the typical representative of this exclusive system is the "mysterious emperor " who " dwells apart in a kind of sacred isolation, still regarded by his subjects as king of kings and lord of lords, still asking for nothing but that he should be left alone and undisturbed." This is no enemy's account of the Chinese civilisation. The preservation of an unalloyed local tradition in culture and manners is the boast of the Chinaman, even when he has had the opportunity of comparing himself with the best products of European education. Some of my readers may remember the warning of an eminent Chinaman of our own time—Marquis Tseng—to a young Chinese diplomatist who was accredited to a European Embassy. "Your great difficulty," he said, "will be to conceal your contempt for the barbarous ways of the Europeans ; but you must learn to do it, else you will never be successful in your career."

The Catholic Church, on the other hand, has been exclusive, not from choice in time of peace, but from necessity in time of war. The polity she has striven to defend was the outcome not of insensibility to the civilisations around her, but of her own assimilation of the genius and intellect of various places and epochs. Her schools have at different times blended with and adapted to their own purposes Platonic and Aristotelian thought, Jewish and Arabian speculation. "The doctrine of the Divine Word," writes Cardinal Newman, "is Platonic ; the doctrine of the Incarnation is Indian ; of a Divine kingdom is Judaic ; of angels and demons is Magian." The metaphysic of the Schools is Aristotelian ; their natural theology is largely based on the philosophy of Maimonides. The avowed aim of the Roman Church at the Reformation was the preservation of the living organism of the Church universal, which had thus embodied, in its teaching and traditions, so much of the intellectual and spiritual life of Europe and the East. One of its characteristics which impressed such students of Church History as Wiseman and Newman was that very power of assimilation which Dr. Jessopp now denies to it. Cardinal Wiseman has remarked that it reflected in great measure the intellectual character of each successive age ;[1] and Cardinal Newman in a suggestive essay has maintained that from the very beginning the Church constantly claimed and assimilated the truths presented to her by the schools and peoples with which she came in contact.

"Wherever she went," (he writes), "in trouble or in triumph, still she was a living spirit, the mind and voice of the Most High : ' sitting in the midst of the doctors, both hearing them and asking them questions,' claiming to herself what they said rightly, correcting their errors, supplying their defects, completing their beginnings, expanding their surmises, and thus gradually by means of them enlarging the range and refining the sense of her own teaching. So far, then, from her creed being of doubtful origin because it resembles foreign theologies, we hold that one special way in which Providence has imparted Divine knowledge to us has been by enabling her to draw and collect it together out of the world." [2]

The intellectual adaptability involved in this assimilative power was notably shown in the Scholastic movement of the thirteenth century. The peripatetic philosophy and the dialectical method, so fiercely denounced by St. Bernard in his contests with Abelard, so much disliked and suspected by the Fathers, became fused with the very theology of the Church. Aristotle, the *bête noire* of the early Christian doctors, became an authority almost as supreme in philosophy as were the inspired writers in divinity. The natural theology of Rabbi Moyses—as St. Thomas styles the Jewish thinker Maimonides—was adopted in its most characteristic features by Albertus Magnus and St. Thomas Aquinas.[3]

---

[1] This view is developed in the Inaugural Lecture delivered by Cardinal Wiseman in 1862 before the Catholic Academia.

[2] See " Essay on the Development of Christian Doctrine," p. 381.

[3] The extent of the obligations of St. Thomas Aquinas to Maimonides

The Catholic polity, the outcome, on its intellectual side, of the fusion of various phases of civilisation with the unchanging essence of the Divine revelation, was directly attacked at the Reformation. Luther did not, like a Savonarola, or even in his measure an Erasmus, aim at mere reform within the pale of the Church, in the light of the truest spiritual ideas of the time. He attacked the principle of unity. To preserve her very existence the Church had to resist the Reformers *à outrance.* The Papacy was for nearly three hundred years in a state of war.

We have, then, to ask whether an attitude which in the Chinaman is a manifestation of his own rigid and self-contained genius, may not be in the Papal Church the adaptation to a state of war of an organism which is neither unduly rigid nor self-contained ; whether the very traces its theology bears of fusion with the thought proper to many times, places, and civilisations, are not standing records of a character diametrically opposed to that of the self-sufficient and narrow Chinaman. And, further, the very fact that this external appearance of rigidity impresses English critics as so significant, reminds us that the state of war also caused a mutual estrangement which has led its critics to judge by appearances. Strangers form their impression of a bare acquaintance from his manners and incidental words or actions. Friends interpret his incidental bearing by their knowledge of himself. A man who visits Italy for the first time sees two Italians conversing, and fancies that they are in a passion. One who is familiar with the genius of the race knows that no more is indicated by their manner

is drawn out in Dr. Guttmann's "Das Verhältniss des Thomas von Aquinas zum Judenthum," etc. (Göttingen, 1891.)

than the animation which gives piquancy to debate. So, too, it requires a real inner familiarity with the peculiar genius of Catholicism to avoid very grave misunderstanding of its separate manifestations; and the English tradition of three hundred years has substituted for that familiarity both estrangement and prejudice. Catholic doctrines are looked at by Englishmen in the light of an unconscious anti-Catholic tradition. A rigidity due to passing circumstances is assumed to be the very essence of the Church. And the most uncouth account of her dogmas becomes, consequently, the most probable.

I am aware that the consideration which I am suggesting opens a far larger subject than I can hope to deal with in the limits of an essay. But I will endeavour to indicate its general bearing on the question which Dr. Jessopp raises, leaving reservations and modifications for another opportunity. Dr. Jessopp despairs of any approach to reunion, because for reunion mutual concession is necessary, and because the " Chinese" genius of the Roman Church, evinced in the Papal Letter of 1896, " To the English people," shows this to be out of the question. And so far as the kind of concessions spoken of in some quarters is concerned—for instance, the abatement of the papal claim to infallibility, which is a defined doctrine—no doubt he is right.

But what I would suggest is that the real difficulty, while it goes much deeper than anything Dr. Jessopp appears to contemplate, does nevertheless, when it is reached, offer some hope of an eventual solution. When the great mass of Englishmen, who think on such questions at all, regard the Papal Church as " Chinese;" when even a High Churchman like Mr.

Gore[1] looks on the Papal Encyclical on Holy Scripture not only as inadequate, but as absurd; when Carlyle can only describe the modern successors of Abbot Samson as "abominable monks;" when we see in the pages of the late Mr. T. Mozley, and many another, that the doctrine defined at the Vatican Council appears to them not only untrue, but simply preposterous, we are reminded that the differences between us are far deeper than any which controversies on "Anglican orders" or on purely theological doctrines represent. It is the wide difference of intellectual tradition, and (in many cases) of ethical principles, which really separates us. These form the context whereby dogmas are explained, and cast a reflected light on the doctrines themselves.

If, on the other hand, much which makes the modern Englishman regard the Papal Church as "Chinese" is due to a state of things in that Church which was exceptional and temporary—which made it for a time markedly unsympathetic with contemporary thought; if much more is due to misunderstanding on the part of those from whom it has been so long estranged; and if many of the causes which have led to this double estrangement are gradually ceasing to exist, there may be hope for a great modification in their mutual relations in the future. It is obvious that if such a doctrine as Papal Infallibility was maintained, long before it was defined, by men of such moderation as Newman and Fénelon—if it was regarded by them as the condition marked out by common sense and experience for making the unity of the Church a reality and not a mere name—it cannot be the preposterous tenet which it appears to the average

[1] Now Bishop of Worcester.

Englishman. It may be true or it may be false ; but it is not likely to be absurd. It has evidently meant one thing to Fénelon, another to the typical Englishman. And this instance is representative of many another. Two corporate bodies, in England especially, for centuries as much separated as different races, have not only come to have fixed habits of thought at variance with each other, but have to a great extent lost both the language and the opportunities which should enable them at least to make clear the points of divergence, and to explain that context of their tenets which makes the views on either side consistent with common sense and even with sanity. The language spoken, the whole intellectual equipment, the class of ideas exercising the mind on either side, have become largely distinct.

But if Cardinal Newman is right in maintaining that assimilation with the thought surrounding it is a normal process in the Catholic and Roman Church, and if the proverb " History repeats itself" is true, there may be in this department hope for very far-reaching change both within the Church and without ; of a far wider assimilation of contemporary thought within, of the consequent diminution of prejudices and misconceptions,—still often so great as to be almost unintelligible to Catholics—without.

This change would, then, involve two elements— increased individualism among Catholics, issuing in a fusion of Catholic thought with the intellectual movements of the time, and a consequent growth of the recognition among those without the Roman communion of the nature and power of Catholicism.

Let me endeavour to explain my meaning more clearly. The Catholic and Roman Church accepted at Trent (as has already been said) the state of siege. The compromises fondly hoped for by such as Erasmus were definitely rejected. Under the circumstances, nothing short of compromises of principle would stay the popular clamour, and to these she could not consent. She decided that rigid definition, and the concentration of her own forces, were the only course, if vital principles were to be effectively defended. Her work became primarily militant. Organised zeal and skilful debate were at a premium. The intellectual element, properly so called, was necessarily for a time sacrificed for the controversial and the devotional. Acute polemic, intense and united *esprit de corps*, the spirit of the martyr, and, above all, absolute military obedience, became essential to the preservation of the organism against the general attack.

In the time of siege, court-martial supersedes trial by jury; the cultivation of the arts is less important than the training of good soldiers; the workmen who had been occupied in building museums and lecture halls are drawn off to repair fortifications, which, though indispensable for preserving the city, are useless for the general culture of its citizens. The length of the siege is likely to be the measure of the completeness of the transformation from the industrial and peaceful to the military state, of the concentration of all the forces in the city on its defence, and of the neglect of those merely intellectual or artistic or scientific pursuits which make a full and refined life. The very success of the defence will depend on energy being diverted from the merely intellectual to the practical. And success must be at the cost of destruction among its buildings, and injury to life and limb among its inhabitants. When the siege is raised we do not find a perfect commissariat, exuberant health among the soldiers, intellectual activity, theatres and lecture halls and museums the centres of interest, but rather full hospitals, buildings which sadden the eye of the architect, a sternness of discipline in daily life which would seem barbarous in time of peace ; and we find, probably, on the other hand, intense *esprit de corps* and deep enthusiasm among an exhausted remnant.

Dr. Jessopp's own article should be a warning that analogies are often very partial. But, up to a certain point, what has here been said helps us to understand the intellectual position of the Church in communion with the Apostolic See since the Reformation, and more especially of the Catholic body in England. Its very constitution, among ourselves, its Vicars Apostolic and missionary priests, were for many years reminders that it sojourned in a hostile land. The war once declared, the greatest minds on either side became necessarily intolerant, pardonably unfair. Sir Thomas More, so strong an advocate of toleration in the *Utopia*, was known as a persecutor, and held it to be his only possible course, as Chancellor, in the anarchy which was characteristic of one phase of the Reformation. The genius and breadth of Milton's mind did not prevent his excluding " Papists " from his scheme of toleration on the score that they were idolaters. Besiegers and besieged, as time went on, became, in their separation, ignorant of each other's character ; and the intellectual virtues of justice, candour, and even the Christian virtue of charitableness became less in place than the more military qualities of *esprit de corps*, skill in the war of words, prompt obedience to orders.

The future priests were withdrawn by the Council of Trent from the universities, and each Bishop was exhorted to establish a seminary for their training as disciplined soldiers of the Church. The Jesuits— those wonderful Janissaries of the Papal Army who arose to defend the ancient order—represented in their military character, and in their very name—"the Company of Jesus"—the genius of the crisis. They surveyed the theological field as well as the field of practical discipline and personal piety. Dogma and philosophy were thus largely removed from the free discussions of the universities, and consecrated to the controversial requirements of the ecclesiastical institutes which were fashioning soldiers of debate and martyrs for the faith. The gradual analysis and further explication of theological truth, due to the sifting by the schools of the traditionary theology, in the light of the thought of the time, gave place to that defence of existing positions which is exacted by the needs of polemic.[1] The deep truths and ancient traditions, which the Church was pledged to preserve, for the moment needed some other protection than the normal process of being gradually analysed and developed by living intellects within the Church. They could not be left to derive growth and nourishment freely from the intellectual life of the age, as plants do from the surrounding light and oxygen. The speculation abroad was perverse and unfair. Contact with surrounding thought and its attendant analysis might easily lead to corruption

[1] The historical method of Petavius and the labours of the Bollandist Fathers are reminders, however, that we owe a far larger intellectual debt to the Jesuits than is represented by their contributions to contemporary controversy.

and destruction. The truths had to be placed in
safety in their existing state of development. They
had to be promptly encased and iron-bound in
formulæ. And a consequent change took place in
their intellectual treatment. The pressing need was no
longer to develop them and in part assimilate them
with a friendly or neutral environment, or to exhibit
their compatibility with philosophies to which they
were, at first sight, in calm intellectual contrast; but
to defend and protect them from passionately hostile
forces. The normal co-operation, so eloquently described by Cardinal Newman, between liberty of thought
and authority, often became dangerous when the whole
claim of authority was being assailed in the name of
liberty. Intellectual exercises became primarily controversial. The truths were safely sheathed in the
definite *formulæ*, and the *formulæ* were defended by
polemic. The hesitation attendant on the endeavour
after perfectly accurate intellectual vision might be as
fatal as cowardice. Clear, strong, definite dialectic
was the most serviceable intellectual weapon, and it
was enlisted in the defence of precisely predetermined
conclusions. What Tennyson has called "the clash of
'yes' and 'no'" was of necessity the familiar sound.
The *formulæ* of the Protestants often, no doubt,
admitted of an orthodox interpretation; Catholic
formulæ could be and were travestied as to their
meaning. Newman has interpreted "justification by
faith" in a Catholic sense; and the word "transubstantiation" has been perverted by its opponents, and
made to signify that our Lord is carnally present,
instead of sacramentally, on the altar; and other
such instances could be given. This is now admitted
on all sides. But at that time the stand had to be

taken, the watchwords accepted, the banners raised, and the finer intellectual discriminations postponed to a time of peace.

Above all, authority, the very principle at stake, and the essential requisite to combined action, became necessarily in practice more prompt and absolute. Tyranny is among the greatest of dangers in time of peace; in time of war the pressure of the peril to the community acts both as a guiding and restraining force on the ruler, and as a motive in soldiers and followers for preferring the chance of some injustice to the risk of any insubordination. Again, debate and dispute, the very life of civil constitutions, the normal means of giving citizens a share in public affairs and in determining the fortunes of the country, the safeguard against injustice, and against the sense of injustice, are fatal in time of war. At such a time all must act together, and generally all must act promptly. Authority is rightly appealed to constantly. There is need for a dictator. The assertion of private opinion may be not only useless but dangerous. Such is the necessary consequence of material war; and it is true in its measure of a mental war between theological parties.

The result is a tendency to close all questions and rule them, at least provisionally, in one sense, for the sake of union and concentration against the foe. Theology becomes controversial in its form, and more and more precise, logical, and uniform in its statement —its immediate utility being not a wider intellectual vision, but a more successful controversial application. Thus we find the Protestant controversy actually incorporated in many modern Catholic text-books. Dogma is explained by its anti-Protestant limitations.

The refutation of a position whose very essence is the disloyalty of private judgment naturally leads to private judgment in general being held in suspicion : and this has often generated a rigid uniformity among theologians at variance with the freer atmosphere of the palmy days of Scholasticism. The mediæval glorying in differences of opinion, and the clash of intellect among Catholic thinkers themselves, between Thomist and Scotist, Dominican and Franciscan, disappear in large measure from contemporary theology. The sanctity of the time issues in something very unlike St. Thomas Aquinas, with his intellectual width and individualism and assimilative genius. St. Ignatius, St. Francis Xavier, St. Philip Neri, St. Charles Borromeo are the embodiments not of intellectual assimilation but of a great spiritual movement. The effective adherents of such a movement display enthusiasm for corporate action ; a tendency to look to Authority to decide all things—to await "orders" like disciplined and well-drilled soldiers, and ask no questions. Those who hesitate at such a time to be prompt in obedience are naturally and rightly charged with disloyalty. The most zealous look mainly to the correlative advantages of ethical discipline for the individual, and effective defence for the body politic. The Jesuits were, as I have said, the ideal embodiment of this military obedience. "The prevailing sin of the time," says an able writer, "was disobedience. The members of the [Society of Jesus] had to aim at becoming the perfect models of the virtue of obedience. The distinguishing traits of a perfect Jesuit formed the antithesis of a thorough Protestant."

It is not difficult to see how this state of things gradually issued in an intellectual condition which must to the world at large appear rigid and even antiquated. An organisation cannot, like an individual philosopher, sift and discriminate constantly in intellectual inquiry. Its individual members may be free to do this work, or they may not. A general rule must exist for general guidance. And while in the Middle Ages, when the authority of the Church was acknowledged, a large measure of free debate and free assimilation among individuals was the habit of the hour; while, in Cardinal Newman's words, the intellect then "enjoyed a licentious revel;" the result of the Reformation was to reverse the rule. "The weight of authority," says the writer just cited, "was placed on the side of restraining rather than on that of developing personal independent action," and, we may add, independent thought. Free speculation was safe among friends, but not when there were foes abroad. The genius of the Church of the sixteenth century being in a sense military, strangers being open to suspicion as spies or enemies, a policy of adhering strictly to the officially recognised, though not necessarily the best, intellectual defences became natural and necessary. It was better that a text-book or an argument should be orthodox and antiquated, than that, under the plea of necessary novelty, heresy should creep in, which might spread the spiritual revolt. The Reformers indeed were known as " novatores," and novelty incurred suspicion. To repeat what the Catholic schools had said for years was at least safe, even if it ignored some questions proper to the hour. The necessary development could be effected later on by degrees. But one hasty and false step at such a time might be very serious. The Index may now be in its present form an anachronism; but at an earlier date, in the unsettled state of public thought, to read heresy in any shape was for fickle and weak minds a snare. Catholics often had to choose between admitting habits of thought which might prove a danger to the Church, and foregoing some intellectual advantages. Moreover, the intellectual advantages themselves might be greatly discounted by a false intellectual method. If men are in general only now discovering that, as Heine long ago said, Protestantism is the mother of free-thought; and if the free-thinking method ignores the authority of some of the elements in our nature which are essential in the search for truth, even those who are not Catholics may now recognise that the Church, in deliberately rejecting some of the culture of an age of destructive speculation, was preserving important truths as well as guarding her own existence. And thus it has happened that a natural alliance has revealed itself between a modern transcendentalist like T. H. Green, and thinkers belonging to the "antiquated" Church.

Again, the Church, in Apostolic times, flourished, not in virtue of its philosophical schools, which did not yet exist, but by means of the supernatural zeal and sanctity of the early Christians ; and if in its first great war against the world intellectual weapons were least in request, may it not be so in this later contest ? There is a law of correlation of forces in the spiritual as in the physical order. As light may pass into heat, so, surely, may that energy in the Church which in one age exhibits itself in intellectual activity, display itself, in another, in a special outburst of sanctity St. Philip Neri, St. Charles Borromeo, St. Ignatius Loyola, St. Teresa, in one century ; St. Francis of Sales, St. Vincent of Paul, M. Olier, in the next ;

succeeded by St. Paul of the Cross, and St. Alfonso
in the eighteenth century :—these are only a few
specimens of the great representatives of intense
spiritual devotedness which the military epoch has
produced. Were not these the forces suited to the
time ? Were they not the beacon lights necessary
in an age when intellectual problems were surrounded
by a mist which made it impossible to distinguish their
true features accurately without such lights ? Polemical
and theological work indeed was plentiful ; but share
in the characteristic thought of the age was in large
measure necessarily postponed until a time should be
passed when controversial passions enveloped theological controversy in an almost impenetrable fog.   Individual Catholics as Descartes and Malebranche might
make a deep mark on the thought of the age ; but the
Catholic body as a whole shunned their speculations,
and preserved the systematic and defensive attitude
typified by the Jesuits.

And if the Catholic schools seem only now adjusting
themselves to problems which have elsewhere modified
so much thought and expression in theology, is there
not more dignity as well as safety in a movement which
is deliberate, than in the daily shiftings of position,
which we see all around us, to suit the whims of the
Zeitgeist—Tübingen criticisms, inaccurate versions of
Darwinism, startling views as to the early status
of the four Gospels which such a work as Tatian's
Diatessaron promptly explodes ?   Deliberation speaks
of care as well as of slowness.   If a Papal Encyclical,
even in our own day, reaffirms the time-honoured and
technical doctrine that there is no " error " in Scripture
—preferring to indicate in general terms that this does
not involve its accuracy in things not pertaining to

salvation, rather than to give the weight of an official approbation to some special adjustment of theology to an incomplete science—can we not see in such a procedure the habitual prudence of a Church surrounded by intellectual enemies? Is there no value in the sense of the sacredness of tradition which refuses to break with the patristic formula that the Scriptures " do not err," leaving its reconciliation with modern criticism to be worked out gradually, as far as possible by the application of old theological principles, instead of uniting with those who, in their alarm, throw the whole cargo overboard, and invent brand-new terminology and doctrines? Such revolutions do not come natural to the Church of the ages.

The siege lasted for upwards of two centuries and a half. Protestants of the sixteenth and seventeenth centuries were succeeded by Febronians and Jansenists in the eighteenth; and these were in turn reinforced by infidels and deists in their war against the Papacy. We need not tell over again the story of the depths to which the Papal Power had sunk at the end of the eighteenth century, or of the confident prophecies when Pius the Sixth died, and again when Pius the Seventh was in exile, that the Papacy was finally doomed. The state of war, the estrangement of the Church from the characteristic intellectual movement of Europe, had probably reached its furthest point at this time. The Zeitgeist was simply irreligious. The Church appeared to the eager *philosophes* a fossil remnant, finally deprived of the vital principle which can modify by assimilation.

Then suddenly arose a new state of things. When Europe began to shake its limbs after the removal of the Napoleonic fetters and to reconstitute its life, the Papacy found allies in unsuspected directions.

Philosophers, poets, historians adopted a Catholic tone. The Romantic school won by their writings a general admiration for mediæval Christendom. Chateaubriand, the Schlegels, Novalis, Fouqué, and many another, with whatever faults of sentiment, showed the still living power of Catholicism ; and a halo of perhaps, in some cases, unpractical romance replaced the contempt of an earlier time. Many very considerable thinkers, writers, and artists in Germany either became Catholics or, at all events, adhered to the Catholic movement with sympathy and a sense of its value. A glance at the recent past convinced many thinking minds that the change in alliances represented facts, and that the old war-cries had come in many cases only to represent words. The battle in which everything was at stake was no longer between Rome and the rebels, but between religion and anarchy or infidelity. While De Maistre said " submit to the Pope," non-Catholic statesmen and diplomats from Bunsen to Bismarck have come to feel the importance of joining with the Papacy in the defence of civil society.

Of this last tide there has been ebb and flow. The forces of the Revolution have come to the front in 1830 and 1848, and again more than once in our own time. The recruits of the Papacy have been considerable. The Catholic revival has on the whole maintained its ground. Catholicism is—notably in Germany—a power which few could have anticipated at the beginning of the century. In America its growth has been very noteworthy. In France we have the marked diminution among the educated of the Voltairian spirit, and the growth among thinking minds of a sense of the benefits of Catholicism. In Italy, too, the cause of religion is held by the best

witnesses to be distinctly advancing. In Belgium the
revival has long been specially remarkable for its
completeness.

At the outset of this movement, at a time when
the extraordinary transformations which had been
effected by the great revolution and the succeeding
wars made the marvellous seem comparatively likely,
there were thinking minds—and those not of Catholic
enthusiasts—which regarded the course of events as
a simple victory for the Papacy, and as portending a
return of all Christians to union with Rome. A. W.
Schlegel, who never actually joined the Catholic Church,
wrote as follows to M. de Montmorency—at a time
when the conversion of Stolberg, Frederick Schlegel,
and their friends was a recent event :—

" The Protestant system does not satisfy me any longer. . . .
I am convinced that the time is not far off when all Christians
will reunite in the old faith. The work of the Reformation
is accomplished ; the pride of human reason, which was
evident in the first Reformers and still more in their successors,
has guided us so ill—especially during the last century—that
it has come into antagonism with itself and destroyed itself.
It is perhaps ordained that those who have influence on the
opinions of their contemporaries shall publicly renounce it,
and thus assist in preparing a union with the one Church of
former days."

And in the midst of this general tendency to
sympathy with Catholic ideals, we have had a section
of our own countrymen, considerable from the days of
the Oxford Movement for their talent and zeal, maintaining that those ideals are essential to the life of the
Church of England itself. We have the majority of
the Anglican clergy upholding the Apostolical Succession as a doctrine of the English Church, and even

treating its denial as an insult. Thus Dr. Jessopp
himself speaks of the denial of a priesthood to the
English Church as equivalent to the denial that her
ministers have any position which is from their own
point of view valid. We have the large majority of
cultivated Englishmen showing a true veneration for
the Catholic piety of a Fénelon, a St. Francis of Assisi,
a St. Teresa, a St. Francis of Sales, whose lives and
works find editors and readers among widely different
schools of thought. We observe an increasing sense
of the power of the doctrine of the Real Presence, not
as a matter of theological consistency, but in influencing
that ethical life of individuals which goes to form the
moral character of a nation.

Such signs of the times cannot but be welcome to
that society which has for three hundred years defended
the Catholic ideals against all the rest of Western
Christendom. But when we find our neighbours
calling on the Papacy now at last to abate its pretensions, to regard itself as an effete or defeated power at
the very moment when many of the main principles
for which it fought show greater signs of renewed
influence, in the religious world, than they have done
for three hundred years, a sense of astonishment and
even of the ludicrous arises. It is easy in the present
hour of freedom to avow admiration for the beauty of
Catholicism. But what society was it which actually
defended Catholic ideals through general obloquy, and
in spite of the scorn of the would-be intellectual, when
the rest of Western Christendom had abandoned them?
Were those ideals as a fact to be found flourishing and
operative in the Church of England a century ago?
It is no disputed question of history, but a matter
which was twenty years ago in the memory of large

numbers of living people, the lament of Newman and
Pusey, the boast of the Bishops who " charged " against
Tract 90, that the mass of Catholic doctrines and ideals
had been kept in practice by the Roman and lost in
practice by the Anglican Church. We may have the
utmost sympathy with the wonderful movement through
whose power they have risen from the dead in a
Church whose members so long gloried in the name
of Protestant. But how far the adherents of the *via
media* actually succeeded in preserving them in the
decisive struggle is notorious. Keble himself did
not venture to maintain in 1837 that the Apostolical
Succession was an essential doctrine of the English
Church.[1] When Cardinal Wiseman lectured in 1835
at Moorfields, how many religious Englishmen outside
the Roman communion rejected private judgment
exercised on the Bible, as their guide in religious
belief, and appealed to the Church ? If the idea of
the Church as the storehouse of accumulated Christian
wisdom and the guardian of the " deposit of faith " is
of deep philosophic importance, as many suppose, to
whom do we all owe its preservation ? If the men
who look at the scars and wounds among the defenders
of the Roman Church, and to its diminished importance
and extent as contrasted with the days of Innocent the
Third, speak in unqualified language of its defeat, are
they quite sure that they are using the right word ?
Civil war, no doubt, whatever its issue, is likely to
leave a large section of the nation apart from the victorious side, and may decimate the victors. And there
is (in the present case) an ever-increasing proportion

---

[1] See A. P. Stanley's letters in connection with F. Oakeley's
ordination, referred to in " W. G. Ward and the Oxford Movement,"
p. 471.

of persons to whom the points at issue are of no deep interest, and who are simply external to the conflict, and to be reckoned neither among victors nor among vanquished. But when we find the more religious minds among the educated returning more and more to the very principles and ideals which Rome kept, at a time when, on the whole, every one else abandoned them, we should perhaps be slow to speak confidently of her defeat. And if Görres, Schlegel, Stolberg, and the scores of able and cultivated German Protestants, who threw their intellectual life into the stream of Catholicism, owned that Protestantism was dead and the Papacy victorious, while the English Protestants who returned to the advocacy of Catholic principles declared that the ideals which had triumphed with them were (potentially at least) what their fathers had always maintained, can we be astonished at those who smile and say that it is an instance of Englishmen not knowing when they are beaten ? Can we even be surprised that the descendants in England of those whose lives were ruined by fines and disabilities, or who were martyred for adherence to Catholic doctrines, should be slow to understand that those who persecuted or killed them belonged to a Church which for the most part potentially agreed with them ?

Be this as it may, and passing from the theoretical to the practical, it is tolerably evident that at the present hour there can be no direct approach to corporate reunion between Rome and any considerable section of Englishmen. The divergences and misconceptions are too deep and extensive. The approximation, though in some quarters very real, is chiefly ethical and devotional. The basis for an intellectual agreement is non-existent on both sides.

Catholics have not yet, as a body, mastered accurately, or at all events sympathetically, the Anglican position. Anglicans have as a body lost that conception of the nature of the unity of the Church which existed before the Reformation. And without it there can be no sufficient force to make them feel the anomaly of their isolation, or to view reunion with the Apostolic See as a duty. Nothing short of this sense will give the requisite energy to surmount the many difficulties of the situation.

But does this mean that the state of war is to continue? Surely not. If the long—and in its early years ever-deepening—estrangement, which bars the road to reunion, was due to the state of war, to the emphasising points of difference until they obliterated points of agreement, may not a gradual change be wrought by sympathy and co-operation—by dwelling on points of agreement until they have brought about that mutual good understanding which will reduce points of difference to their normal proportions? And—which is more important—if the divergence has been due to an anti-Catholic "psychological climate," may not the new sympathy with Catholicism alter that climate, and work an intellectual change by a movement primarily ethical? If obstacles to reunion have obviously accumulated since the reign of James the First, when so much of the Catholic *ethos* remained in the popular mind, may not the revival of Catholic sympathies gradually remove those obstacles? Present reunion and war are not exhaustive alternatives. A sense of brotherhood with our fellow-Christians, a determination to work with them where we can, to be absolutely just where discussion of differences is necessary, to prefer

co-operation in doing good to needless disputation,—
this is a programme, not indeed of reunion, but of
rapprochement.

The tradition of three hundred years cannot on
either side be cancelled in a generation. Even among
that party which is most eager for the restoration of
a Catholic superstructure in the Established Church,
a large remnant of the anti-papal tradition inevitably
remains. Increased co-operation and *rapprochement,*
while they would bring to light and develop our points
of agreement, would also further the cause of mutual
good understanding by making clear the nature and
extent of our real divergences. And it would be found
that one which chiefly bars the road between the
advanced Anglicans and ourselves is our difference as to
what is meant by the Catholic Church. If the Catholic
Church means only the aggregate of Christian bodies
which have preserved in their orders the Apostolical
Succession, and have considered themselves to hold
primitive doctrine, it is obvious that Monophysites,
Donatists, and even Arians, at different times, reason-
ably claimed to be Catholics. The Catholic Church,
which disallowed their claim, is consequently (according
to the Roman tradition) the realisation of an idea
distinct from this. Whatever may be the difficulties
attaching to the ideal of an exclusive Church, it was
on its preservation that Rome staked everything at
the Reformation ;—on preserving the reality of a single
polity, at once international and universal, and yet
with power to determine authoritatively the conditions
of membership. The very meaning of reunion varies
with the sense in which the phrase " Catholic Church "
is understood.

Until the full significance of this divergence

has become clear, controversy is at cross purposes. Laborious appeals to history are made on the Anglican side to determine what doctrines are primitive, while the Roman Church upholds the constant tradition of definition by the Church in every age, which implies that the primitive form as ascertained by history is *not* necessarily the ultimate or the more exact form of expression ; that the later explains the earlier, as the fully developed limb expresses the purpose and symmetry of what appeared vague and indeterminate in the fœtus. The appeal to primitive expressions as the norm whereby the expressions of the later Church are to be *limited*, violates the conception of the Church which Rome has ever maintained as the historical one. Again, the fœtus is not looked at with the same eyes by one who considers it as the first manifestation of what becomes later so much more definite, and by one who examines it with the best of microscopes but with no such guide to its ultimate shape. And so the Catholic and Anglican must often look at Church History with different eyes.

To one, then, who holds the Roman view of the nature of the Church, much of the ablest Anglican argument from Church History appears to be beside the mark ; it seems to him to ignore the qualification which even Vincent of Lerins gives to his famous *dictum*, that doctrine may so develop that its earlier may be to its later form what the child is to the man.[1] On similar lines triumphant conclusions against Newman's view of the Papacy are drawn by Anglican

[1] "Ut quamvis," St. Vincent adds, "unius ejusdem hominis status habitusque mutetur una tamen nihilominus eademque natura, una eademque persona sit." (See "Commonitor." ed. Klüpfel, Vienna, pp. 199 *seq.*)

critics from the difference of its position in the early and later centuries, while this very difference was essential to the argument of Newman's " Essay on Development." [1] A principle of regarding the explicit statements of early Christians as final expressions of dogma is adopted in regard to the papal supremacy, which, if applied to the doctrine of the Trinity, would commit the Church irrevocably to Arianism or similar heterodoxy. [2]

On the other hand, Catholics have perhaps, at all events until recently, shown an inadequate appreciation of the peculiar state of things which made men like Bishop Tunstall for years uncertain that to remain within the English Church after the breach with Rome was to part company with the Church Catholic. And by insufficiently recognising such irregularities in the working out of an idea as history must disclose, they may have furnished some excuse for a casuistry which has turned comparatively brief anomalies into precedents for all time. An anomalous state of things may justify individuals ; perhaps a generation : but an anomaly can never become a general law for permanent action.

Heated discussions, then, are a waste of labour, until such divergences as these are clearly appreciated.

---

[1] " The regalia Petri might sleep, as the power of a chancellor has slept ; not as obsolete, for they never had been carried into effect, but as a mysterious privilege which was not understood : as an unfulfilled prophecy. . . . As the Church grew into form, so did the power of the Pope develop ; and wherever the Pope has been renounced decay and division have been the consequence. We know of no other way of preserving the *sacramentum unitatis* but a centre of unity " (pp. 150 *seq.*).

[2] This point is worked out by Abbé Duchesne in his essay on " Les Témoins antinicéens du Dogme de la Trinité," Amiens, 1883. He cites the still stronger view of Cardinal Newman in the same direction. According to Duchesne, the language, though heretical, falls short of Arianism.

Personal intercourse, on the other hand, with Catholics in general must gradually issue in a truer understanding. Catholics, by frequenting the universities, and by mixing with their fellow-citizens and working with them for the commonwealth, will lose that attitude, belonging to the days of persecution, which has had so large a share in creating the general impression that the Papal Church is " Chinese." When they have learnt to make themselves understood in word and in act, we may find out, for the first time since the struggles of the sixteenth century, how far the English character is still susceptible of being influenced by Catholic principles as such, without those associations which have coloured them in the past, which have made them seem to Milton idolatrous or to Dr. Jessopp Chinese. And even apart from ulterior results, the cause of religion must benefit by the hearty co-operation of all the most earnest religious life of the country in vindicating the reality of the supernatural and the power of prayer.

I have ventured to urge this view of the case the more definitely, that it seems to be clearly indicated in the late Pope's Letter to the English people, to which I have already referred. I scarcely think that any dispassionate reader of the letter can doubt that by its very form, and especially by the emphasis with which it sets forth certain Catholic practices which are distasteful to Englishmen, it shows that reunion was not in the eyes of Pope Leo an immediately practical matter. And yet it seems equally plain on the surface that the letter is intentionally a step in the direction of recognising that the " state of siege " is past—that it is designed to invite Englishmen to look on their Catholic countrymen as fellow-workers for the good of their country, and to encourage among Catholics a feeling of brotherhood with those who are separated from them. The virtues of " our separated brethren," if this account is true, are emphasised with a very practical purpose. As long as it seemed to many on both sides a duty to preserve an attitude of direct hostility, it was quite obvious that the misunderstandings, unfairness, bigotry, due to what I have called the state of siege, must last. The bulk of Englishmen necessarily retain a considerable remnant of the "No-Popery" sentiment which was fashioned so assiduously in the course of centuries ; and Catholics largely preserve the intellectual traditions of their forefathers. When people have been fighting hard for generations it is not of much use merely to *tell* them to be friends, and to conduct their discussions dispassionately. But let them work for a common cause, on the importance of which they are agreed, and the sympathy on one point may pass to a better understanding on others. When we see around us a civilisation in which belief in theism and immortality is becoming perilously weak and vague, in which Christian education is threatened, in which a positive caricature of forces destructive of social order shows itself in Anarchism and Nihilism, there is surely enough for all lovers of religion to work for together, while they agree to differ on further questions, pending, at all events, the arrival of that calmer and more sympathetic temper which would make discussion more fruitful. By such a course we should be spared on both sides many heated and able assaults on positions which nobody holds, and laborious arguments built on premises which are the very points really at issue.

And if such a change of attitude on both sides appears to some a small thing, from which it is visionary to expect so much, the present writer differs very widely from such readers. A mere " feeling " or an " attitude " may seem a small thing in words ; but in fact its potency is tremendous. " Caste feeling," " race feeling," " sect feeling," are responsible for many of the saddest pages in history, the more so when they have tainted and disfigured the nobler zeal with which they have attempted to blend. Each is essentially barbarous and prolific of injustice. A national " feeling," persistently feeding on all rumours congenial to it, led to that monstrous interpretation of every word or act of the " papist" which gradually gave its extravagant intensity to the English " No-Popery " cry. And a temper of justice and kindness may be equally potent in clearing the air of prejudices, and enabling at least those who care to see things truly and justly to do so.

The polemical spirit substitutes heat for light, and renders assimilation and approximation almost impossible. Controversy is no doubt in all ages an occasional necessity. But it can hardly be fruitful in persuasion, as distinct from mere defence, unless a temper of sympathy has first ascertained accurately the real points on which the opposite parties are agreed and those wherein they differ. Then, and not until then, it becomes compatible with assimilation. Then we may hope that it will not merely rejoice the already convinced, but will rather be a step towards that exacter exhibition of truth which commands attention and conviction on all sides.

And if the preceding remarks have in them any measure of truth, it would seem that it is the growth of this temper of fairness and sympathy on all sides, by mutual co-operation against our common foes, irreligion, vice, anarchy, infidelity, which will eventually lead to a real reunion if it is ever to be attained. Nothing else can give a true knowledge of the degree of union already existing, and the degree of divergence yet remaining. Nothing will tend more to increase the former and diminish the latter. And the present writer may express his conviction—though he cannot from the nature of the case expect many readers to share it—that such a course would lead ultimately to an estimate of the possibilities of Catholicism which, to the fixed prepossessions of the present generation of Englishmen, appears simply utopian.

III.

UNCHANGING DOGMA AND CHANGEFUL MAN.

TAKING up the tune to which an eminent agnostic sang some years ago, representing every discovery of science as attended by "the groans of a strangled theologian," Dr. Mivart, in two essays which have become famous,[1] has chanted a pæan on the victories of science over divinity, not only over that despicable body the Roman Curia, and over the Roman Congregations, but over Popes and Councils and the whole theological school—nay (by implication), over Lutherans and Calvinists as well. For certainly the opposition to Copernicanism was far more uncompromising among Protestants than among

[1] "The Continuity of Catholicism" (*Nineteenth Century*, January, 1900), and "Some Recent Catholic Apologists" (*Fortnightly Review*, January, 1900). This criticism of Dr. Mivart's position was written during his lifetime, and I could have wished in republishing it to have entirely suppressed its polemical form. I have gone as far as possible in this direction by omitting the first few pages. But some parts of Dr. Mivart's essays are of permanent importance, as outspoken and concrete exhibitions of a form of liberal Catholicism which appears to me agnostic in principle, and which, nevertheless, the unwary might accept as identical with such theological developments as are called for by modern research. My criticism would lose all actuality if I did not refer to them. But I should wish my words to be regarded as impugning a way of reasoning rather than attacking the reasoner himself. Personally I have great doubts as to these two essays representing deliberate and well-weighed conclusions.

Catholics. The *De Revolutionibus Orbium* was dedicated to a Pope, and denounced by Melanchthon—the mildest of the Reformers. But the writer of whom I speak never for a moment inquires how far there may have been good reason, or at least some reason, for opposing anything which afterwards proved true. He never places himself in imagination in the position of the men whom he criticises, with their antecedents and circumstances, but projects the present on to the past, and applies triumphantly the wisdom which has come after the event to demonstrate the ignorant folly of those who lived before the event. Thus the conduct of the Roman authorities is described by him roundly as " ridiculous," as a " humiliating and disastrous failure," as " disgraceful." Had he understood the principles of that historical criticism whose conclusions or hypotheses are to him simply dogmatic bowstrings for strangling the theologians, had he regarded the persons he criticises as human beings and not as abstract embodiments of the anti-scientific temper, he must have realised that they were not likely to be fools, and did not behave like fools, regard being had to the circumstances of the time. But the historical method, though its conclusions are useful to him as an instrument of assault, is most uncongenial to a mind which, in its theological and philosophical reasonings, is purely, and almost touchingly mediæval, and in temper has the controversial *animus* which invented in the eighteenth century the famous *e pur si muove*. The result is a very curious psychological study ; but of light on a complex and difficult subject, nothing whatever.

The writer proceeds to find out that individual Catholics have been more submissive to the teachings of science than the theologians, and that the theologians themselves have eventually followed suit, and abandoned their former principles. They have given up belief after belief in obedience to science—not according to fixed rules ascertainable by the study of history as normal to theological development, but by a simple process of implicit obedience to scientific men and historical critics, which has no natural limitations. It plainly follows that Catholics may eventually, as he intimates, give up belief in the Virgin birth of our Lord, or for the matter of that—so far as the present writer can see—in the Incarnation itself.

The unfortunate result of this line of thought is that it throws confusion over what is really a difficult problem, which occupies the minds of nearly all thinking Christians at present.

To believe in the Christian revelation, yet to believe in a scientific view of the world so unlike that accepted by its first teachers,—that is part of the problem. Can we show that, in separating the revelation from the inaccurate science of those who expounded it, we are not emptying it of all meaning? that the change is in the human adjuncts, not in the Divine message? Is it possible to maintain that Christianity still supplies the key to the meaning of life, and therefore, gives the highest knowledge, though the medium through which it has been viewed by man in the past, and expounded by its teachers, has now been so largely changed by advancing science? May it be that scientific agnosticism has fallen into those very errors of exaggeration, and of dogmatism outside its own sphere, which science has brought to light in some of the mediæval theologians? Success is apt to turn the head, and to destroy the sense of proportion. A Senior Wrangler once, it is said, gravely acknowledged public plaudits in a London theatre which were really bestowed on the Prime Minister. Science, on this view, is led by success to forget its true place. It has so extensively changed the secular outworks of divinity, that it claims simply to dictate to revelation itself. In mediæval Christendom a similar phenomenon was sometimes apparent in the divines who then lorded it over the world of thought, as the men of science now claim to dominate that world. The theologians of those days taught the world its physics, as, within our own memory, Huxley and Tyndall claimed to determine our theology.

To believe, then, in the Christian revelation, and to believe that it is a salutary check on the anti-theological extravagances of men of science, and yet to believe in the methods of modern science and criticism, and to see in them a salutary check on the excursions of theologians beyond their province —is not this a tenable *via media ?*

Had Dr. Mivart investigated this position in detail, looking fairly at the point of view of each of the parties concerned, his work might have been helpful. Or, again, had he professed to state the case frankly for considering that science has really dethroned the Christian revelation, he might have helped us in getting at the truth. But when a writer professes to be saying the best that can be said for Catho- licism and Christianity, and at the same time repre- sents them as without any stable principles, and as almost exclusively consisting in superstitions which must one by one be entirely dropped at the bidding of critics and scientists, he does not help us. It is a principle of justice that counsel should be heard for the defence. Dr. Mivart himself volunteers to assume the office, but apparently without having read his brief, or, at least, without having understood it.

I do not propose here to institute a full examination of the large subject he has raised. And I shall purposely keep clear of the most knotty points in which traditionary theological positions conflict with the positions now fashionable among modern critics and scientists, because an adequate discussion of them cannot be brief. Moreover, the passions aroused by contemporary controversies obscure the distinct recognition of principles. When people are disagreed as to the weight of the scientific or critical evidence for a position which, if true, would modify current theological opinion, the argument inevitably drifts to the discussion of that evidence, and away from the definition of the principles visible in the Church's past action in her relations with advancing thought.

My object here is to attempt to show how, in the past, such changes as have taken place in the beliefs current among Catholics have been reconcilable with the *semper eadem* of Catholic doctrine. The lessons of the past may be applied by individuals for themselves to the problems which interest them in the present.

Dr. Mivart has, then, it seems to me, simply ignored the principle manifest in the history of the past changes in the accepted theological teaching to which he refers—the principle which Newman expressed when he said of a belief which is retained in new relations and circumstances, that "it changes with them in order to remain the same." A revelation of changeless truth had been made to restless, changeful man, whose media of apprehension and

modes of expression were ever altering. No philosophy was revealed. No science was revealed.
Yet the Christian message could only be handed
on explicitly in terms which included both. Once
we realise the instances of this phenomenon which
the first few centuries of the Christian era were
enough to disclose, we are enabled to get order from
Dr. Mivart's chaos.

The changes brought by modern science are only a
repetition (*mutatis mutandis*) of the changes brought
by ancient philosophies. It was not the Divine revelation which changed. It was man with his equipment for its explication and expression who changed.
We find his restless attacks and comments and the
reply of the living Church in each age ;—new phrases,
new formulæ, new philosophical methods. The
Church acted by resistance and assimilation. The
resistance meant that she would not submit to be
dethroned—whether by gnostic Hellenism in the
third century or by agnostic science in the nineteenth ; that she guards the true view of life which
successive speculations would sweep aside and replace.
The assimilation meant that she is ready to express
the revelation in terms of human philosophy and
science, provided that its essence is guarded. Thus,
at the time of Irenæus, we find the dangerous flood of
Greek speculation opposed by the Church. Yet by
the time of Nicæa its ideas and terminology, and in
part its method, have gradually been in great part
accepted. We see neo-Platonism and the Church at
daggers drawn in the days of Porphyry and of Julian
the Apostate. Yet long passages from Plotinus find
their way later on into approved and even official
works. Aristotle is regarded as the arch enemy by

the Fathers. "I do not know," writes Cardinal Newman, "which of them could endure him."[1] Yet in the pages of St. Thomas Aquinas his philosophy is used to express nearly all dogmatic truth, and his Metaphysic was later on incorporated in the definition of transubstantiation.

The changeless dogma has from the first been a living truth with practical relations to changing man. A stone remains unaffected by the growth of its environment. And, like the buried talent, it works no good to any one. A living man retains his life—and therefore his identity with his former self—only by responding to changing conditions. The old analogy of religion to the growing boy who becomes a man yet remains the same, had a profound meaning. A growth of theological science, changes of explication, at times radical changes of method, such as we witness in comparing the theological works of the Fathers with those of the Schoolmen, were inevitable. They answered to the evolution of thought and of civilisation. And those of Dr. Mivart's examples which have real importance are the outcome of this same phenomenon which is visible from the very beginning. If the Church is truly *semper eadem* we must look for the operation of this undying principle in our own age as well as in its predecessors. It is only the unreflecting observer,—one who regards his own time as a fixed norm of absolute truth, without antecedents and sterile for the future,— who is disconcerted by its appearance. Such is often the view of the man in the street. But one looks for something better in educated inquiry.

It would appear, then, that the Catholic doctrine

[1] See "Idea of a University," p. 470.

is now as stable as it ever was in principle; and that
the changes in theological opinion from age to age are
not, as Dr. Mivart supposes, a new discovery made
by him. They do not represent a blind and unlimited
obedience on the part of Catholics to the opinions of
scientific men. They are more accurately regarded,
not as changes in the meaning of dogma, or changes
of dogma, but as changes in its explication. They
are instances of growth in our understanding of what
practically follows from, or is involved logically in,
dogma; or of increased precision in our discrimination
of the essence of dogma from its form; or of the
readiness of the Church to express dogmatic truth in
the terms supplied by the science or thought of the
day; or of all these phenomena. That certain changes
result in the practical detailed belief of Catholics is
undeniable.[1] We do not now necessarily believe, with
St. Thomas or St. Gregory, that hell is in the bowels
of the earth. We do not believe that the Aristotelian
physics explain the resurrection of the body. But the
change is no series of dissolving views whose claim to
continuity lies solely in their being gradual; in which
we can trace no vital connexion between the successive pictures and no underlying identity in the dogma.
It is a change which necessarily follows in our apprehension of mixed propositions in which physical
science and matters cognisable by reason are mingled
with the truths of faith. The latter are unchangeable,

---

[1] Of course, the theologian will rightly tell us that the changes do not
affect what is *de fide*. This is exactly what I mean by saying that the
changes are not in the dogmas, but in their explication. A residuum
remains unchanged, and that is *de fide*. But it may take a long time to
determine in detail exactly what that residuum is. And theologians may
make great mistakes on the subject in periods of transition. The Roman
theologians, as we have seen, considered Copernicanism to be contradictory, not to an *opinion*, but to a dogma *de fide*.

the former may change. The explanation of propositions whose meaning depends on both, must change with the changing element. Dogma proper does not teach physical science or philosophy. It may be expressed in terms which imply either or both. But it is the dogma and not the science which is revealed and cannot change.

Therefore, in strict theological language, there is no change in the meaning of *dogma.* There is a change in the explication of dogmatic propositions[1] which are in one age expounded according to mediæval science, in another according to later discoveries. Theology is very jealous of speaking of a change of meaning in dogmas lest the phrase should seem to imply a change of meaning in Divine truth. It prefers to speak of a change in the inferences drawn from them; and this custom has wise reasons. Nothing is gained by banishing technical expressions, which have their own utility, provided we do not draw inferences from them as though they were not technical. We might as well accuse of quibbling, or disingenuousness, the lawyer who says, " The king can do no wrong," as the theologian who says, " Dogma cannot change its meaning," or " There is no error in Scripture." With dogma, as with the teaching of Scripture, there is theologically no error and no change. But the concrete belief of those who held that Scripture teaches Copernicanism to be false, is not identical with ours.[2] Nor is the belief of those who thought

---

[1] " Dogma, in its theological sense, is a truth contained in the word of God, written or unwritten—*i.e.* in Scripture or tradition—and proposed by the Church for the belief of he faithful."—*Vide* " Catholic Dictionary," article " Dogma." The dogma of the Incarnation was elucidated by many successive dogmatic propositions.

[2] I mean, of course, by identical, *wholly* the same. A part of the

that hell was in the bowels of the earth and that
Christ in His Ascension went up to a place above
a stationary earth and beyond the blue sky of a
summer's day, the same as that of those who think
otherwise.   We still believe that the Bible is the
Word of God, Who cannot err, and that the wicked
go to hell, and that Christ "ascended into heaven."
But we explain these beliefs in the terms required by
a newer science and a new view of the physical
universe.

There is, then, a very real change in concrete
belief.   And to those—probably the majority of uneducated Christians—who have never reflected on
the origin of such concrete beliefs, and have identified them with the dogmas taught through their
medium, the stability of dogma may seem, for
the moment, imperilled by a marked change in its
scientific explication.   But consideration restores the
balance and shows the change to be in the colour
of the human glasses through which dogma is viewed
by man.   Reflection shows, moreover, that the change
is but the new application of a principle which is
itself *semper eadem*.

This principle, indeed, was not entirely forgotten
in Galileo's own time in reference to Copernicanism
itself; and Bellarmine (as we know) said that, if Copernicanism was proved, Scripture must be interpreted
in a new manner, in accord with the Copernican system.
But it is one thing theoretically to acknowledge a principle, quite another fully to realise that it must be actually
applied, not only in explaining the past, where the mind

belief is different.   The analogy of a technical legal principle holds only,
of course, so far as it is an instance of technical and not popular phraseology.   Both must be understood in the sense in which the experts
explain them.

is accustomed to it from long habit, but if necessary to newer problems. If we are to judge by the language of Galileo's condemnation, the average Roman theologians did not look steadily at the possibility which the more far-seeing genius of Bellarmine contemplated.

There are many still who do not sufficiently remember the past to apply its lessons to the present; who admit principles theoretically, but do not realise what they involve. The problem of reconciling Catholic dogma with advancing science, and the two ways of regarding it, were excellently stated—long before Dr. Mivart wrote—by a French prelate, the late Monsignor D'Hulst. It is inevitable, he maintained, in his presidential address to the Catholic International Scientific Congress of 1888, that the points of contact between science, which is always moving, and faith, which is ever the same, should be constantly changing. The question is this: Is the traditionary explanation of a dogma identical with the dogma? Or is it only the way of stating the Catholic position natural at one stage of scientific knowledge, impossible at a later stage?[1]

---

[1] " Si la foi est immobile, la science ne l'est pas. C'est la gloire de la parole divine d'être toujours semblable à elle-même. C'est l'honneur de la pensée humaine de n'être jamais contente d'elle-même et de reculer sans cesse les bornes toujours étroites de ses connaissances. Mais entre deux termes contigus, dont l'un est en repos, l'autre en mouvement, il est inévitable que les points de contact se déplacent. Si le déplacement se faisait toujours au nom d'une certitude absolue, l'accord serait facile entre croyants ; car autant ils sont convaincus qu'une proposition révélée n'a rien à craindre des constatations scientifiques, autant ils sont prêts à affirmer qu'une proposition démontrée n'encourra jamais le démenti autorisé des juges de la croyance. Ces deux axiomes représentent les deux faces d'une même véritée enseignée en termes exprès par le Concile du Vatican et par toute une série d'actes pontificaux, et qu'on peut résumer en cette formule ; *le dogme catholique ne saurait être pris en défaut par les faits.* Mais le problème est moins simple que cela dans la pratique.

The whole question then is : What is the true *explication* of the dogma ? It is the ignoring, by Dr. Mivart, of this important element which is at the root of his confusion. He regards dogmatic propositions as exhaustive expressions of reality,[1] and consequently the changes in their explication are to

" La science, en effet, arrive rarement d'un bond à la certitude. Elle procède par l'hypothèse, s'essaie aux vérifications expérimentales et s'achemine à travers des probabilités grandissantes vers le terme désiré de l'évidence discursive. Encore si cette marche était régulière et constante. Mais non. Il y a des tâtonnements et de fausses manœuvres ; il y a des chevauchées hors de la route ; *magni passus, sed extra viam ;* il y a des hypothèses qui jouissent longtemps d'une certaine faveur et que de nouvelles recherches obligent d'abandonner. Tant que dure leur crédit provisoire, bon nombre d'esprits trop prompts à conclure les confondent avec les dires absolus de la science, et pendant ce temps-là on se demande comment les mettre d'accord avec l'enseignement chrétien, " Les uns disent, ' Le désaccord est manifeste, c'est l'hypothèse qui a tort.' Les autres répondent, ' L'hypothèse est bien appuyée, c'est vous qui interprétez mal la croyance. Ce que vous prenez pour l'enseignement catholique n'est qu'une façon d'entendre cet enseignement, façon bien naturelle tant qu'on n'avait pas de raisons d'en chercher une autre, mais qu'il faut abandonner à la demande de l'expérience.' Sans doute, si l'autorité suprême intervient pour fixer le sens indécis du dogme, le dissentiment fait place à l'unanimité. Mais il est rare que cette autorité se mêle ainsi aux virements de bord de la science. Gardienne prudente de la parole sacrée, protectrice bienveillante de l'activité humaine, elle attend d'ordinaire, se contentant de surveiller le mouvement et de condamner les excès de part et d'autre. Pendant ce temps-là, deux tendances se manifestent parmi les catholiques ; celles des hardis, qui sont parfois téméraires ; celles des timides, qui sont parfois arriérés. Et là encore la situation se complique et les reproches se croisent. Les hardis prétendent que ce sont eux qui sont prudents, parce qu'ils réservent l'avenir et épargnent aux théologiens la nécessité de s'infliger plus tard à eux mêmes un désaveu. Les timides répondent que ce sont eux qui méritent la louange décernée aux braves, parce qu'ils témoignent moins d'appréhensions devant les attaques de la science, plus de confiance dans la victoire finale de la conception traditionnelle. Encore une fois, Messieurs. ces divergences sont inévitables, et vouloir les prévenir serait interdire aux croyants de penser."

[1] It is on this view that Dr. Mivart's whole argument is based, and he states it in words quoted by me later. Elsewhere he states its contradictory, which seems to me additional evidence that he has not mastered the problem he is dealing with.

him, not the attainment of greater precision and the development of dogmatic expression according to a definite law ascertainable in hstoiry, but the gradual succession of dissolving views, exhibited at the bidding of the man of science on the canvas of theology. He ignores the fact that the whole history of dogma, during the first centuries of the Christian era, was that of the adding of defined propositions to explain more clearly the limits of their predecessors ; that, consequently, single propositions never professed to be exhaustive. He ignores also the fact that dogmatic mysteries confessedly exceed all human language and conceptions. Propositions which either deal with the mysterious, or are partly indeterminate, cannot be ultimate, unequivocal expressions of reality. Yet Dr. Mivart treats fresh limitations of their conceivable meaning, designed to prevent their misapplication, as dishonest subterfuges. To limit the meaning of *Extra Ecclesiam nulla salus* by the doctrine of " invincible ignorance" and of "the soul of the Church"—though the limitation is only the detailed application of principles already recognised in theology,[1]—is to Dr. Mivart a change to new teaching. And to deny this is dishonest.

For Dr. Mivart, then, there is no "sens indecis du dogme"—to use Monsignor D'Hulst's phrase. To say that a proposition is true in one sense and not in another is quibbling. Professing adherence to a Church which has continued to define further and further for 1900 years, he quarrels with the statement that a single formula is not an ultimate position

---

[1] It will not be forgotten that so representative an apologist as St. Justin had taught as early as the second century that all people leading good lives (μετὰ λόγου βιώσαντες) were really Christians, whatever their religious profession.—" First Apology," 46.

intellectually, and that therefore we often cannot say of it, *apart from further explication of its sense*, that it is absolutely true or untrue.   He states his own (as he supposes) opposite view as follows :[1] " I, on the other hand, earnestly contend that every statement duly analysed must be true or untrue.   For what is truth ?   It consists in an accurate correspondence between an act of the intellect (normally, and especially a judgment) and some objective existence. So far as any assertion conveys to us an idea which corresponds with objective reality, it is ' true,' and so far as it diverges from that reality, it is ' untrue.' "

Surely a moment's reflection shows that this passage simply misses the whole point at issue.   It confuses what a proposition is to an ideal intelligence, which knows the reality and can compare it with the proposition, with what it is to us.   The whole point of the passage criticised by Dr. Mivart is that there are propositions concerning things which so far transcend human intelligence that the propositions can *not* be compared by us with the objective reality ; that however fully an ideal intelligence can know exactly how much in them corresponds with objective reality and how much does not, our intelligence cannot know it.   In other words, certain propositions represent mysteries which we cannot fully understand. Dr. Mivart replies that, duly analysed, and compared, they are seen to correspond to intelligible truth, which is undeniable.   But the point is, that the analysis and comparison, though possible to God,

---

[1] *Fortnightly Review*, January, 1900, p. 29.   I should observe that a definition may of course be *final* so far as man is concerned, though from the limits of human language and of human thought on Divine things it does not reach the ultimate analysis as known to God.

may not be so to man. This astonishing confusion lies at the root of the whole of Dr. Mivart's
argument.

Religious philosophers from St. Thomas Aquinas
to Cardinal Newman have regarded the position
rejected by Dr. Mivart as quite fundamental. Human
language has to be used of Divine things. Terms
properly applicable to the finite creature are, in many
theological propositions, used of God Himself. The
real facts corresponding to propositions containing
these terms may be, doubtless, within full reach of
our apprehension as applied to the visible creation,
but they have only some analogy to the truth, when
used of what is Divine. "Are things said concerning
God and concerning creatures said in the same sense
(*univoce*)?" asks St. Thomas Aquinas. He replies
that the terms (*nomina*) are not used in the same
sense; neither are they used in a wholly divergent
sense (*equivoce*). But they are used in an analogical
sense (*analogice*). A term used in reference to man
"in some sense describes and comprehends the thing
signified. It does not do so when it is used in
reference to God; but it leaves the thing signified
as uncomprehended, and exceeding the signification
of the term." "No term," he adds, "is used in the
same sense of God and of creatures."[1] In the same
sense writes Cardinal Newman. He sums up his long
treatment of the subject in the Sermon on "Development" in this one sentence: "Dogmas are symbols of
a Divine fact."

The element of mystery—taken as including all
the unknown particular determinations of a general
dogmatic proposition—is responsible for nearly all

[1] Vide the "Summa," Pars prima, Q. xiii. Art. 3.

changes and developments in the explication of dogma. There is an unknown residuum of Divine truth or of scientific fact which leaves room for mis-understanding. It is the attempt to make more deter-minate the expression of purely theological mystery—to secure it from the misrepresentation of the heretic —which leads to dogmatic development. It is the attempt to express its consequences or details in terms of contemporary science which leads to changes of current teaching, as scientific advance negatives formerly received conjecture.

The process began, in the region of theology pure and simple, with the highly mysterious truths con-cerning the Trinity and Incarnation. That Christ is true God and true man has been the unchanging doctrine of the Church. But the speculations in Greek philosophy on the part of the gnostics and others raised many questions as to what precisely this dogmatic truth involved. Arianism followed. Then came the gradual further explication of the mystery in terms of the Greek philosophy itself.

Here we have two facts to be considered : (1) The dogmatic propositions, even when they are all formu-lated, are only analogies to the reality and not adequate to it; (2) their formulation was gradual, nor was the explication of later ages known to earlier ones. Although the sense of the Church is to be regarded as ever the same, its most exact theological analysis and expression in response to a particular heresy was a matter for discussion the nature of which and the outcome of which could not be foreseen until the heresy arose. The terms of this further explication depended on the philosophy of the time. Transub-stantiation was not philosophically expressed until

after the mediæval acceptance of Aristotelian terminology. The revelation was given once for all.
That was not (as the Vatican Council reminds us)
a matter of philosophical ingenuity. But the propositions in which it was gradually embodied were
defined after much contest to meet various emergencies and to exclude the successive heresies which arose.
Nor was the true explication always obvious. The
term *homoousion* was some years before the Council of
Nicæa set aside by a representative body of theologians
as savouring of Sabellianism. They denied that it
was the true explication of the Catholic doctrine *vis-
à-vis* to Arianism. It was not plain to the Fathers of
Antioch that it did represent the mind of the Church.[1]
Yet at Nicæa, further discussion caused it to be
approved and defined. Apollinaris denied in effect
that Christ was perfect man. His denial was found
heretical, and Theodore of Mopsuestia, adopting the
Catholic doctrine that Christ *was* truly man, passed
on to exaggerate the limits of this doctrine, and
denied that Our Lady could be "mother of God."
" It is madness," he wrote, " to say *God* was born of
the Virgin. Not God, but the temple in which God
dwelt, was born of Mary." Here the vindication of
the Catholic doctrine that Christ was true man led
him to a deduction which he defended as logical, but
which was really false. And his doctrine issued in
the heresy of Nestorius. The definition of Ephesus
registered a further point in the defined analysis of
the mystery. But this definition, in turn, proved
inadequate to guard against exaggerations of the

---

[1] Newman compares this apparent vacillation to the difficulty a man
may have in expressing his own view—though he may *have* a most real
view, without being able in a moment to analyse it.

newly-defined dogma. The definition that Mary was mother of God and the doctrine of *homoousion* were invoked by Eutyches to defend the belief that Christ had only one nature. And the subsequent definition of Chalcedon was required further to secure from perversion the theological expression of the mystery.

The definitions which express the mind of the Church are thus successive. That mind is only gradually defined. In 1869 there were still Catholics in the communion of the Church who denied that the doctrine of Papal Infallibility was in accordance with the mind of the Church. The definition of 1870 set such doubts at rest. A further element in the mind of the Church was explicitly determined. We could conceive exaggerations of the limits of Papal Infallibility which might be condemned like the Monophysite exaggeration of the limits of *homoousion.*

Thus development in the explication of *purely* theological mystery comes of reflection, *vis-à-vis* to contemporary controversy, on the original revelation. Such explications the Church has not hesitated to define (on occasion) as part of the deposit of the faith, thereby cutting off philosophical explanations which clashed with the revealed mystery.

Let us now take a class of instances where the mysteries involved are not religious but scientific— where the unknown elements arise from our imperfect or defective conceptions of the physical universe. Take the passage of the Creed : "He ascended into Heaven, and sitteth at the right hand of God the Father." Here, again, the whole question for explication is : How far, and in what sense, does the proposition correspond with objective Reality ? Obviously the boy who regards it as a declaration that Christ

went up through the blue firmament to a place called
" Heaven," and is now sitting on a throne, means one
thing by it, while he who declines to assent to more
than that Christ left the earth and passed to His
Father in a manner which we cannot understand,
takes a very different view of the *manner* and *degree*
in which the proposition corresponds with objective
Reality. The boy explains it in the terms obviously
suggested by metaphorical language, his own scientific
culture raising no objection to this simple explanation.
Yet both believe in the same essential doctrine,
although their explication of it is different. The
advance of secular knowledge makes the boy's explication difficult or impossible to accept. But the proposition is still regarded as true, though science has
excluded the erroneous scientific explication. Thus
a false theological explication of a purely theological
mystery is excluded by a theological definition. A
false physical explication is banished by a definite step
of *scientific progress in the race, or of culture in the
individual.*

The same principle applies in the dogma of the
"Resurrectio Carnis "—"I believe in the resurrection of
the body." All may agree that the same body will rise
at the last day, but when we come to give the explication of this statement, to define how it takes place,
and so corresponds with objective Reality—when we
ask, What is the same body ?—the explication of
St. Thomas Aquinas, based on the physics of Aristotle,
will be one thing, the explication which modern science
permits will be another. Here, again, the mystery is
scientific, and science may point the onward path.

So, again, as to the doctrine of eternal punishment.
Theologians attempted to ascertain and express its

relations with the world known to physical science.
They asked : Where is the "everlasting fire"?
St. Gregory the Great and St. Thomas Aquinas
debate whether the fire is within the bowels of the
earth or in some unknown part of the earth—not
necessarily beneath its surface. The former is regarded as more probable from a text in the Apocalypse
—which, however, is an anti-Copernican text. The
modern explication, since Copernicanism has entirely
changed our views of the universe, must be widely
different.

Let us, to fix our ideas clearly, consider somewhat
more fully the dogma of the "resurrection of the
body." Let us go to the "Summa Theologica" of St.
Thomas Aquinas, and read its explication in the light
of mediæval science. We are reminded, as we read
the pages, of the frescoes by Orcagna in the Campo
Santa at Pisa, or of the pictures of Giotto. Each
stage of the process is set before us. The details of
the fire which is to consume the world are given.
The question is discussed: "Is the voice of the
trumpet the cause of the resurrection?" Again:
"Will it be in the night?" "Will it be sudden?"
Equally we are made to see what the risen bodies of
the elect will be like—their agility, their transparency,
their subtlety, their impassibility. The actual process
of the resurrection is described. We find each body
regarded as reducible to a definite heap of ashes.
"Ashes" is used, we are told, partly (from the heathen
custom of cremation) to express the substance into
which the body decomposes, partly because the fire
which will burn away the *fomes peccati* will really
reduce the remains of the body to ashes. We find
the axioms of a philosophy which combined physics

with metaphysics quoted as determining that the
various limbs will rise, that the "nails" will rise,
that the "hair" will rise, that certain "humours of
the body" must rise as being part of its perfection
and integrity ; that other "humours," as part of the
corruptible element (tending to death), will not rise ;
that those tending to life, but only to the life of *others*
(as "milk") will, again, not rise. The question as to
the identity of the risen body with the body as it has
been in life is discussed, and it is explained that the
very same dust and ashes will rise again, and that
probably each portion will go to form the same part
of the body as in life "so far as the essential and
organic parts are concerned ; though perhaps not in
the case of the accidental parts as the nails and the
hair."

Without denying that the careful student will find
many facts and principles in these pages which he
can express in modern language—(indeed, modern
theologians have adopted portions of St. Thomas's
treatment)—or that the ages of faith may have shed
a light on the future which we should be unwise
to lose sight of, it is equally clear that all that part
of the explication of the dogma which turns upon
mediæval physics must now be abandoned, as it has
been abandoned, in the Catholic schools. The underlying assumption that the material particles belonging
to one man's body are his own definite property for
life has now given way to the knowledge that they
are constantly changing. Therefore we know that
in whatever the identity of the body at different
periods in life does consist, it does not consist in
the identity of its physical component atoms. The
dogma of the resurrection of the body remains

unchanged. Its scientific explication necessarily changes as scientific knowledge advances.

All defined dogmas, then, are regarded as immutably true; yet their explication is gradual, and their full explication is often beyond us. So far as this explication depends on theology, theology yields a negative advance—excluding heresy by definition; so far as it depends on science, the advance of science yields a similar advance—excluding conjecture by ascertained fact. This view of the case is what Dr. Mivart regards as shuffling, but it appears to the present writer to be common sense. St. Thomas asks if terms whose meaning answers exactly to nothing in the thing are necessarily empty, and he replies "No," because they may express our *relation* (*habitudo*) with Reality. This is expressly said of the knowledge of God, but it equally applies, for a similar reason, to the knowledge of many things so far out of the reach of our experience that we cannot have more than an approximate and analogical conception of them. For practical purposes, for the ascertainment of our practical relations with truth, it is enough to know that Christ went to His Father, that the body somehow will rise again, that the wicked shall for ever be punished, that we have in Scripture the Word of God, without our being able to reduce to exhaustive analysis all that is involved in these doctrines.

The theological doctrine of the inerrancy of Scripture is an example in which both the principles I have indicated have to be considered—the principle of theological analysis and that of the scientific criticism. What is the real mind of the Church?—the abiding belief behind the change which has come to pass since Copernicanism was regarded as involving "error" in Scripture? Undoubtedly the *communis sensus* of Catholics in Galileo's time was that the inerrancy of Scripture involved by logical consequence the falsity of Copernicanism. "Most certainly," writes a well-known Ultramontane theologian, "all Catholics who in Galileo's time laboured to 'think with the Church' would have rejected Copernicanism as anti-scriptural." [1]

The change which our own day has witnessed has resulted from two causes: (1) the scientific advance, which has made Copernicanism a matter almost of demonstration: (2) the concurrent and partly consequent reflection, which is still taking place, on the limits of the Catholic teaching concerning the inerrancy of Scripture with a view to its reconciliation with known facts.

The first of these causes needs no further comment here. As to the second, reflection made it clear that the strongest statements made by theologians as to the literal truth of all Holy Writ had never been consistently upheld—that they had been of the nature of general statements of a technical principle. That there is no "error" in the Bible must be understood as a theological statement whose explication is not at once obvious, and not as popular slang. Many of the Fathers and theologians who have thus spoken of Holy Scripture, have also understood portions of the narrative figuratively. Dr. Mivart treats as a good joke—what is really an instance of this significant fact—that Cardinal Cajetan regarded the story of the formation of Eve not as history but as allegory.

As to the further explanation of the inerrancy of

---

[1] *Dublin Review*, July, 1871, p. 141.

Scripture it has been given in various ways. To the present writer the following appeals most forcibly. The root-principle of the doctrine and its real meaning are best approached by considering the way it is generally stated, and the defined dogma from which it is derived. It was defined at Trent that God is the Author of Scripture, and the conclusion at once follows that "He cannot be the Author of error." But this does not mean that He cannot utilise ideas due to the imperfect knowledge of a rude age in conveying to it great truths. As the only way to teach a child is through the immature and inadequate ideas and knowledge within its comprehension, so too with the human race in its scientific infancy. I teach my tiny child his first lesson in history by picture-books. He takes each detail of the picture as literally accurate. Thus there is incidental error, mixed with the truth he learns. The parent is not the author of the child's error, which he is doing his best to diminish. This appears to be substantially what Leo XIII. contends in a famous passage in the Encyclical *Providentissimus* on Scripture—a passage which materially qualifies the apparently more stringent views put forth in the rest of the Encyclical. To use, in the Book of Josue, or elsewhere, the *communis sermo*, the figurative language intelligible at the time, in the scientific childhood of the race, was not theologically to be the Author of error ; although, if interpreted literally, the language of Scripture was erroneous.

Thus the language of the Scriptures was anti-Copernican and not literally true, without detriment to the fact that God was through the Scriptures teaching truth and not falsehood, diminishing rather than creating error. The Catholic dogma did not change. But man's understanding of its practical consequences did very considerably change, and he had to explain it differently. For to the Roman theologians of 1616 the dogma in question included the view that Copernicanism not only was erroneous, but involved nothing short of heresy.[1]

And this further analysis of the dogma has (providentially as it seems to some) enabled us to face recent critical research, which would have led to a far rougher break with traditional explanations, had these not been already to some extent modified owing to the Galileo case.

For example, a writer who is at once a learned theologian and an accomplished man of science— the Rev. Dr. Clarke of Chiswick, a member of the Pontifical Commission on Biblical Studies—has thus summarised, in answer to Dr. Mivart, the lines on which he has attempted in his writings to reconcile the document-theory of Genesis with traditional Catholic principles :—

"Writing in defence of the theory, I appealed to the presence of real or seeming contradictions, *e.g.* to the single couple of birds in Gen. vi. 19 and the seven couples in Gen. vii. 2, as one among many indications that the account of the Deluge consists of quotations from distinct documents, It was, of course, rejoined by representatives of the conservative school that if this was a contradiction, the inspired writer must have asserted what was not true either when he said there were two couples or when he said there were seven. I answered : (1) that when the Encyclical declares that there is nothing false in the Bible, the meaning is, not that, *e.g.*, 'There is no God,' which we read in one of the Psalms, is true, but that nothing which the Bible, properly interpreted,

---

[1] This is expressly stated in the Decree of 1616 against Galileo.

vouches for is false ; (2), that an author avoids not only a contradiction, but even what looks like one, in his own statements ; and (3) that, if one document said seven and not two, while the other said two and not seven, the sacred author cannot but have perceived the contradictory character of the statements, and must, in quoting them, have intended no more than to lay them side by side before his readers.   The following question was consequently put : ' If, in addition to the statements in the Bible which are vouched for and are true, there are in it unvouched-for statements which are or may be false, how are the two kinds to be discriminated ? ' I replied that, though when one author cites another, the *primâ facie* inference, the inference to start from, is that he regards the other as an authority to be followed, this provisional inference does not always hold good, and does not do so where, for example, he extracts two divergent accounts. If he gives only one account we have still to consider whether and to what extent he or other inspired writers, or the Church in her doctrinal definitions, build on it in matters of faith or morals.   We have also to take into account the context, the author's style and manner of writing, and the literary methods of his time, together with whatever else is relevant.

"If this is shuffling and dishonesty, I have to plead guilty to both.   As it is not, I repudiate the accusation.   But Dr. Mivart is a physical scientist (in the old sense of ' physical '), and the Bible is the essential teaching literature of religion. He has, it seems to me, ignored that it teaches as a literature, not as a text-book."

But these are the views which made Dr. Mivart most angry.   Here are his words on the subject, written to the *Times* of February 1, 1900—

"Ecclesiastics . . . have profoundly disgusted me by simultaneous assertions and denials.   [They] try to play fast and loose with what they profess to regard as most sacred, saying that certain things must be believed while yet they may be disbelieved ; that it is necessary for salvation to hold with the Fathers and doctors of the Church and also

that there is no occasion really to do so ; that the decrees
of Trent and the Vatican must absolutely be accepted as
they are meant, and yet that they may be explained away."

This, I must be allowed to say, is simply the view
of a mind which fails to realise that theology must
ever preserve the record of the swayings to and
fro of theological opinion in the past. To make it
perfectly simple would be to destroy its roots. A
system which embodies the records of 1900 years of
controversy among the subtlest minds, under the
varying intellectual conditions, and with the various
culture of so many successive ages, cannot be anything
else than highly complex in expression. Moreover,
it cannot be in every case easy of interpretation. All
the reasons which make the statute-book complex,
which give the lawyers trouble in applying it to
concrete cases, apply here, and many more, as the
ground covered is far wider. Once it is admitted
that not a revelation in secular knowledge, but
only a revelation in faith and morals, was given
by God, yet that it had to be translated into
practical maxims and practical information for the
benefit of the world,—had to be made living and
operative, in every age, to be expressed in harmony
with the mode of understanding the world belonging
to that age—it becomes clear that the best statements
of religious truth must have been *accompanied* by
much which was inaccurate. Such accompaniments
found their way into current expositions insensibly
and automatically. And although a perfect intelligence could have done what Dr. Mivart wishes,
could have kept entirely separate the truth from its
accretions, human beings could do no such thing
except by the aid of repeated *fresh* revelations.

Human reason can effect this separation only step by step. Where a step is taken by a definition of the Church, where an accretion added by individuals is ruled to be an heretical perversion, .the Divine "assistance" is regarded as securing that definition from error, but no more. The normal process of arriving at the truth (under Providence) is the process of reflection on the primitive revelation, and it is the business of the theologian explicitly to register its results as each fresh heresy is felt to involve explicit opposition to some part of the "deposit." There is no fresh revelation to meet the emergency. Where, on the other hand, the accretion is that of false science, it is scientific discovery which gets rid of it.

In both cases it is almost inevitable, from the nature of the human mind, that, as thought advances, opinion should sway to the right and to the left; that a heresy or error in one direction should evoke a strong statement in the opposite one; and that when this is taken in too absolute or maximistic a sense by individuals the contradiction made from a different point of view should appear to some to be inconsistent with the previous ruling or definition. It might most plausibly have been argued in the fourth century, by one whose attention was concentrated on the error of the Docetæ which denied Christ's humanity—by one who was earnestly vindicating Christ's true humanity—that the phrase "Mother of God" was a return to Docetism. So in effect argued Theodore.

This tendency to reaction is not without its counter-part in scientific speculation. Our fathers witnessed the change of opinion from the days of Pritchard's book on Man to those of Darwinism; from the days when it was considered bold to oppose the view that man so far differs from man that they cannot come from a common stock, to the days when men of science claimed a common ancestor for a man and an ape. In both cases—in theology and in science—the pendulum sways far on each side. We now, seeing the past more clearly in its true perspective, can trace the line of advance. The hands of the clock move unerringly onward, though the pendulum goes from side to side. But those who look only at the present minute, who watch only the swinging to and fro of the pendulum, undergo a puzzle similar to that of Professor Huxley's celebrated "death-watches," which could find no other purpose in a clock than to tick. They need to trust the "wider teleology" of the Church, and to realise its patience and its eternity. Although the modifying of language and shifting of points of view may make the pendulum of orthodox argument seem to go sometimes very near to heterodox language on either side, though theology may at moments seem to stagger, it nevertheless advances with growing coherence. Thus in the grace controversy Thomists were roundly accused of Calvinism, and Molinists of Pelagianism. The policy of partial toleration has really secured the belief in freedom requisite for moral effort, without attempting to dispel the impenetrable mystery of predestination. Only a totally unhistorical view can regard the resulting subtleties as disingenuous. Casuistry is unnecessary to the angels. The only way to make it unnecessary to man is that he should boldly sin. So, too, we avoid theological subtlety either by the direct vision of things Divine or by absolute agnosticism.

From another point of view Dr. Mivart's objection seems to me an instance of the objection of every practical man with limited imagination to all technical

sciences. How well Sir Walter Scott has drawn the
long-winded, prolix, and pedantic lawyer, with his list
of precedents and his Latin quotations! Or take
Manzoni's Dottore Azzecca-Garbugli in the *Promessi
Sposi*, to whom Renzo goes for advice in his trouble.
The obvious instances given in such caricatures show
mainly the tiresome prolixity of technical law. The
technique of an elaborate science overwhelms a small
man—as Saul's armour was too much for David. He
becomes a slave to the letter. Yet, after all, it is only
from the legal expert that we can get a safe opinion.
We must endure the fools of the profession. We
may smile at them. We cannot afford to despise the
science, or to regard its subtleties as unnecessary.

But the case is similar with Dr. Mivart's own
science—medicine. Its deductions from the *data* of
scientific observation are often as inaccurate as those
of the theologian from the *data* of revelation. Most
of us have had bitter experience of terrible blunders
asserted confidently by our doctor as truths, supported
perhaps by all the technical apparatus of proof. Yet
which of us does not feel that our best hope of health
and of knowledge in such subjects comes from the
medical profession ?

People will and do ask : Where are the changes in
current opinion to end ? What security have we that
the most cherished beliefs will remain ?

Here it may be observed, in the first place, that
many of the changes hardly touch the practical religious life. They startle—as Copernicanism may
have startled the practical man—but after the first
shock, their actual remoteness soon becomes evident.
The Ptolemaist soon found that the moving earth did
not shake him, that he did not tumble off it, and, that

for all the purposes of everyday life, his old plane astronomy was still sufficient. Its practical teaching remained true, though its theoretical explanation was changed. In all branches of knowledge ultimate explanations of what is practically known by experience, or by reliable testimony, are what least affect us in everyday life. If the wicked go to hell, it matters little whether hell be in the centre of the earth or no. Ultimate beliefs and convictions, indeed, do matter, and here the question becomes partly speculative. These must, indeed, have their fixed and unchangeable element. But this element he who holds that the Church is from God has in abundance. The fact that our knowledge of the physical universe is constantly deepening, that, therefore, our account of it is ever changing, does not make a sensible man sceptical of its ultimate reality or of the reliability of his senses. Each step of knowledge displaces some imperfect conception, but we are conscious that the changes are a movement towards fuller knowledge. So, too, that Divine truth is intellectually inexhaustible throws no doubt on its Reality.

And the limits to possible change—even by way of explication—are sufficiently clear in those central truths which are at the very heart of religion. Of such mysteries as the Trinity, the Incarnation, we understand little, and can never understand all. But they must ever remain with no part abrogated. Of others, as the Resurrection and the Virgin birth, we as little understand the physical mysteries they involve. They do not profess to be scientific explanations of revealed truths. They are not taught by theologians by way of explanation, but by the Church as facts, and facts they must remain for us—

inexplicable, but certain. Our ultimate belief in them
stands or falls with our belief in the Church. For
their full explanation we must wait " until the shadows
flee." Mysterious facts—but undoubted facts—they
must ever be for us here.

Once again it will be objected that the subtle explanations and distinctions which this view of the case
involves are unsuited to beliefs designed (inclusively)
for the man in the street. I answer that the *theory*
of knowledge must be subtle, even of our knowledge
of a table or a chair. It has in every department,
and from the beginning, given trouble to the best
philosophers. For *practical* knowledge, the Church
provides by the " Schola Theologorum " and the living
exponents of the Church's manifold tradition—the
parish priest, the preacher, the confessor. So Nature
provides for the unspeculative man by bidding him
trust his senses which represent a sufficient practical
knowledge of the sensible world—although the man
of science has a more accurate knowledge of it, and
although it may well be that the angels conceive of
the world much more perfectly than we do. Their
knowledge may as far exceed ours as the knowledge
of the man with five senses exceeds that of the blind
man who has but four. The principle on which priest
or theologian is trusted, is that the approved thought of
the Church exercised on the Divine Revelation ought
to guide the practical belief of the many. The man in
the street must trust the experts. Private judgment
falls between two stools. An unskilful individual reasoning on one-hundredth part of the evidence is not likely
to be right. The ordinary theological text-book, and
the educated priest, on a large number of questions, can
give an explanation representing the general consent

of Christian thought within the Church. On newer and more difficult issues they will probably be better informed than the man in the street, even if in evil days the text-book may be behind the best theological thought of the time. It ought not to be. But it may be. The determination to be safe renders the official mind slow, and may make it, in this or that instance, lag behind the strenuous and restless speculations of these latter days.

Such, then, in rough outline, has been the Church's mode of action in guarding the mysterious unalterable revelation, and at the same time making it intelligible to changeful man at the various stages of his history—in the changing conditions of custom, thought, and secular knowledge of successive ages. The method of the Church has been tested, and found in the long run, to be adequate. Its principles are ascertainable in history. The exact nature of the compound between the changeless and the changing elements which our grandchildren will see in the future we cannot tell. But we believe that the Church will eventually be adequate to its task—of preserving the revelation inviolate, and of effectually showing it to be credible to man at every stage of scientific culture and growing knowledge. To say this is only to profess the faith of a Catholic. Our present task is to work together as members of the Church in applying its principles to the present ; in keeping the faith still itself—not with the identity of the fossil which has ceased to have living relations with its environment, but with the identity of a living being who continues to be himself, and preserves his life by assimilating what is wholesome from without ; who asserts his own distinctive individuality, and influences his neighbours

by means of that strength and development which
are so largely derived from the extrinsic conditions of
the social and intellectual life of his own time.

NOTE.—A critic who has read these pages objects that I have not kept
carefully apart those theological conclusions which may change and
those truths *de fide* which are immutable. I have inserted some notes
to meet his objection. But to a large extent the very difficulty I am
dealing with is that the distinction in question cannot always be securely
applied in a period of scientific transition. What one generation of
theologians regards as heresy—that is, opposed to what is *de fide*—the
next may consider as being opposed only to an opinion which may,
after all, prove false. We cannot be too often reminded that Galileo's
theory was by the Roman theologians of 1616 declared to be not only
erroneous but heretical.   "It was generally received," writes Cardinal
Newman, "*as if the Apostles had expressly delivered it both orally and
in writing, as a truth of Revelation,* that the earth was stationary."
The advance of science and of theological analysis *subsequently* changed
this general opinion.   The distinction of 1616 between what was heretical
and what was merely erroneous proved to have been a blunder.   And we
may blunder again if we allow theological presumption, that a conclusion
to which the science or criticism of the day points is heretical, always to
blind us to evidence that it may be true.

IV.

THE FOUNDATIONS OF BELIEF.

MR. BALFOUR has explained for us, in the Introduction to his book on the " Foundations of Belief," that the work is designed " to recommend a particular way of looking at the World problems, which, whether we like it or not, we are compelled to face." And the attitude he recommends, while forming a basis for the study of Theology, is brought into relief by contrast with what he calls Naturalism, the leading doctrines of which are, "that we may know phenomena and the laws by which they are connected, but nothing more. More there may or may not be, but if it exists we can never apprehend it." This system is, he adds, practically identical with what has been called Agnosticism or Empiricism. And yet, if one were to look for Mr. Balfour's intellectual ancestors, I believe that it is among the founders of Empiricism that they would be discovered. The Empirical School took its rise, as did Induction, in a protest against indulgence in speculation at the expense of fact. The father of Empiricism, John Locke, had been perplexed and discouraged in his undergraduate days by the futile subtlety of the scholastic method pursued at Oxford. "True knowledge," he wrote, "first grew in the world by rational observation . . . [but] man laboured by his imagination to supply what his observation and experience failed him in; and when he could not discover by experience the principles, causes, and methods of Nature's workmanship, he would needs fashion all these out of his own thought, and *make* a world to himself, framed and governed by his own intelligence."[1] The consequence was that "the most acute and ingenious part of man became by custom and education engaged in empty speculation." This tendency is apparent in the exhaustive accounts of the Universe given by the later Schoolmen—accounts based on principles which they dispensed themselves from proving, on the plea that they were "innate." It was this method of reasoning that Bacon styled the *intellectus sibi permissus;* and, like Bacon, Locke protested against it. He insisted on rigid observation of the actual capacities of the human mind in place of indulgence of the speculative imagination; on the humble search for what knowledge the constitution of our nature permits us, in place of the "vanity" of supposing that our "narrow weak minds" could "penetrate into the hidden causes of things," and understand "this great and curious fabric of the world, the workmanship of the Almighty," which in truth "cannot be perfectly comprehended by any understanding but His that made it." But, on the other hand, Locke was no Agnostic. The man who should acquiesce in scepticism because he recognises the limitations of human knowledge he compares to one "who would not use his legs, but sit still and perish because he had no wings to fly."

Mr. Balfour's temper and method are, up to a certain point, very similar. He shows the same deep

[1] Fragment, "De Arte Medica," 1668.

sense of the limitations of human knowledge, the same aversion to dogmatism, the same conviction of the futility of mere "brain-spinning," which he compares to a man walking nimbly on the deck of a ship, and congratulating himself on his successful locomotion, while all the time the ship itself may be making its way rapidly to shoals and rocks which will bring it to inevitable destruction. And by means of another nautical simile he indicates his own method, —that of studying diligently the universe of fact, intent on missing no glimpse of real light which it may afford, by which we may guide our path, instead of inventing an ideal system which has no correspondence with the perplexing world in which man's lot is actually cast. "If we have to find our way," he writes, "over difficult seas and under murky skies without compass or chronometer, we need not on that account allow the ship to drive at random. Rather ought we to weigh with the more anxious care every indication, be it negative or positive, and from whatever quarter it may come, which may help us to guess at our position and to lay out the course which it behoves us to steer."

How, then, if Mr. Balfour's spirit is in great measure that which originally animated the Empiricists, has it come about that the Empirical philosophy is one principal object of his attack?

One reason is that the later Empiricists themselves became speculative dogmatists.

Locke began, as we have seen, by protesting against unreal theorising and arbitrary assumptions. He proposed to scrutinise the limits of our faculties of knowledge. He found that a large number of our ideas really resolve themselves into the products of

sensible experience.   The analysis of experience was
to him what the extensive observation of physical fact
was to Bacon.   It was safe ground.   It was clear
that at least all convictions which could be resolved
into products of experience were true, whatever else
might be due to prejudice or illusion.   He treated
the mind as a *tabula rasa* on which was gradually
traced a network woven by sensation and the mind's
reflection on its sensation.   But with Hume the innate
love of human nature for speculative systematising
returned.   Locke had never limited human certainties
to the knowledge of phenomena.[1]   His statement that
all knowledge comes from experience did not exclude
God from our knowledge.   Hume arbitrarily limited
the meaning of the statement in question, and made
it the point of departure for the freest speculative deduction.   He transformed Empiricism as understood
by Locke, into Naturalism as explained by Mr.
Balfour.   Berkeley had led the way in the negative
portion of his system of Idealism.   Hume developed
this side of Berkeley's teaching, and reached a
scepticism, highly speculative in that he adhered to
rigid deduction from his own arbitrary interpretation
of Locke's system, and neglected the facts which his
very reasoning process must presuppose,—a scepticism which he combined with the dogmatism involved
in his argument against miracles.

The successive phases of more or less dogmatic
Empiricism need not be traced here.   The same
temper was visible—though in a lesser degree—in
J. S. Mill's attempt to reduce our knowledge, even

---

[1] Locke's ideas of reflection, and his ontological certainties, "God
the world, and the soul," are, it need hardly be said, instances of his
departure from thorough-going Empiricism.

our mathematical knowledge, to the inseparable association of ideas. A more marked instance of it is the
application by Mr. Herbert Spencer of the Evolution
theory—which in Darwin's hands was so cautiously
treated, with so much hesitation as to its details, with
such wide observation of facts—to form a complete
and symmetrical system of philosophy. Both these
systems are as arbitrary and dogmatic in what they exclude from the sphere of our knowledge, as had been the
Scholastic "innate" principles in what they included.

Thus has come about the curious phenomenon
that systems, primarily associated with two eminent
representatives of that scientific temper which resents
dogmatism and excessive speculation as diverting attention from the world of fact, have been applied and
transformed to support conclusions replete with the
very dogmatic and speculative character which was so
repugnant to their authors. The detailed theories of
Mill and even of Herbert Spencer have perhaps lost
credit, but the tendency they represent is still abroad.
Mr. Balfour opposes to it a rigid application of the true
laws of induction. The all-solving principle—whether
of association or of evolution—is (as a principle of
universal application) a dogmatic assumption based
on an insufficient induction. In Mr. Balfour's own
words, it "leaves large tracts and aspects of [the
human] consciousness unaccounted for."

Mr. Balfour appeals, then, in the first place, to a
wider and completer process of mental observation.
He examines our various convictions and conceptions,
—be they prejudices or truths, illusions or elements of
real knowledge,—never allowing himself to assume
the genesis of what is complex from what is simple,
in consequence of an *a priori* presumption (latently

dogmatic) that such a genesis must be ascertainable. He recognises the mysterious as a fact in our consciousness no less than the simple. To profess, for the sake of consistency, to unify things which are really distinct, is as dogmatic as to invent for the sake of professing to know. If what is at first sight mysterious on closer scrutiny *does* resolve itself into a disguised complication of simpler and lower elements, well and good. This is a fact to be accepted and reckoned with. If, on the other hand, the more you look at it the less such a resolution appears possible, if instead of a manifestation of something lower and simpler than itself, it appears to have its source in something higher and *more* mysterious than itself, that is equally a matter of observation of which the true inductive philosopher must take account. Thus Mr. Herbert Spencer, in the course of his highly symmetrical disposition of mental phenomena and their causes, explains the ethical instincts as the outcome of qualities which have helped individuals or tribes in the struggle for existence. Mr. Balfour, on the contrary, opposes to his procedure—which is obviously based on the strongest presumption that the facts of the case ought to square with his theory —the true inductive method of close observation of the phenomena in question. Is such an account the lawful result of observation? How can it be reconciled with the sentiments of moral approbation, of sin, of remorse? Can you fashion a conscience which is really like the human conscience from Mr. Spencer's principles; or do you get only something which stands to conscience much in the same relation as Hans Andersen's clockwork nightingale, with its one mechanical tune, stands to the nightingale in our

woods with its free and living song? Is an account
of art which divests the artist entirely of the character
of a seer, an interpreter of some great Reality, consistent with convictions of our nature which have at
least as good a claim on our attention as those simpler
elements which are made the basis of so far-reaching
a generalisation? These are the questions which
Mr. Balfour asks in effect; and so far he is recalling
the Empiricists to their own principles. He is pointing out that they in their turn are theorising and
dogmatising; that they too are ignoring, in their
impatience for symmetrical theory, the full variety
and puzzling complexity of the world of fact.

But, after all, both Empiricism and Induction, while
they represented a step forward of the utmost importance to philosophy, shared at one time or another the
fate of nearly all great movements of thought. They
both seized upon truths which had hitherto been
neglected; and they both neglected truths which had
hitherto been recognised. If even Locke undervalued the rational element in experience, Bacon did
so equally in scientific investigation. "He was so
afraid," wrote Dean Church, "of assumptions and
'anticipations' and prejudices—his great bugbear was
so much the *intellectus sibi permissus*, the mind given
liberty to guess and imagine and theorise, instead of,
as it ought, servilely submitting itself to the control of
facts—that he missed the true place of the rational
and formative element in his account of Induction";
and his system, as he designed it, was, in the words
of the same writer, "as barren of results as those deductive philosophies on which he lavished his scorn."[1]
Beginning on the side of the observer, protesting

[1] Dean Church's "Bacon," p. 245.

against the mediæval tendency to pose as a God
and imagine a scheme which has no ascertainable
counterpart in reality, he was slow to appreciate the
methods whereby a Newton or a Galileo could inter-
rogate Nature by experiment, and even leap with a
fair prospect of success to great generalisations.   The
experimental methods have received their best analysis
in Mill's "Canons of Induction."   The first conception of great and fruitful hypotheses must ever
be the special prerogative of genius.   The character
of such hypotheses differs utterly from that of the
mediæval assumptions, in that our Newtons and our
Darwins, instead of measuring the world by their own
minds, spring to the method of Nature herself, are instinctively guided by previous familiarity with Nature,
and await verification by experiment.   But it differs
also from Bacon's own system not only in its use of
experiment, but in its tentative trust of the highest
semi-conscious intellectual processes as an ultimate
means of ascertaining those very facts which Bacon
explored only by the light of direct observation.

What the method of a Newton adds to Bacon's induction Mr. Balfour in parts of his work appears to me
to add to the Empirical methods.   Passive induction
was sterile; passive scrutiny of the consciousness
had from the first an Agnostic tendency.   In both
cases positive illusion was avoided; in neither were
all available indications of truth utilised.   Mr. Balfour
perceives the necessity of not merely passively observing, but of interrogating our consciousness, of
finding out the presuppositions of coherent experience,
of guessing at the underlying laws, of framing, provisionally at least, great assumptions on insufficient
evidence, to see if perchance their truth or falsehood

will become clearer in the very act of using them as working hypotheses. The verification of a great hypothesis is a kind of questioning and cross-questioning of Nature. Her awful silence in the presence of the unperceiving gives way before those who know how to put the questions. By a succession of replies, each of which is simply Yes or No, she discloses significant truths. So too Mr. Balfour cross-questions the psychological world. He takes, for example, the plausible assumption of synthetic evolutionism as to the genesis of the human faculties. Mr. Spencer began the process of examination, and gained, as we all know, answers up to a certain point satisfactory. Mr. Balfour proceeds to cross-question. He asks if, on the supposition that the Human Reason finds its ultimate origin—as naturalistic advocates of evolution have supposed—in a purely reasonless concourse of atoms, it can have that correspondence with objective fact which we inevitably assume. He elicits in detail the kind of knowledge which (even waiving this initial difficulty) arises on the naturalistic hypothesis in the course of evolution—only that knowledge which is necessary for the preservation of the species. He asks Psychology if the forces contemplated by Mr. Spencer can possibly account for the mass of our rational knowledge, and Psychology perforce answers No.

That he gains an equally positive answer in respect of the hypotheses which he considers on the affirmative side cannot be said. We remember that Newton long refused to consider the law of gravitation established, because of a slight discrepancy between the pace at which, according to the best information available, the moon fell through space, and that at which a stone would fall from the same height.

For sixteen years he continued his observations, which at last resulted in the discovery that the distance of the moon had been miscalculated. Thus the discrepancy was at last removed, and the hypothesis verified. Mr. Balfour appears in his book to be still pursuing the double process—considering on the one hand the consequences of the great spiritual hypotheses of Theism and Christianity, which he has invoked to account for the facts, and on the other hand ever enlarging his observation of the facts themselves in their inner significance and detailed analysis. Still the conclusion suggested by him seems at first sight to carry out the lines I have indicated. Naturalism has failed to account even for the power of the human reason to give us "any general view of the phenomenal world," let alone its powers of reflecting "with sufficient precision remote aspects of reality." The only possible explanation is that the world is the "work of a rational Being" who made "*it* intelligible, and *us*, in however feeble a fashion, able to understand it" (p. 301). And it is suggested that in some degree we share the attributes of the Rational Author of Nature (p. 76). Again, he draws a similar conclusion from the failure of naturalistic evolution to give a sufficient account of conscience. It offers only the explanation suggested by the genesis of conscience in the course of evolution, which genesis has no ethical character. Mr. Balfour supplies the deficiency by postulating a Divine purpose working *through* evolution as an instrument, so that "in the region of Design it is only through the later stages that the earlier can be understood" (p. 325). These presuppositions, necessary for the scheme of human knowledge, and yet outside the sphere to which Naturalism limits that knowledge, are accepted much as the postulates of science are accepted —notably the existence of an independent external world. The ground of their acceptance the author expresses provisionally, and with hesitation as to the adequacy of the terms, as the " satisfaction of a need." The relation between a need and its satisfaction "is something different from that between a premise and its conclusion," but "equally remote from that between a desire and its fulfilment." It has not the logical validity of the first nor the "casual, wavering, and wholly subjective character of the second."

I have given what appears to me to be the true account of Mr. Balfour's method as a whole ; but a great deal of his work has a more destructive character than I have indicated. On lines familiar to readers of his " Defence of Philosophic Doubt," he sets him-self to prove not merely the inadequacy of many of the processes which we have been accustomed to consider as rational, but their misleading character. The reader finds himself carried on from criticism of a purely Naturalistic account of the origin and capa-cities of human reason to what seems very like a destructive criticism of the rational capacities of mankind. " So far as empirical science can tell us anything about the matter," he writes, " most of the proximate causes of belief and all its ultimate causes are non-rational in their character." While it is perfectly plain that Mr. Balfour holds that an ultimate rational cause of which Empiricism knows nothing does give a rational source to the processes whereby we come to believe, it is not equally plain that he gives sufficient ground for supposing that man can

find in the scrutiny of his rational nature itself any
guarantee for the accuracy of such an opinion.   Some
readers may feel that the processes of the human reason
are so far discredited by him, in his detailed examination,
as to make them appear unequal to aspiring to decide on
the very cogent considerations which Mr. Balfour also
presents in favour of a belief in a rational origin of our
own reason—an origin which ensures some correspondence between the subjective and the objective.

Indeed we have in these portions of his work—
notably in the chapter on the Philosophical Basis of
Naturalism—indications of a line of argument which,
while consistent with the *terms* of his conclusion
(already quoted), really differs from the argument I
have indicated, and changes the import of that conclusion.   Not only is Empiricism viewed as incomplete in these parts of the book, but the Empirical
methods which in their place we are all in the habit
of using, are regarded as misleading.   Scientific and
psychological analyses are shown to lead simply to an
impasse.   Instead of being brought by Locke's method
of close scrutiny of the consciousness to a higher
estimate of the rational capacities than Naturalism
contemplates, Mr. Balfour here reaches a lower.   Instead of a Reason so wide in its sweep that it suggests
a Source higher than any which the evolutionary
processes themselves disclose, we have a reason
observably self-contradictory where we are in a position to scrutinise its operation.   Instead of the perception, by a process outstripping logical analysis, of
the necessary presuppositions of the logical processes
themselves, we have non-rational instincts contradicting analysis.   Instead of rising to an ultimate
Rational and Ethical cause by a survey (in which

Reason, latent and explicit, takes an active share) of all that is noblest in the nature of man—by a process higher though less capable of verification than mere analysis (just as sight travels to the vast world of fixed stars, though its information is far less precise and far harder to verify than the information which sight and touch together give us of the properties of a stone), we invoke a Divine guarantee, in our despair, to justify beliefs which all examination shows to be simply non-rational. In place of the "need" for a God of Reason and Goodness being tantamount to something like a rational necessity suggested by the highest rational insight, we have, in the words of Tennyson's despairing infidel, only "the guess of a worm in the dust and the shadow of its desire."

I fully share Mr. Balfour's desire to face facts frankly ; and were the result of an accurate investigation of the rational processes what this line of argument implies, it would become us to resign ourselves to the inevitable. But I believe that the case is otherwise. Moreover, it appears to me that the two lines of thought, neither fully developed, but both suggested in the work before us, are really inconsistent. I shall therefore, as I conceive, be furthering Mr. Balfour's main argument if I can show that his disparagement of the human reason is based on an insufficient examination of the psychological facts to which he appeals.

I propose, then, with this object, briefly (1) to consider one or two instances of his disparagement of the human reason in its analytical processes ; (2) to examine his proof that Authority as a non-rational cause is responsible for a multitude of beliefs popularly ascribed to Reason ; and (3) to indicate the bearing of my conclusions on the main argument of his book.

We find, as I have intimated, instances scattered up and down this volume, in which Mr. Balfour dismisses the analysis of rational motives for belief as unproductive, and falls back upon non-rational causes of belief. One of his justifications for this procedure is that our conclusions appear constantly to be more certain than our premises. " In all [branches of knowledge]," he writes, "conclusions seem more certain than premises. . . . In all of them ideas so clear and so sufficient for purposes of everyday thought and action, become confused and but dimly intelligible when examined in the unsparing light of critical analysis."[1] What, then, is the value of a proof which seems less certain than the thing to be proved ? Take, for example, the judgment " I see a brown chair." Nothing could appear simpler or more certain than such a judgment. Yet, when we investigate the process whereby we reach it, we find that science tells us of an immensely complicated process, culminating in the incidence of certain ethereal undulations on the retina, and the stimulation of the optic nerve, and metaphysic raises the whole problem of Idealism. Mr. Balfour makes the investigation on lines somewhat similar to Berkeley's in his famous dialogues between Hylas and Philonous. Mr. Balfour's inclination, in the face of the difficulties which the process brings to light, is to sweep away the complicated web of scientific and metaphysical subtlety ; to refute Idealism almost as Dr. Johnson did by kicking a stone, and to say simply that we must assume a correspondence between the mind and the external world, both being the creation of a Higher Reason, which designed that there should be

[1] See p. 283.

a correspondence between the microcosm and the macrocosm.

I have already intimated my opinion that this method unduly disparages the powers of that very Reason which is our means of perceiving the necessity of looking for its source in a Higher Reason. I believe that the clue to a truer solution of the difficulty under consideration will be found in a work published fifty years ago, and yet in many ways peculiarly suited to the phase of thought revealed in the book before us. John Henry Newman, when at the height of his influence at Oxford in the later thirties and the early forties, was struck equally with Mr. Balfour by the fact that our conclusions so often appear more certain than our premises. He made an inquiry very similar to Mr. Balfour's into the Testimony of the Senses. He probed the analytical reason, and came to the conclusion that, when left to its unaided resources, its chief power is simply to reveal to us the difficulties of our condition.[1] Like Mr. Balfour, he was struck by the insufficiency of the current Natural Theology and evidential works on Christianity. Like him again, he instituted a comparison between the external world which is the postulate of Science and those supernatural beliefs which are the basis of the spiritual, devotional, and moral life. Mr. Balfour suggests that, so far as empirical knowledge goes, we might have other senses which would reveal to us the real nature of the external world far better than our existing ones. Newman entertained this hypothesis more positively and seriously. "What," he wrote in one of his University Sermons, "if the whole series of impressions

[1] University Sermons, 1st edition, p. 353 : " Reason can but ascertain the profound difficulties of our condition."

made on us through the senses be . . . but a Divine economy suited to our need, and a token of realities distinct from them, and such as might be revealed to us, nay, more perfectly, by other senses as distinct from our existing ones as they are from each other ? " [1] And he suggested that, similarly, those tokens of the supernatural world which are set before us in theology may be an economy, representing to us great truths, of whose existence and relation to ourselves and our conduct they make us aware, but of which, as they are in themselves, our present faculties can have no adequate cognizance.

One thought which runs through these remarkable sermons is the very one which haunts Mr. Balfour, that alike the ultimate analysis of *what* we believe and the ultimate proof of by what *right* we believe elude us ; and yet we continue to believe, and (in many cases) to retain an undiminished certainty that we are justified in believing. But Newman's very statement of the case, in this volume and elsewhere, shows that he conceives its solution as lying in a direction to some extent at least different from that indicated by Mr. Balfour. He states the case almost popularly in a letter to a friend written in the year 1840. " The human mind," he wrote, " in its present state is unequal to its own powers of apprehension ; it embraces more than it can master." [2] This view of the matter is developed in the University Sermons and the Essay on Assent. He expressed his meaning more exactly years later in his contention that the mind is often " swayed and determined by a body of proof which it recognises only as a body and not in its constituent parts." The

---

[1] University Sermons. New Edition (Longmans), p. 347.
[2] Letters and Correspondence (Longmans), vol. ii. p. 311.

difference between this line of thought and Mr.
Balfour's—with which it coincides up to a certain
point—is that Newman, instead of tending to reject
the process of analysis as giving no guarantee of the
soundness of our reasoning, merely on the ground that
the analysis cannot be carried far enough to justify
fully the certainty of the previous conviction, maintains
that this inequality is the normal state of things and may
be easily accounted for. The analysis may be carried
far enough to give a presumption, more or less strong,
—often a reasonable conviction,—that the mind has
done its work correctly ; and the fact that it cannot be
carried further, instead of discrediting its value and
showing the cause of conviction to be non-rational, is
merely an instance of that inequality between our
powers of " embracing " and our powers of " mastering "
which an investigation of the mental processes themselves will quite sufficiently explain.

That this is so in many very simple instances is,
I suppose, indisputable. The conviction which each
individual has of the fact of his own birth, or of the
fact that England is an island, rests (with nine-tenths
of us) on considerations which are felt by the mind as a
body of proof. Two things are evident on a moment's
reflection : (1) that we shall find the *full* analysis of
the proof difficult or impossible, (2) that we should
not be less certain of either fact if we failed in our
attempted analysis, or more certain if we succeeded.
This at least shows that the mind as a fact does
pronounce with absolute confidence, being determined
in its conviction by its latent consciousness of a *mass* of
proof, which is not sorted or analysed into its component
parts. Yet the latent mass of proof *is* proof ; and the
conviction is *not* a merely non-rational instinct.

Another fact which is evident on consideration is that the full body of proof in each case comprises a multitude of experiences. And one of the very difficulties of analysis results from the fact that a large store of past experiences and latent considerations, such as the constant succession of indirect verifications of the belief that England is an island,—a belief which was first simply instilled by a schoolroom lesson or by looking at the atlas,—its confirmation by various authorities, its consonance with the rest of our knowledge, the absence of any experienced fact which would be consistent with its denial, the reasons (drawn from experience) of the significance of this absence, and the rest, so accumulates in its effect as to *act* almost like an instinct; while, from the limitations of the consciousness, as much as from defect of memory, its full rational strength can never be represented in words. The full analysis of the proof is not simply the logical statement of its character, but in addition the full record of experiences in part forgotten. To represent its cogency we must give both an analysis of all the kinds of verification the belief has received, and all the instances of each class. Still in such a case a very little thought will show that the absolute confidence which is in reality due to the mass of experiences, whose character and details are mostly forgotten, does arise from motives which warrant it; although we do not expect or even care to trace them with any completeness. We can appraise the body of proof with sufficient accuracy for our purpose, by the double process of observing its spontaneous effect, *as* a body, on our own convictions, and of very partially investigating its details. One further point : if we ask ourselves the questions raised by Mr. Balfour as to the metaphysical problems involved in all statements about concrete fact—if we ask, in reference to the statement " I was born," what is meant by the " I," what is involved in the belief in my body as independent of my consciousness and the like,—we at once see that our certainty of the proposition has no reference to such questions. The certainty is practical and in some sense relative. Whatever answer the questions receive, however little we "master" the ultimate analysis of what we are saying, doubt thrown upon its meaning in no way affects the practical certainty with which the mind " embraces " the judgment that " I was born," or that " England is an island."

Had Mr. Balfour fully realised these psychological facts, I believe he would have considerably modified portions of his chapter on " The Philosophical Basis of Naturalism." To deal adequately with this question, I should have to examine the position taken up in his " Defence of Philosophic Doubt." But I may sufficiently indicate the direction of my criticism by referring to an argument advanced in his present work. Its treatment will necessarily involve the introduction of a few pages dealing with controversies both more ancient and more technical than I could wish ; but some reference to this part of Mr. Balfour's work is necessary to explain the bearing of my remarks.

Mr. Balfour institutes an examination of the theory that our knowledge of the external world is an inference from the phenomena of sensation ; that when " I am in the act of experiencing a tree in the next field, what . . . I am really doing is inferring from the fact of my having certain feelings the existence of a cause having qualities adequate to produce them. . . . The process of inference is so rapid and habitual that we are unconscious of performing it." In the course of his criticism we find a remarkable passage which brings into relief the fallacy which, as it seems to me, underlies his whole treatment of this question. Scientific observers, he points out, have been under the impression that they were observing not their own sensations, but external objects. If our knowledge of the external world is really an inference from sensation, that impression has been an illusion. Yet but for this illusion we should never have had science.

"We have not merely stumbled upon the truth in spite of error and illusion, which is odd, but because of error and illusion, which is odder. For if the scientific observers of Nature had realised from the beginning that all they were observing was their own feelings and ideas . . . they surely would never have taken the trouble to invent a Nature (*i.e.* an independently existing system of material things) for no other purpose than to provide a machinery by which the occurrence of feelings and ideas might be adequately accounted for. To go through so much to get so little, . . . to pile world upon world and add infinity to infinity, and all for no more important object than to find an explanation for a few fleeting impressions, say of colour or resistance, would indeed have seemed to them a most superfluous labour" (p. 118).

The whole force of this criticism appears to depend on an inadequate appreciation of the form of Idealism against which it is directed. Mr. Balfour has elsewhere spoken of the "extreme simplicity of the reasoning on which Idealism rests." I cannot but think that his conviction of its extreme simplicity has made him fail to enter more than partially into the psychological facts to which it appeals,—facts which none of us can afford to treat lightly, although we may differ among ourselves as to their exact interpretation. What, according to any credible form of Idealism, men of science are observing is surely not either "fleeting impressions" or their own "ideas" in the *popular* sense, as Mr. Balfour's argument seems to imply. It is rather that definite system revealed by past experience, which, as we know it only in terms of our sensible experience, only yields relative and not absolute truth, but which, nevertheless, is coherent and permanent. This system is made up of "ideas" only in the most strictly technical sense. The effect of Mr. Balfour's phraseology depends on its implying primarily an examination by scientific explorers of their feelings *in the present*, and on their drawing, in the present, inferences to a cause adequate to producing them. Surely this is psychologically quite inexact. The inference both to the existence of a coherent system, and to its representing something external, has been, surely, the gradual and unconscious result of an *accumulation* of experiences in the past,—constant experiences from the first dawn of consciousness of the interaction of our own activities, muscular, sensational, locomotive, of which we are the authors, with coherent effects produced by something existing, in Berkeley's words, "independently of my mind, for I know myself not to be their author." [1] Scientific observation, though made *by means of* present sensation, is not an examination of present feelings, nor is it made "to account for fleeting impressions." The present sensations are interpreted by the product of past sensible experience, which is habitually in our mind. They presuppose that product, and only bring

[1] "Works," edition of 1784, p. 160. Cf. also p. 202.

before us aspects and instances (it may be new aspects and instances) of the coherent system which past experience has revealed to us. To this system Berkeley himself was ready to give the name "things." "In common talk," he wrote, "the objects of our senses are not termed ideas, but things. Call them so still, provided you do not attribute to them any absolute external existence." But that they discernibly *represent* an external existence, Berkeley was equally emphatic in asserting. It is this coherent system, habitually regarded as representing something external, and not either "feelings" or "ideas" (in the popular sense) or "fleeting impressions," which the men of science are engaged in investigating *by means of* their present sensations.[1]

No doubt, if we suppose a man suddenly endowed with senses for the first time, and tell him forthwith to examine his own feelings as a road to physical science, the proposal seems as absurd as Mr. Balfour intimates. He must first learn to stand and to walk, and to realise his constant relations with something which gradually becomes most coherently, though only relatively, known to him. And it is this knowledge which science proposes to extend.

These remarks hold good *mutatis mutandis*, if we maintain with modified realism that our perception of the primary qualities is immediate, or if we hold it to be an inference that such a quality as extension, as being revealed to the consciousness in sensations of different kinds, has in it an objective character.

---

[1] Mr. Balfour shows elsewhere some appreciation (though very partial as it seems to me) of the facts to which I refer. But it remains true that the apparent force of the passage I am criticising depends on their being forgotten.

In each case the analysis of our consciousness, instead of being as Mr. Balfour says "essentially inconsistent" with our spontaneous conviction, corresponds with it as far as it goes. The analyses alike of the different schools of thought go far enough hand in hand to give at least a good indication of the premises on which their common practical conclusion rests — that there is an external Reality which is known to us more or less relatively through the senses.[1] And this is the spontaneous conviction of the unphilosophical mind—except that the question as to the relativity of sensible knowledge has simply not occurred to it.

This, of course, does not touch the Metaphysical question as to the *nature* of the "thing in itself;" but it would as little paralyse scientific investigation to believe from its commencement that we can only know the external Reality in terms of its sensible effects,—of what is revealed in sensation active and passive,— as it weakens our belief in the geographical truth that England is an island, or our interest in the fact, to have it brought home to us that (if so be) we have no knowledge of what we mean by England itself, except in terms of our sensible experience. Science, whether geographical or astronomical, is not on this hypothesis undertaken, as Mr. Balfour says, "to account for" our impressions, but to extend the knowledge, relative though it be, which has been begun by our past sensible experience in the manner already indicated. Its conclusions are exactly as relative as all sensible knowledge is.

[1] Newman does not treat exhaustively in any of his published works of the nature of the inference to an external world. But he says expressly that we know "nothing at all" of "substance or of matter." ("Apologia," p. 239.)

And certainly facts do not show that Idealism *has* diminished the interest of its upholders in physical science. Kant's awe at the "starry heavens" was none the less that he considered space to be only a "form of thought." Berkeley's eloquent description of the planets and fixed stars,[1] and of the truths which astronomers have to tell concerning them, coexisted with thorough-going Idealism. The study of Nature is not likely to seem valueless because we cannot with our present faculties know the position which our relative knowledge of it will hold in the world of Reality, beyond "our bourne of time and place."

I should be inclined to say that the discovery of the relativity of physics is somewhat parallel to that of a further relativity within the sphere of physical science itself. The "plain man" thinks he perceives the external world immediately, and the "plain man" thought in Galileo's time that he saw sun and planets moving. When he is first told that he has been wrong, he is thrown into confusion, and thinks that his informant has upset some deep conviction.[2] He views plane astronomy as based on "error" and "illusion." But when he has fully taken in the import of the new standpoint, he sees that the mariner can still guide his ship by pre-Copernican observations, and that the sundial may with advantage remain where it stands. And so, too, it is with the discovery that

---

[1] In the second of the dialogues between Hylas and Philonous.

[2] I need hardly say that if Mr. Balfour merely means that primitive scientific explorers could not *apprehend* the consistency of Idealism with their own experience—that is to say, could not take in what Idealism *meant*—their rejection of it would not have been persistence in "illusion," but adherence to relative truth, the relative character of which they did not recognise, in preference to a misapprehension which would have been positive error.

physical science is relative, and that we cannot now be in a position to decide what it tells us in terms of absolute truth. It does not make science uninteresting, or change our conviction that we are learning much from it; though doubtless there may be in such a discovery a certain lessening of the freshest enthusiasm, parallel to that which advancing life, with its lessons as to our limitations, brings in so many spheres of interest.

We may apply our parable by pointing out that Mr. Balfour's *reductio ad absurdum* of the cosmothetic Idealist's basis for science applies word for word to the Ptolemaist's belief (in the fifteenth century) in the teaching of pre-Copernican plane astronomy. We have the "singular spectacle of a creed which is believed in practice for one set of reasons, though in theory it can only be justified by another; and which, through some beneficent accident (*sic*), turns out to be true, though its origin and each subsequent stage of its gradual development is the product of error and illusion."[1] Surely the truer account in both cases is that the coherence of science was due neither to a beneficent accident nor to illusion, but to the truths (relative though they were) on which the investigation was based. I may add that Mr. Balfour's failure to keep apart the questions of the accuracy of scientific conclusions and of their relative character leads him to use the word "truth" ambiguously. The conclusions may be quite accurate and yet not *absolutely* true.

The main difference, then, between Newman's method and Mr. Balfour's would appear to be this —that Mr. Balfour, contemplating the supposed

[1] See p. 117.

inferential process primarily as a *present* inference to
an adequate cause instead of an inference based on
a *complexus* of past experiences, finds it unsatisfactory
and shadowy, dismisses it, and looks to a different
region for the basis of our conviction; tracing that
conviction to an instinct, and our justification in
trusting it to the fact that it supplies a need. The
line of thought indicated by Newman, on the other
hand, leads us to find in the inferential process far
more,[1] because it leads us to contemplate it in its true
strength as a complicated record of latent reasoning
from varied experiences, of reaction of the activities
of which we are conscious, on something existing
independently of our minds, which gives gradually a
homogeneous and most definite conception of certain
leading attributes of that something so far as its powers
of affecting us are concerned.   The process of the
analysis of experience, which to Mr. Balfour is more
or less beside the mark, becomes, in Newman's system,
valuable, although incomplete.   It indicates sufficiently
the ground for the fundamental postulate of science
considered as relative; while, according to Mr. Balfour,
it is inconsistent with the beliefs to which science owes
its existence.   Mr. Balfour's method seems to give
no protection against the fear that an instinct which
appears simply to contradict all attempts at rational
analysis is purely illusive.

But if, on the other hand, we are able, when we
investigate the grounds of our spontaneous decision,
to see that they are in large measure rational, we
have at least some warrant for trusting the decision

---

[1] I do not forget that according to Newman there *are* cases where
the mind (notably of a man of genius) traverses a path which analysis
cannot sufficiently follow to justify it at all.

even where we cannot follow its analysis; just as
the doctor concludes from his soundings, which give
him direct information on only a few critical conditions of the action of lungs and heart, that they
are really as a whole performing the vital functions
satisfactorily, and that they will keep at work all that
complicated machinery, quite inaccessible to observation, which is involved in the continuance of human
life. The assumption is that the rational nature, when
healthy and normal, makes for truth as the vital
functions make for life; and this assumption, which
is confirmed by analysis, where analysis is possible,
we make in every act of reasoning. Analysis is not
to be rejected as Mr. Balfour tends to reject it, because
it does not attain to completeness. It may give an
excellent indication as to whether the mind is on right
or on wrong lines by its partial observation of the
processes of the living reason; and it may even point
to a process being normal, while it incidentally discloses difficulties which it cannot resolve,—as the
dissector may understand the working of a function
as a whole, and yet its actual performance may involve
the expansion of some muscle to an extent which
seems absolutely impossible on scrutiny of the dead
tissue.

I pass to the consideration of Mr. Balfour's treatment of Authority. He carries his attempt to maximise
the extent of the non-rational causes of belief, and to
minimise our obligations to the human reason, into
one of the most remarkable and valuable chapters of
his work, the chapter on Authority and Reason. I
cannot but think that here, too, his observation of
psychological facts has been somewhat at fault. We

find the same tendency to insist exclusively on one aspect of a truth, and to ignore the latent workings of the human reason. He is concerned primarily with pointing out the falsity of the popular conception (p. 201) that Reason "is a kind of Ormuzd, doing constant battle against the Ahriman of tradition and authority;" and that "its gradual triumph over the opposing powers of darkness is what we mean by progress." Mr. Balfour points out how large a share Authority has and should have in forming the convictions of the individual; how essential it is, both for his own preservation and for that of the society in which he lives, that he should accept the mass of convictions which form the basis of the action of the body politic. For the individual, he maintains, to examine for himself the exact evidence on which "rests every positive enactment and every moral precept which he has been accustomed to obey," and to act on them only in proportion as he is satisfied with the result, would be fatal. "To say," he writes, "that such a community, if it acted on the opinions thus arrived at, would stand but a poor chance in the struggle for existence, is to say far too little. It could never even begin to be; and if by a miracle it was created, it would without doubt immediately resolve itself into its constituent elements."

That this obedience (at least provisional) to established authority is of the highest importance, and that many disregard it in maintaining the supposed right and duty—the absurdity of which is not too strongly emphasised by Mr. Balfour—of each individual to make up his mind on all subjects by his own "free speculative investigation," is beyond question. It may be remarked, by the way, that this was largely recognised by the parent of the doubting philosophy which paved the way for modern Rationalism, by Descartes himself; who advocated (in the third section of his "Discours de la Méthode") "une morale par provision," which included the duty of submission on the part of each man to the laws and customs of his country, and to the religion in which he had been brought up, and of following in practical life the most moderate and most generally received maxims.

But Mr. Balfour goes much beyond this. In the first place he is concerned with pointing out the current exaggerations as to the importance of Reason and to show the "comparative pettiness of the *rôle* . . . played by reasoning in human affairs." He passes—at times almost insensibly—from the place occupied by Reason in determining individual conviction, to its place in determining the convictions of the race; from protesting against the common exaggerations of the sphere of private judgment, to protesting against exaggerations as to the scope of Reason in the corporate judgments of the community. And his occasional identification of the two leads, I cannot but think, to inaccuracy of thought. He states the "current theory," which he is opposing, first, as the theory that "every one" should sift the reasons for his own convictions, and in the same paragraph as the theory that "Reason only can be safely permitted to mould the convictions of *mankind.*" Yet the *reductio ad absurdum* to which he proceeds,—of supposing every man, woman, boy, and girl as instituting an independent examination into the justification of social and ethical rules of the community—is obviously conclusive as a criticism of the one theory, irrelevant as against the other. Again, a little later, he

speaks of current exaggerations of "the importance of
Reason among the causes producing and maintaining
the beliefs, customs, and ideals which form the groundwork of life"—a phrase which obviously suggests
beliefs and customs of a nation or of mankind; but
his illustration, while extremely apt in reference to
the individual, is not so in reference to the race. He
gives the analogy of a boy who worked the steam-
engine in its early stages, by pulling a string at stated
intervals, by which operation the valve was opened
which admitted the steam into the cylinder. The
boy, he says, probably "greatly magnified his functions, and regarded himself as the most important,
because the only rational, link in the chain of causes and
effects." This illustration without doubt is analogous
to the self-satisfaction of an individual who exaggerates
the importance of his own Reason in carrying on the
processes of daily life. But if we apply it to the
share taken by human Reason in general in determining the customs which are the groundwork of life,
we find that most of the very important process which
to the boy was independent of any rational exercise,
was for the race the result of its own inventive Reason.
A word inserted into the sentence in which Mr. Balfour
points the analogy would make this clear. "So do
we stand," he writes, "as reasoning beings in the
presence of the complex processes, physiological and
psychical, out of which are manufactured the convictions necessary to the conduct of life." Add after
"psychical" the words "and rational," and it becomes
clear that the argument and illustration serve to show
not the small place which Reason occupies, but which
the reasoning of one individual occupies in the
process.

This leads us to remind ourselves that the reasoning of one generation naturally issues in conclusions which form the "groundwork" of social life for individuals in the next. And in this way a very few achievements of the individual Reason come to affect the whole race; and the successful struggle of Reason against Authority in one generation may issue in a change in the "groundwork" of social life, which is due to Reason, although it does not necessarily affect all individuals through the medium of their own reasoning faculties. To take up Mr. Balfour's "steam-engine" illustration and complete it: the passenger who in our own time enters the train with the conviction that it will carry him from London to Brighton in an hour, owes this conclusion in part at least to the properties of a mechanism which embodied the results of the reasoning of Watt and his successors. On the other hand, the motley array of postboys and stage-coach drivers who, as our grandfathers have told us, used to gather together at the Feathers' Inn at Wadesmill and drink confusion to the intruder, were obviously representatives of the established Tradition and of the Authority of customary belief. Their historic refrain—

> "No boiler so large or so hot,
> Can rival the speed of the Tantivy trot,"—

was the voice of Tradition and of the Authority in possession, while their rivals, if they expressed their sentiments with more of scientific cogency and less of that poetic enthusiasm which is characteristic of primitive beliefs, were, relatively at least, the representatives of Reason. Here we have an instance in which in a few years the victory of Reason over

Authority introduced absolutely and universally, for every individual, true conclusions hitherto entirely unknown.

But we may look at this instance from another point of view. We may regard it, not as the opposition between Reason and Authority, but rather as the opposition between blind trust in traditional Authority and an intelligent use of scientific Authority—for Watt and his successors inherited the scientific conclusions of their predecessors.

And this brings me to the second point in Mr. Balfour's comparison between the provinces of Reason and of Authority, in which he appears to draw a conclusion more adverse to Reason than his own premises warrant. Confining ourselves to the question as to the respective shares of Authority and of Reason in determining *individual* belief, let me observe that at first he contemplates these two powers as causes of belief, right or wrong, and, as we have seen, bases his decision in favour of Authority greatly on the impossibility and absurdity of each individual investigating the social convictions which are the groundwork of life. But it is plain that individuals differ infinitely among themselves as to how far this surrender of their private judgment to the decisions of the community is based on Reason. In the uneducated, as in young children, the cause of belief may be simply blind submission to the influence of Authority. In the older and more educated it is far more a *rationabile obsequium*. And yet the rejection of the absurdity of private judgment (which is the central point of his argument as he first states it) is at least as characteristic of those who trust Authority because they perceive such a course to be reasonable, as of those who trust it blindly. That is to say, it is as characteristic (at least) of those for whom Authority is (in Mr. Balfour's language) a reason for belief as of those for whom it is merely a cause and not a reason. Mr. Balfour, observing that with this class of cases Reason precedes Authority as a cause of belief, dismisses them from the list of the beliefs due to Authority. He classes them as due to reasoning from "Authorities." "Authority, as I have been using the term," he writes, "is thus converted into 'an Authority' or into 'Authorities.' It ceases to be the opposite or correlative of Reason. It can no longer be contrasted with Reason. It becomes a species of Reason." Yet a moment's consideration will show that by this statement he very seriously curtails the list of beliefs which the argument with which he had set out would assign to Authority. It is obvious that a large amount of that trust in Authority which is natural and necessary to the social life of the community, is open-eyed and reasonable. We trust to our wine-merchant to get us good wine ; but in choosing one rather than another we are guided by reasons drawn, perhaps, from the quality of the wine which he has supplied to our friends. We trust ourselves to the care of the railway train ; but if we hear of a dozen fatal accidents on one line in a single week, we shall be slow to travel by that line. If, then, we hand over to the side of Reason and dismiss from the ranks of Authority all cases where our trust is based on reason—if with Mr. Balfour we distinguish between Authority and "Authorities," and place them in opposite scales—much less is won for Authority by the argument than would appear from the statement of the case with which Mr. Balfour had set out.

Mr. Balfour points out with subtle observation the unconscious action of Authority. When we appear to be reasoning, we are really affected by a " psychological climate," by the intellectual preconceptions of the age, by the views of an influential person, by early prejudice. Our conclusion is really determined, not by the reasoning to which we may ascribe it, but by the Authority of which we are unconscious. This is true and most important. But I think that he fails to note that Reason often acts latently as well as Authority. He speaks of turning non-rational causes of belief into reasons by " explicitly recognising" that the Authority causing our belief is trustworthy (p. 220): but I think he insufficiently recognises how often it has been implicitly both reason and cause before it became a reason explicitly.

Let me take a simple instance of this. I go to my banker for guidance as to investing a sum of money. I do so, so far as I am aware, simply because my father always went to him. I have not chosen him. He suggests distributing the money through many securities. I am somewhat inattentive to details, as I habitually leave such matters entirely in his hands. I vaguely remember the names of the stocks, and that is all. Later in the day I see in the newspaper that Australian banks are in a very bad way. This calls to my mind the fact that one of my investments was a deposit in the Bank of Australasia. I at once question the wisdom of the investment, and write to my banker. Thus it becomes obvious that, however vague and shadowy, there was a basis of reason for my trust in the banker,—the implicit assurance that " he knows all about such investments." The news in the paper brought the latent motive to light by throwing doubt on its consonance with fact.

It is obvious that if this explanation be true its effect is far-reaching. There is some latent reasoning process of this kind in nearly all the trusts which make up the daily habits of life. Baker, butcher, lawyer, doctor, are all trusted with some latent motive of the reason. Be it observed that the question here is not of right reason. The question at issue is whether among causes of belief, true or false, Authority, legitimate or illegitimate, or Reason, right or wrong, is the cause of the greater number. And it appears to me that if all instances where there is a trust based on reason are described as instances of reasoning from "authorities" and placed on the side of Reason rather than on that of Authority, the working out of this distinction removes the large proportion of beliefs which at first sight are attributable to Authority back again to the side of Reason.[1]

If I pursue this question further, it is not for the sake of cavilling at what, after all, is partly only a form of expression—for Mr. Balfour does not appear to contemplate latent reasoning as reasoning at all. It is rather to get at the practical difference involved in Mr. Balfour's statement of the case and my own. Some of the practical consequences of Mr. Balfour's view may be seen by considering an amusing simile in his book, whereby he illustrates the statement that the influence of Rationalism, which would at first sight seem to be a form of the influence of a process of reasoning, is often in reality for individuals

---

[1] It is quite true that we may allege (as Mr. Balfour says) different reasons at different times for the same conviction ; but this does not surely prove that it is really due to Authority and not to Reason. It may prove—a not uncommon case with women—that we do not frankly recognise the *real* reason influencing us ; but it does not *necessarily* prove that there is no reason.

the influence of Authority. Rationalism, though it began in reasoning, has come by degrees to form a "psychological climate." It often influences the individual, not in virtue of the antecedent reasoning which he has not, it may be, apprehended, but by its contagiousness as a temper of mind which has come into existence through that reasoning. Mr. Balfour suggests that, "like a schoolboy's tears over a proposition of Euclid," beliefs due to its influence may be "consequences of reasoning, but not conclusions from it."

This is very true and very important up to a certain point. Yet the fact that Rationalism is, what the schoolboy's tears are not, the embodiment of a reasoning process in the race (even though an inexact one), makes a great difference even in the mode of its action on individuals. If it affects them largely as a "climate," it also affects some of them in varying degrees through their reason, as they enter into the line of thought and the historical causes to which it was in the first instance due. And thus it is that persons of philosophic minds can make some stand against the influence of a "psychological climate," which, even if ineffectual at the time, in the long run may purge it of its exaggerations. This has come to pass in our own time in the case referred to by Mr. Balfour, of the rationalistic incredulity which so long discredited Mesmerism. And this instance is typical of many others. It really shows the connexion between Mr. Balfour's two omissions. His omission to recognise fully the share taken by Reason in framing the beliefs which the individual may accept on Authority leads him to do insufficient justice to the tendency of individuals in varying degrees both to travel back along the lines of reasoning whereby their ancestors or teachers may have come to their conclusions, and to have an instinctive sense of the watchful reason and criticism of the race, which protects social customs and beliefs from going very far astray.

These considerations hold good even in the more limited sphere of party allegiance and permanent adherence to a religious sect. However much is due to the mere influence of contiguity with others who profess the creed in question, religious or political, there is generally some degree of mental assimilation of the characteristic trains of thought on which it rests, and I believe—which is passing to a further and separate question—that by reflective minds, even where no idea of independent inquiry enters, all religious creeds are adhered to in virtue largely of the true elements they contain.[1]

[1] In the last section of his chapter Mr. Balfour states his position in a way which, while it comes nearer to recognising some of the questions here raised than the earlier part, seems still to show that he does not clearly separate the province of Reason in forming individual conviction from its province in forming corporate convictions which may act on individuals as Authority. Speaking of the action of Reason in producing belief, he writes : " Of its immense indirect consequences, of the part it has played in the evolution of human affairs by the disintegration of ancient creeds, by the alteration of the external conditions of human life, by the production of . . . 'psychological climates,' we can in this connexion say nothing. For these are no rational effects of the reason ; the causal *nexus* by which they are bound to reason has no logical aspect." This, as I have pointed out, is partly (though not wholly) true in respect of the action of such results of reasoning on this or that individual, but it is not true if we consider the human race as a whole. And that Mr. Balfour still has in his mind the action of Reason on the race as a whole we see in the very same paragraph, where he says, "To Reason is largely due the growth of new and the sifting of old knowledge," etc., which, though quite true of the race, is not true of the individual, who in many cases simply acquiesces on authority in the sifting process carried on by competent minds.

While, then, I sympathise to the full with Mr. Balfour's exposition of the absurdity of supposing that the individual is to form or could form an independent judgment in many matters where the community supplies him the machinery of its own customs and principles ready to hand; while I recognise the force of his exposition of the large share taken by Authority, often unconsciously to ourselves, in moulding our convictions; while I agree that this is at least in many cases beneficial; while I go so far as to admit that, for the majority, total emancipation from this subtle influence of Authority is utterly impossible, even in cases where it is desirable, and that even for the few it can only be partial—for there are inmost habits of the critical intellect which have been largely fashioned by Authority—I should say that this is as much as the evidence warrants. Mr. Balfour, if he appears to establish more, does so in virtue of the omission of distinctions which are essential. Beyond these limits his scathing attack on Reason is, if I am right in my observations, both destructive of his own methods and untrue to fact. His last words are in keeping with this undue extension of his theory. He finds our chief superiority over the brute creation " not so much in our faculty of convincing and being convinced by the exercise of reasoning, as in our capacity for influencing and being influenced through the action of Authority." Had he said of intelligently surrendering ourselves to trustworthy Authority, I should have no quarrel with him. But as a great deal of the capacity of being influenced by Authority of which he speaks is common to ourselves and the brutes, his statement, as it stands, does not carry conviction.

It is well to keep Reason in its place, and to find out its limitations, and the absurdities in which it lands us if it makes excursions on its own account instead of submitting to proper guidance. But if we depreciate Reason too much, we paralyse it. Not merely philosophic scepticism, but practical inaction is reached. An uppish man of real ability is often made far more useful by a certain amount of snubbing, which teaches him the necessity of working in harmony with others and the value of self-distrust. But the point may be reached at which he becomes disheartened and useless : and so with Mr. Balfour's treatment of Reason. Teach it, if you will, its own limitations, the necessity of submission, the danger of a spurious originality ; but do so in order thereby to make it more reverent, more alert, to ensure its efforts being better and more profitably directed. I believe most of our convictions to be due, not to what Mr. Balfour calls in the latter part of his chapter Authority, but to what he terms Authorities, trust in which is not absolutely blind or without a reasoning element ; and I believe the highest characteristic of man, the development of which would be most helpful to him, to lie not in blind submission to Authority, but in cultivating that finer and truer estimate of the province of Reason which Mr. Balfour so eloquently vindicates in his *exposé* of the folly of private judgment, which should make it sensitively alive alike to its weakness in isolation, and to all the signs by which it may determine in what direction it should look for trustworthy Authority in the judgment of its fellows and of the society in which it finds itself.

More than eighty years ago another statesman raised

the question here discussed by Mr. Balfour ; but his conclusions, up to a certain point remarkably similar, involve a far fuller recognition of the rational element in the surrender to Authority. Vicomte de Bonald, the first half of whose long life was spent in the France of the eighteenth-century philosophers, and who had witnessed alike the decay of Faith and the deification of insubordination in which their teaching culminated, published his work, " Les Connoissances Morales," in 1818.   Partly owing to the somewhat fanciful conclusions drawn in the latter part of the book, it is almost forgotten ; but its earlier pages are very instructive.   Like Mr. Balfour, M. de Bonald noted how small a share the individual Reason takes in the carrying on of social life.   " We are guided," he wrote, " by the habits which we find established in society.   We have no reason to conform our action to them but the example of others.   We make no use of our Reason—of that Reason of which we are so proud."   He further maintained that what we do instinctively in respect of daily habits, we ought equally to do in respect of the moral convictions on which the society rests.   If the man who refuses to eat until he has analysed for himself the whole physiological process involved, and thus assured himself that it is reliable, will die in the interval, so the society whose members postpone obedience to its ethical convictions until they have examined them critically, will perish.   Further, the examination is necessarily to a large extent futile, as a man owes many of the ideas which he uses as tests in his criticism to that very society the basis of whose structure he is criticising.   His action thus becomes both a vicious circle and an irrational revolt.   " He places himself by the very act," writes Bonald, "in a state of revolt against the society. He assumes to himself, a single individual, the right of reforming what is general, and he aspires to dethrone the universal Reason to make his own particular Reason reign in its stead, that Reason which he owes entirely to the society." And if one man has the right to do this, all have; experience shows that if men examine independently they often do not agree: thus the universal application of this method—which fortunately common sense has prevented—would mean the absolute destruction of social order.[1]

But while this view of the case marks strongly the truth which impresses Mr. Balfour that the individual Reason is a disintegrating force, M. de Bonald's conclusion is not so adverse to the importance of Reason in human affairs as that of the English statesman. "If," adds the French writer, "human Reason, the Reason of each of us, is so noble and precious a faculty, if it is the light which enlightens us and the Authority which governs us, what Authority is there more imposing, what light more brilliant than the universal Reason, the Reason of all peoples and all societies, the Reason of all times and all places." The Reason, then, of the race does much; the Reason of the individual, *if used in isolation from, or still more in opposition to, the Universal Reason,* can do little or nothing.

I now reach my third point—namely, the inquiry

[1] "Tout périt dans la société, lois et mœurs, pendant que l'homme délibère s'il doit admettre ou rejeter les croyances qu'il trouve établis . . . telle que l'existence de Dieu . . . la distinction du bien et du mal," etc. "Recherches Philosophiques sur les Premiers Objets des Connoissances Morales." Par M. de Bonald. A Paris, Chez Adrien Le Clere, Quai des Augustins, 35. 1818. (Vol. i. p. 110.)

as to how and where the foregoing considerations, suggested both in my own criticism of Mr. Balfour and in M. de Bonald's treatment of the subject, may help us to supplement Mr. Balfour's own remarks.

In the first place, a good deal of what Mr. Balfour says as to the small share of reason in the conduct of daily life, applies in a very different degree to the uneducated and to persons of reflective habits. In some of his observations he seems to contemplate a very extended suffrage. Living as we do in society, the intellectual insight of the thinker, like the spiritual insight of the Saint, benefits his fellows; and thus even apart from the question of social traditions, which have approved themselves by their practical success, the community is far more enlightened and its habits far more superintended by Reason than would appear from considering instances of the inertness of Reason which might be more or less true of 999 men out of 1000. The thousandth man makes his genius or sanctity permeate the society. Thus, in considering the part played by Reason, it is necessary either very explicitly to treat of this difference between minds, and of this far-reaching influence,—this power of the Saint or of the genius in awakening other minds, and drawing from them an echo which would seem beyond their spontaneous exhibition of rational insight—or to make, as Bonald does, the distinction between the Universal Reason, which, as being largely determined by the men of genius, includes this power, and the individual Reason. Newman lays down the groundwork for the distinction, of which I speak, so far as it applies to religious subjects, in his account of Faith and Wisdom,[1]—both

[1] "University Sermons," p. 276 *seq.*

of them distinct from rationalistic reason, Faith being
the more or less instinctive trust of the many, Wisdom
the property of the few reflective and spiritual minds.
I conceive the ideal of the Mediæval Church to have
been somewhat similar, however insufficiently it was
carried out. The ancient traditions and the original
Revelation were sifted and applied by the Saints and
Doctors of the Church, and the results communicated
as the teaching of the Church to the many, who could
indeed receive it and in varying degrees enter into
the collective Wisdom which determined it, but could
not for themselves have ascertained it. Thus the
reasonable basis of a belief would necessarily mean
two distinct things,—for the whole body, the premises
used by the collective Wisdom and Sanctity of the
teachers; for the individual, the grounds he has for
trusting that his teachers are imparting the outcome
of that Wisdom and Sanctity.

As I have said, I am speaking here of the ideal
and not of its historical realisation. But, as an ideal,
this is at least analogous to the part played by Reason
in fashioning a very large number of the secular convictions of human society; directly for the few, though
the medium of Authority for the many. And I should
be inclined to view it as an illustration of Mr. Balfour's
own statement that there is hardly such a thing as
unaided Reason for individuals.

But, again, while the simultaneous communication
between unequal minds has so much to do with
the matter, there is also Bonald's other factor in
the Universal Reason—the Reason "of all times."
Allowing fully for the futility of a vast amount of
thought in every age, there is surely, within certain
limits, a lesson to be learnt from the evolution of

thought. "Psychological climates," which represent
the characteristic thought of different periods, do not
succeed each other at random.   Their very exaggerations witness to the underlying Reason at work.
If scepticism succeeds credulity, if a speculative age
is followed by an age which will not trust itself
beyond an experience which is almost within reach
of the blind, we see the human instinct for truth at
work, though passion and prejudice constantly con-
vert what should be a correction into a reaction.   In
spite of the see-saw of exaggerations, a distinct line of
advancing truth can be traced.

And again we have, by extending our view to the
workings of the human mind *semper et ubique*, a far
larger field for our induction; and this gives
Mr. Balfour's own argument from human needs a
proportionately greater force.   The needs of the race,
never ceasing to display themselves, and the religious
instinct of man in history, supply a far more urgent
exhibition of the need for religion than the capricious
experience of the individual, or his own observations
of his living fellow-creatures.   Of the perversities and
eccentricities characterising many of the systems in
which the religious instinct has found some expression, something shall shortly be said.   But the
constant display of the need, and the highest products
of its satisfaction, are noteworthy.   The wonderful
results, in the stories of heroic devotedness and
sanctity in the past, of faith in the power and aid of
God, make Mr. Balfour's argument far stronger than
any which most of us could derive from our own halting
Faith and inconsistent lives.   "Idle gleams to thee
are light to me," says the holy Sage in Tennyson's
poem, when the dissipated sceptic complains that his

religious aspirations are "idle gleams" which "come and go." That is to say, what to the sceptic was indistinguishable from what Mr. Balfour calls "a desire," was to the Sage a "need."

But this survey leads us to look back further along the lines of evolution; and in so doing we get an additional presumption from analogy which strengthens the foregoing argument. Consider the gradual development of sensitiveness to the environment, which, by a series which can be traced with tolerable completeness, brings the living being first to the vaguest consciousness of what is not itself, then to more distinct relations with other beings animate and inanimate, involving the increased differentiation of the senses, and soon leading to what is the first symptom of a sense which is destined to place the inhabitant of this small planet in immediate relations with that vast natural universe which is known to astronomers. The earthworm has, I believe, no rudiment of a special organ of vision, yet he will move in response to the light if you turn a bull's-eye lantern on him. The story of the advance from earthworm to man is a suggestive one.[1] It is a story of the gradual unfolding of the sentient organism to what is in some sense a great Reality outside it. At each stage in the advance, the germ of what is to be ultimately a means of wide

---

[1] "In the lowest forms of animal life the whole surface is sensitive to light, and organs of vision have no doubt arisen in the first instance from limited areas being especially sensitive to light in conjunction with a deposit of pigment. Lens-like structures . . . were subsequently formed; but their function was not in the first instance to throw an image of external objects on the perceptive part of the eye, but to concentrate the light on it. From such a simple form of visual organ it is easy to pass by a series of steps to an eye capable of true vision." (F. Balfour's "Comparative Embryology," ii. 471.)

knowledge is mysterious and uncertain. That very sensitiveness to light which in man gives so definite a perception of his fellow-creatures, made the starfish (in all probability) only dimly aware of the presence of some moving object intercepting the light. We could conceive at each stage the advocate of Naturalism and the advocate of what we will call relative Transcendentalism—if we suppose powers of reflection and discussion to be coupled with sensible endowments so limited,—debating as to whether these new-born feelings were really indicative of something beyond, or merely self-caused feelings consistent with primitive solipsism. We now stand above this process, which has been in great measure accomplished. We see that the relative transcendentalist was right,—that evolution was the gradual unfolding of the consciousness to external Nature. But we are still conscious in ourselves of vague indications of a new insight into a higher and further Reality. The religious consciousness, which includes the sense of "need," gives at least a dim presage of a knowledge of things as much beyond our present comprehension as that which is perceived by the sight of man is beyond what is accessible to the vision of the Cœlenterata. Does not the course of evolution raise at least a presumption that this presage and these mysterious glimpses do in fact point to a further stage on the path to Reality? Is evolution, so long a process upwards to wider knowledge, to turn suddenly and begin a process downwards to mere delusion?

And little as can be gained on the same lines from the wayward history of man during his comparatively brief career, we have at least the rise into definiteness of the Christian Ethics, which have carried further and spread far wider the deep sense which we find in the Psalms of the near presence of the living God, so distinct from the vague and distant Theism of (for instance) the Vedas, so intimate in the personal relations contemplated, and in great measure realised. These relations have been carried into practical and general action by the doctrine of the Incarnation to a degree which without it could never have been possible. If, then, the survey of the early course of ages leads us to look at the religious instinct from the first as a dim sensitiveness to a new world, whose character is shadowed forth in the conscience, giving doubtless, as imperfect senses give, new error as the necessary accompaniment of new knowledge (hence the superstitions and distortions which have discredited the religious instinct), surely we have here, in the later purifying and focussing of the religious ideals, a step at least in the direction of a rational indication both of the truth that what is manifest *is* a new sensitiveness to a new light, and of the nature of the Reality towards the knowledge of which the religious consciousness is advancing.

On the whole it would appear that the strength of Mr. Balfour's main position depends on his faithful adherence, in its interpretation, to the quasi-inductive method on which it is really founded. Where his observations have been patient and accurate, his conclusions are true and powerfully stated. He not only successfully disposes of the claims of Naturalism as a sufficient philosophy, and of the Naturalistic account of ethics and of Human Reason, but he gives the individual good ground to search for what his own reason cannot lead him to by a direct path, in those great religious assumptions without which our nature remains so incomplete, and our deepest needs continue unsatisfied—a process which has some analogy (though but a partial one) to the formation of great scientific hypotheses to explain physical facts.

But it is obvious that utterly blind and stupid guesses at Nature's methods would be quite useless in leading to true results. And so, too, if Mr. Balfour's destructive criticism of the analytical processes (notably in the chapter on the Philosophical Basis of Naturalism) is as valid as he seems to suppose, a reason so misleading, when we can observe it closely, will not seem fitted to suggest, with any prospect of accuracy, the general lineaments of a Life-philosophy.

But here I believe that Mr. Balfour's observation of the relevant facts is at fault. The reasoning processes, if patiently surveyed, do not yield such bewildering results as he supposes. If physical science is clearly understood as sharing whatever degree of relativity sensible knowledge possesses, some of his most startling paradoxes fall; and an adequate recognition of the province of latent reasoning and its tests would still further diminish the force of his destructive criticism. Mr. Balfour's constant dilemma " reason " or " instinct," practically identifying " reason " with complete philosophical analysis, ignores here the third ground of a rational instinct which represents a latent rational process, ascertainable as such.

And as there is a rational as distinct from a blind instinct, so there is an open-eyed as distinct from a blind sense of need. And so understood, I believe

that Mr. Balfour is on right lines in giving as a groundwork for our acceptance of the great presupposition
of theology, a Wise and Holy Author of the Universe,
the satisfaction which that assumption ministers to an
urgent and constant need.

The nature of the justification is at least in keeping
with the character of the assumption. If the need
points to a great Reality, a fuller and higher embodiment and source of those Ethical and Rational instincts
which create the need, it is to be expected that we
should not "know as we are known" by a Reason
so far above our own. A dog cannot understand the
means whereby its master does effectually convey to
it his will, and secure its obedience. We have no
help for it but to surrender ourselves to what are so
far non-rational causes of belief, that we cannot rise
to their apprehension by direct logic ; and the experience of consequent harmony and growth may well be
at least one principal element in the justification of our
trust.

And further, once the bridge is crossed which joins
us to the world of Reality, according to Joubert's
saying, "In poetry I should fear to go wrong if I
differed from poets, in religion if I differed from the
Saints," Authority, whose credentials are discerned
through the rational and moral light, has great value
in carrying us further. Those in whom the sense of
the incompleteness of our nature without religion has
been deepest may well determine the line of advance.

The justification, then, of our religious convictions
solely by the satisfaction they afford to what I have
called a blind sense of need, while it harmonises with
one strain in Mr. Balfour's disparagement of human
reason, and with a pessimistic interpretation of his

saying that "certitude is the child of custom"—a saying which naturally recalls David Hume—appears to me both inadequate and out of harmony with the general drift of his striking book. And so, too, a blind surrender to Authority is an inadequate account of the trust in Authority, the necessity and value of which, in the social and religious life, he so powerfully exhibits. I can accept his analysis and his conclusion only with the reservations I have indicated. Theism as the presupposition of Theology is accepted, on grounds similar to those which justify belief in an external world as a necessary presupposition to science. In neither case can a complete logical proof be given. In both cases our intellectual (and ethical) nature points to their rational *necessity* for the completion of the scheme of human knowledge. The analysis of past experience in the one case and of the phenomena of consciousness in the other indicate a conclusion which they cannot reach. In both cases the last link of the process is outside the province of human Reason, but that is (in the case of Theism) at least in harmony with the supposition that a Higher Power is acting on us, whose evidence is in our own life and growth, but whose proportion to ourselves is not such as to allow that we should hold it in the grasp of our limited faculties.

The directly practical object of Mr. Balfour's book has made it necessary to consider chiefly its main conclusion, and it has been impossible to do this briefly. I regret that the profoundest portions of a work, most suggestive throughout, and in parts very powerful, passages characterised by a philosophical comprehensiveness and wisdom which are not equally apparent in some of the destructive criticisms it contains, have therefore fallen outside my scope. I may instance as an example the admirable treatment of " Beliefs, Formulas, and Realities."

Throughout the book we have a combination, especially suited to our own time, when the temperament of a Pascal is so general, of a deep sense of the difficulties of man's position, and of the need for light we do not possess, with an equally deep sense that a practical acquiescence in scepticism or Agnosticism would be to ignore what is best in our nature. That a great Reality beyond us is the source of all that is highest in us is for Mr. Balfour a central belief which no detailed defeat of the reason can shake.

V.

CANDOUR IN BIOGRAPHY.

"PUBLISH everything. To suppress is to falsify history. The frank, manly, honest, straightforward biographer knows that he would do small service to the character he is portraying by omitting anything. The timid or cunning friends who ask that documents should be suppressed are calling on the biographer to be untruthful. If I bowdlerise, I shall idealise and give a false picture. I will brave the anger of surviving friends. I will have the courage to speak out." This, and a great deal more of the same quality, was urged a few years ago in defence of the biography of an eminent person [1]—the author of which was certainly not open to the charge of "idealising." The biography itself, though in some respects a vivid and graphic work, is, I believe, open to criticism of a kind that would carry me far beyond the considerations above alluded to. But as these considerations have a force of their own, and open a question interesting beyond their special occasion, I shall attempt to make a few suggestions on the theory of biography which they imply. I will examine the theory on its own merits and without reference to any existing exemplification of its possible consequences.

[1] Of Cardinal Manning.

I begin by entirely admitting that the careful student who wishes to form an accurate judgment of a given character should see the whole available evidence. The suppressions of the "astute" or the "timid" are so far prejudicial to perfect truth and accuracy. I go a step further, and do not care to dispute that, apart from letters unintelligible or misleading without explanation of their circumstances, the public may, in the long run, form the truer impression of a man for a very liberal publication of his letters. No doubt the judgment of the general public is far more superficial and liable to bias than that of the best critics, or of those deeply interested in forming a true judgment. But in the long run the evidence will be sifted by the more careful students, and their verdict will obtain with the majority.

Here, be it observed, a tolerably true impression may be gained at some cost. Feelings may be hurt; failings may be brought into prominence, which friends would prefer to forget; faults may be placed in such relief as to give quite an erroneous impression—from the accidental preservation of an undue proportion of letters in which they are vividly disclosed. Still, if choice is to be made between two inaccurate versions of a man's character, one due to the suppression of letters in which faults are exhibited, the other to their over-free publication, the less pleasant is likely to be nearer to the truth. Whether, having regard to the sacredness of a dead man's reputation, it is right to give the world what is slightly unjust rather than what is considerably too favourable is a further question.

Be this as it may, the biography of a man is on an entirely different footing from the mere publication of his remains. It is not a collection of documents, but a narrative, illustrated by documents. The process of sifting the evidence is supposed to have been already gone through by the biographer. The reader takes him as a guide. He knows that the publication of *all* documents is an impossibility. No biography could be endurable which attempted it. Selection there must have been; and he trusts to the biographer's judgment, to his personal knowledge of his subject, to his opportunities of seeing *all* the evidence, that the selection has so been made as to give the various elements of the character justly. The reader does not, in the first instance, sit as a judge or sift critically. He knows that material for so doing is largely inaccessible to him. He accepts the character as it is depicted by the biographer, with the aid of the materials of his choice.

And the writer obviously chooses from his mass of material that which will exhibit the conception of the character which he has been led to entertain by the conscientious study of *all* the evidence available. Two biographers who have formed different conceptions would not choose the same material. If Carlyle and Macaulay had adhered to their respective estimates of Boswell, after reading all his papers and letters, and if each had then proceeded to write the life of Boswell, the letters which would strike each as characteristic would be largely different. To one writer he was a toadying busybody, with a touch of reverence, to the other a reverent disciple with an element of the prying busybody. Many of the letters chosen, and the suggestion in the text as to their relative significance, would differ accordingly. And the impression left on the reader—who, be it ever remembered, does not at first study the matter as a critic, but takes in the general effect of the book as a whole—is likely to be determined by the biographer's own judgment.

In other words, a biography is *not* primarily an accumulation of evidence. It is a picture.

Now, nothing is more striking in painting a likeness than the minute changes which may alter the whole expression. One finishing touch is added to an excellent picture. The casual observer may still say, " Like, very like. The long nose, the lanky limbs, the big eyes—just what I remember." But the intimate friend groans and says, " That line has spoilt the whole picture. It gives a sinister look which tells of a wholly different nature."

This may happen from a momentary lapse in the painter's art. But if so minute a change has so considerable an effect, how extensive must be the powers of the caricaturist, whose aim it is to paint an unmistakable likeness, which shall nevertheless have certain features so exaggerated as to produce a ridiculous effect! His art consists in delineating what is true, but out of proportion. He fascinates by his vividness, and it is often waste of time in the ordinary onlooker to try and hunt out the secret of the false impression produced. Every feature can be defended as corresponding with the original. And it is an endless task to trace in detail the numerous changes in relative proportion which in combination produce so startling a result. No more amusing caricatures are made than by the mechanical process of reflecting a figure in a convex or concave mirror. Here the laws of nature ensure a real correspondence between the reflection and the object reflected. And yet a comparison between the two reflections will show what absolutely opposite effects can be produced from the same "material" by the reversal of its proportions.

It is obvious that a similar result may be obtained in biographical narration. All human characters are made up of the same primary affections and passions; just as all human faces have eyes, nose, mouth, and chin. It is in minute varieties of form and in the proportion they bear to one another that the difference lies. And here is the opportunity for the biographical caricaturist. Turn a man's occasional weakness into a besetting sin, by accumulating instances of it without reminding the reader that five occasions may be spread over fifteen years; depict an odd mannerism as though it were of the essence of his manner; dwell on three instances of resentment and leave barely described twenty cases of generosity—this is the kind of treatment which may manufacture from true items of evidence a grotesquely false representation of a man, both of his bearing and of his character.

And there is another tempting method of caricature. It used at one time to be the fashion in schoolroom histories to make the characters embodiments of some leading quality, of some characteristic marked out, it may be, beforehand, by political or religious prejudice. Becket has been the proud and ambitious Churchman; Queen Elizabeth has been Good Queen Bess; Mary, Bloody Mary. And on the other side Luther has been little more than an insincere sensualist.

A biography on such broad lines would carry its inaccuracy on the face of it. But the temptation remains to make one quality the characteristic to which all others are subordinate. And this is a common means of effective caricature either in painting or

in writing. The Jew is caricatured as being the embodiment of a nose. The vacant fop may be typified
by want of chin. And in literature there is often the
temptation to give the typical miser, the typical spend-
thrift, the typical hypocrite. To do so enables the
author to be more graphic and leave a more definite
impression on the reader's mind than he is able to
leave by observing the true proportions and giving
fully the complex web of human character. You may
even give forcibly a perfectly true aspect. But such
pictures as a whole are utterly untrue to the original.
They stand out in the memory as Dickens's Harold
Skimpole, or Jingle, or Fagin, or Pecksniff, or
Micawber, as vivid and never-to-be-forgotten sketches
of certain aspects of men who, if they ever lived,
were something so much more, that the sketches are
not real representations at all.

A caricaturist, then, seizes true aspects and develops
them out of proportion. A literary caricaturist does
the same for some salient features of character, or
external mannerism in a creation of his own. The
biographical caricaturist does it for the subject of his
biography. And, as Dickens was all the more effective
because, as his friends tell us, he used in real life to
see only the peculiarities he depicted, and to be so
fascinated by them as to neglect looking further, so the
biographical caricaturist is the more vivid and effective
if he writes with conviction, if he sees in the character
he is describing almost exclusively the peculiarities he
is led to dwell on and to depict out of proportion. He
gives the man as he sees him; instinctively selects
material illustrative of the aspect which fascinates him
by attraction or repulsion; interprets everything by
the leading feature; makes a Macchiavelli, or a

Mephistopheles, or an Iago, of one who had in reality many human qualities very evenly balanced.

In fact, he commits precisely the same offence against true art as the idealising biographer, with the addition of an offence against kindliness. The idealiser takes the good traits, chooses instinctively by preference material illustrative of them, neglects weaknesses or faults. The other takes the special characteristics which have amused or struck him ; notes a trace of them in every letter he prints ; seizes with delight and places in boldest relief such documents as really bring these characteristics out; and achieves a result similar to that of the born caricaturist in art, who has from the first *seen* in his subject mainly suggestions of the giraffe, or the peacock, or the hawk ; who instinctively concentrates his attention on the features to which such suggestions have been due—the prominent nose or chin, the long neck, the strut, the lanky legs—and develops 'them with fascinated amusement, until the other features appear to have scarcely any connexion with the character of the face—to be mere appendages, or a necessary background for the significant excrescence. The conviction grows upon the artist that the features which have struck him are the key to the whole face, and he is more and more inclined to treat reduction to proportion as suppression of truth. He defends his sketch with perverse ingenuity. He has done full justice to the other features, he declares. He enlarges on their beauty and significance, though he has, in point of fact, traced them hastily and faintly in the actual picture. He will not reduce by a hundredth part of an inch the uncomely mouth and chin which he has made so large and distinct. They are there in the original man, and on no account will he rob his picture of its realistic details which he has so carefully elaborated. And the chief offence against accuracy being a change of proportion, it is waste of time to argue with him in detail. The inaccuracy cannot be adequately measured in words or figures. No broad statement can be commensurate with the far-reaching error. A tenth of an inch too much here and too little there is only in all two-tenths; the faint colouring or blurred outline elsewhere cannot be described in its exact degree; yet the untrue effect of the whole is grotesque.

All this holds good of biography. The caricature, which is due mainly to a one-sided view of the character, held with conviction, is likely to be at once the most vivid and the most misleading. A memoir of Dr. Johnson is, we will suppose, to be written, shortly after his death. The writer who undertakes to deal with his remains and write his life (Boswell by hypothesis being non-existent) has barely known Johnson. The only time he met him, in 1755, Johnson had eaten too much, was somewhat the worse for liquor, and was extremely rude to one or two of the writer's friends. He has adopted Horace Walpole's estimate of Johnson, that "he may be a very good man at bottom, but is a most disagreeable man at top." The sight of him with his swollen veins after excess in eating and drinking has made an indelible impression. Of his brilliant conversation he knows only by hearsay. He does not deny or doubt it. But all he heard and saw was rudeness obviously joined with drunkenness. He reads Johnson's papers and diaries, noting as most significant the confessions of excess in eating and drinking, the slothfulness, the other faults liberally owned to. The picture takes shape and grows vivid in his own mind. " Here is a man who, from his great talent and reputation, has been idealised by his friends. I have no such prepossession. I will depict the man as I saw him myself. I will extenuate nothing." And the writer is as good as his word.   He gives the picture of a drunken sot, an uncouth bear, rude to every one, hardly human, without sense of propriety. He does not deny that Johnson reformed and gave up drink, that there were better traits in his character ; nay, having read the diaries and letters, he says that the character was in some respects a noble one—when he was sober.   But such admissions are addenda and appendices.   The book is, on the whole, a protest, full of righteous indignation, against idealisation.   It is a picture "of the man as I saw him, as I knew him."   It is not the Johnson whose piercing perceptions, vigour of mind, moral elevation of judgment, wonderful brilliance and wide information, commanding force of will and intellect, have made us almost forget that such a scene as impressed this biographer may have really occurred.   It is a picture drawn from that one evil hour, by one to whom that evil hour is a living fact, and the rest a matter of hearsay or reading.

The friend of Johnson is indignant.   " Where," he asks, " is Johnson's piety ? "   The author triumphantly shows in a footnote the words " in spite of his religious feeling."   "Where is his constant charity?"   The author has set down twenty lines in the seven hundredth page of Vol. II. which give a long eulogium of his charity and goodness of heart.   " But you represent him as unkind in the great bulk of the text, and even in this passage you do not convince the reader that you believe in his kindness, or give instances of it."   Here,

indignation is the effectual retort : "When I acknowledge the faults of the man I am accused of telling
lies, yet when I speak in admiration of him I am told
that I do not say enough. Because I do not give you
a set of goody-goody stories suitable for a saint's life, I
do not satisfy you." "How about his tender love for
his wife?" Two whole pages on it in the seventeenth
appendix. "I had not observed these pages. Still,
the general effect is contrary to the drift of such
passages. You do not give his good qualities due
proportion. Take, for example, his real sense of the
fitness of things, quite inconsistent with this picture of
a mere boor—take his interview with George III., his
visit to the Duke of Argyll?" Five pages, including
both episodes, in the twenty-seventh appendix. The
biographer here becomes effective and even triumphant. "False proportion," he exclaims," is now the
burden of your criticism. How could I emphasise such
a quality more than by concentrating the instances of
it, collecting them together and giving it as a salient
feature in his character? The fact is you want me to
suppress his excesses and sottishness. This I will
never do. His was a noble character, and will not be
served by such unworthy subterfuges. He was a downright and truthful man, and would be the last to
sanction such suppressions himself."

We have our Boswell, and such a book would do
Johnson no harm. But had it given to Englishmen
their first idea of Johnson, it might have taken years
for the proportions to be set right—for the *evidence* in
the book itself to have corrected the *picture* in the
book. Appendices seventeen and twenty-seven would
eventually be reached by some literary Columbus,
would be enlarged upon in their bearing on the rest.

A fresh key would be thereby supplied to letters hitherto read for the sake of their incidental illustrations of blunt rudeness. Confirmation of the new view of Johnson would come from the book itself, read under the influence of this new suggestion. Further confirmation would be given by the anecdotes and letters supplied by surviving friends. The current of opinion would be changed, and the secret of the one-sided biography analysed.

But, meanwhile, the unpleasant picture of the original biographer may have been reproduced by reviewers without the favourable admissions which even his own text supplied, to qualify the painful effect of the whole ; and for a generation Johnson would have lived for the popular mind a vivid figure, painful to his surviving friends from the very authenticity of the anecdotes against him so carefully collected, and the rude letters preserved. The picture would, for the time, remain in the public mind as the true Dr. Johnson, whom his friends had invested with a halo which the evidence produced had for ever removed.

I will only add that, such being the power of the biographer from his own erroneous or prejudiced judgment to turn the picture derivable from a man's writings into a caricature, in which the proportions are distorted, it has naturally been the custom to leave private papers to be dealt with by a friendly hand. To obtain a true likeness is difficult. It is nearly impossible that one who is not a friend should so far understand those remarkable traits which make a man worth writing about as to execute a true likeness. And though many a friend will give an idealised portrait, it is certainly juster to the dead that the selection and description should be carried out on the principle of illustrating good qualities at the cost of giving insufficient space to bad, than of illustrating faults in such lengthy detail as to leave little space for anything else. The latter method can give no real picture of those qualities but for which the biography should not be written at all. Neither course is satisfactory; but if omissions are to be called "suppressions," and to be regarded as uncandid, it is hard to understand how a biography is more candid which is written on the principle of omitting nothing which tells against a man, than one which leaves nothing unsaid which would tell in his favour. Luckily the latter class is the commoner. The fault of ignoring weak points is popularly criticised; while that of giving them the most prominent place is less commonly considered, because fortunately we have not yet reached the time when many persons are ready to write the life of a good or eminent man, without feeling before all things interested in depicting those qualities to which his goodness or eminence has been due.

VI.

TENNYSON.

A REMINISCENCE.

"DORIC beauty" is the phrase by which the late Mr. Huxley once expressed the special character of Tennyson's conversation—with its terse simplicity and freedom from artificial ornament : "and yet," he added, "on hearing the first few words one might only say,—'Exactly, this is the man who wrote the "Northern Farmer."'"

My first recollections of Tennyson date back as far as 1869, or earlier. As a boy, living near him in the Isle of Wight, I was somewhat in awe of the mysterious figure, whom I often saw in company with his friend and neighbour, Mrs. Cameron, or at times with my father, tall and thin, enveloped in a huge cloak, walking rapidly, with a slight stoop, on the Beacon Down or in the Freshwater lanes. He seldom spoke to me in those days, although I was intimate with his second son, Lionel. I think it was the report of a careful study I made of the Holy Grail, in Rome, in the year 1879, which changed this. On my return to England our acquaintance was at once on a new footing. I stayed with him at Aldworth in the following year : and thenceforward walks and talks with the poet were frequent.

There were several things which struck me for the first time after I came to know him better. One was, that even at a time when I was walking with him often, and enjoying the real intimacy which was my privilege, his shyness on first coming into the room, before we started for our morning walk, remained. One had noticed it less when it appeared to be only the slowness of a man of a certain age to talk to a boy. But to the very end it was the same, even with those whom he was most frequently seeing. How familiar the picture yet remains! One waited, perhaps, in the ante-room at Farringford for a few minutes before he appeared. And when he did so there was the far-off look in his eyes, something between the look of a near-sighted man and a very far-sighted man;—due, no doubt, partly to defective vision, but conveying also a sense that his imagination was still occupied with itself, and that his mind was not yet "focussed" on the world immediately about him. I have known him stand for several minutes, after a half-absent "How d'ye do?" in this dreamy state, with his curious look of high-strung sensitiveness, before he began to talk. And if one waited silently for him to speak, one might have to wait in vain. To tell him an amusing story was the best means of breaking the spell. The gleam of humour came to his face at once, he broke into laughter, left the regions of mental abstraction, and probably at once capped the story himself.

If a stranger had come to see him, the shyness and abstraction might last longer. I remember once going to Farringford with a friend—a true worshipper of his genius—and after the first words of greeting he seemed to be entirely in the clouds;

until, after long waiting, we hit upon a device to
arouse him.   A picture by Edward Lear hung in the
room, and under it were four lines from the " Palace
of Art : "—

> " One seem'd all dark and red—a tract of sand,
>   And some one pacing there alone,
> Who paced for ever in a glimmering land,
>   Lit with a low large moon."

We were looking at the picture, and I said to my
companion : "Read the lines."   She read them,
giving them a kind of metrical jingle.   In a moment
Tennyson, who had been standing alone at the other
side of the room, stepped rapidly across, seized her
arm, and said : " Don't read them like that," and went
on with his deep, sonorous voice to read or rather
chaunt them himself, with the roll which was so well
known to his friends.

When once the spell had been thus broken, the
absolute freedom and naturalness of his conversation
came on those who had not seen him before as a
surprise.   And no doubt the impression left on some,
of his being difficult and holding himself aloof, came
partly from meeting him on occasions when the first
shyness failed to pass away.

The earliest walks I remember with Tennyson
were large parties.   Six or eight would often go with
him ; and he himself talked with one at a time,
changing his companion occasionally.   But from about
1882 onwards I frequently went out with him *tête-à-
tête.*   And it was then that he waxed most earnest on
problems connected with Metaphysics and Religious
Philosophy.   Before we started there would be a good
deal to distract his attention.   First there was the
unloosening of the dogs who were to go with us.

Don and Duke in earlier days, and later the beautiful stag-hound Lufra or the graceful Karenina, are an inseparable part of the picture of those walks that lives in the memory. And conversation was from time to time suspended while he dealt condign chastisement for their occasional misdemeaniours—the chasing of a sheep, or the fighting with another dog.

As we crossed the "careless-ordered garden" he would call attention to some little alteration or addition, in which he was sure to be keenly interested. "Did you ever see a cypress growing as a creeper before ?" he asks, as he points to a dark tree nailed against a wall. "We have *crucified* that tree to make it grow thus." We stop again at the tennis-lawn :— "The rabbits look on the chalk-line as marking out charmed and forbidden ground." And he traces with his stick the minute disturbances of the turf which his watchful eye has noted near the outer line of the court, nowhere passing within it. A hundred yards outside the Park gates we pause at the shop of Rogers, the naturalist, who has been stuffing a heron or a monkey which one of the Freshwater sailors may have given him, and the poet will study it with keen interest. Then the walk is resumed, but before we have gone far along the road to Freshwater Bay some tree or plant will again stop him. Then he suddenly breaks off with : "But what is the good of speaking to you about this ? You are as bad as your father, who noticed nothing, and did not even know his own fields from mine. You once took a lily of the valley for a snowdrop."

And then the conversation passes to literature, or personal reminiscence, or poetry, or metaphysics. But soon the sound of the cuckoo, perhaps, brings it

back :—" Do you hear that note ? It differs from
what we heard a week ago. If you want to remember
when to listen for the cuckoo learn the lines I learnt
in Lincolnshire as a boy." And he repeats the old
verse :—

> " In April he opens his bill,
>   In May he sings all day,
>   In June he changes his tune,
>   In July away he does fly,
>   In August go he must."

Conversation never flagged : neither did the rapid
pace at which the poet walked—except when he
would stand still for a minute to tell some story
with particular emphasis. I remember his humorous
satisfaction at Aldworth in 1881 because he and I had
distanced Mr. (now Sir Richard) Jebb and another
friend, who were detected sitting down to rest some
hundred yards or more behind us. " I am over seventy
and he is not forty, yet I can outwalk him," Tennyson
said. The remarkable suppleness of his joints remained until a year before his death, and at Christmas,
1891, as we came home from our walk, he climbed a
difficult gate without help ; and as we approached
Farringford he ran—literally ran—down a hill, as he
had often done in earlier years. He was then eighty-
two years old.

Before passing to some of our talks on matters of
deep and permanent interest, I must give as their
setting some sayings and stories on various subjects
which I noted down between the years 1884 and
1887 ; and I will put together as though belonging to
one walk sayings which really belong to several.[1]

---

[1] This applies also to small incidents already given, some of which
occurred at Aldworth, some at Farringford.

His companion had been reading Browning and had found "Sordello" somewhat difficult. This confession amused Tennyson. "When 'Sordello' came out," he remarked, "Douglas Jarrold said to me: 'What has come to me? Has my mind gone? Here is a poem of which I can't understand a single line?' Browning," he added, "has a genius for a sort of dramatic composition and for analysing the human mind. And he has a great imagination. But a poet's writing should be sweet to the mouth and ear, which Browning's is not. There should be a 'glory of words" as well as deep thought. This he has not got. In his last work he makes 'impulse' rhyme with 'dim pulse.'" He spoke of Browning's love of London society: "I once told him he would die in a white tie, and he rather liked it."

This led to a discussion of Goethe's saying: "Es bildet ein talent sich in der stille." Some poets seem, he said, to find solitude necessary. I remarked that Arthur Clough in his Oxford days shrank from general society. "I knew him well in later life," Tennyson said. "He once travelled with us in France. He was a delightful companion, but was rather wanting in the sense of humour. He had great poetic feeling. He read me his 'In Mari Magno,' and cried like a child as he read it." I spoke of Clough's friendship with some of the Oxford Tractarians, and of their separation owing to Clough's movement towards religious negation. This led Tennyson to tell me of a talk he had with George Eliot on the subject of her negative religious views: "How difficult it is to repeat a thing as it really happened! George Eliot had this conversation with me at Aldworth, and the account of it which got into

print was that I disputed with her till I was red in the
face, and then roared, 'Go away, you and your
molecules!' The real fact was that our conversation
was 'sweet as summer,' and at parting I shook her
hand, and said very gently, 'I hope you are happy
with your molecules.'" He spoke with admiration
of George Eliot's genius and insight into human
character, but maintained that she was not quite so
truthful as Shakespeare or Miss Austen:—"The
character of Adam Bede is not quite true to human
nature. It is idealised. I am reported to have said
that Jane Austen was equal to Shakespeare. What I
really said was that, in the narrow sphere of life which
she delineated, she pictured human character as truth-
fully as Shakespeare. But Austen is to Shakespeare
as asteroid to sun. Miss Austen's novels are perfect
works on a small scale—beautiful bits of stippling."
His companion remarked that Macaulay's well-known
comparison probably meant no more than this. We
thus passed to his impressions of Macaulay himself,
and these he gave with grim humour :—"I only met
him once. I was introduced to him in the Fifties by
Guizot. Macaulay bowed and went on talking to
Guizot, addressing no word to me. Then he turned
to me, and said, 'I am very glad to have made your
acquaintance,' and walked away. He did not show
much sign of being glad to make my acquaintance."

I told him Jowett's account of a talk with
Macaulay : that it was as though Macaulay were
delivering a lecture to an audience of one person.
This led to a comparison of Macaulay's monologue
with Carlyle's. Of Carlyle he said : "He was at
once the most reverent and the most irreverent
man I have known. I admire his estimate of

Boswell, and hate Macaulay's. Mrs. Carlyle was a most charming, witty converser, but often sarcastic. She never spoke before her husband, who absorbed the conversation." I asked, " Did he not listen to *you* when you talked ? " " In a way," he replied; " but he hardly took in what one said. Carlyle was at his best, *rollicking* at the Ashburtons' house—the Grange. He and Lady Ashburton were the life of the party. Those parties were very interesting, and Lady Ashburton was a woman of great brilliancy. She liked Carlyle, but I think at that time, if she had a favourite, it was George Venables. Carlyle had a great feeling that we needed a strong man in England. 'Our Cromwell is being born somewhere,' he used to say."

This led us to speak of our modern statesmen. He seemed disposed to agree with Carlyle, and would not accord to any the title of a really great ruler. Speaking of Mr. Gladstone, he said : "You cannot rule, as he thinks he can, with a silk glove. You must have an iron gauntlet ; though you need not always make people feel the iron." He went on to contrast Gladstone and Disraeli, doing full justice to the gifts of the former as an orator, and to the latter's "diplomatic craft:"—"The great fault of Disraeli's character was that he was scornful. Gladstone is genial and kindly." He was very grand on contemptuousness. It was, he said, a sure sign of intellectual littleness. Simply to despise nearly always meant not to understand. Pride and contempt were specially characteristic of barbarians. Real civilisation taught human beings to understand each other better, and must therefore lessen contempt. It is a little or immature or uneducated mind which readily despises.   One who has lived only in a *coterie* despises readily.   One who has travelled and knows the world in its length and breadth, respects far more views and standpoints other than his own.   He quoted these lines of Wordsworth's with strong admiration :—

> "Stranger, henceforth be warned, and know that pride,
> Howe'er disguised in its own majesty,
> Is littleness, that he who feels contempt
> For any living thing, hath faculties
> Which he hath never used ; that thought with him
> Is in its infancy."

The conversation passed to Lord Palmerston, and thence to the Italian movement of '48, with which Palmerston was in such close sympathy.   Tennyson told a story *à propos* to the craze for revolution in Italy at that time, which gives some idea of the kind of humour in which the poet delighted.   Constant little revolutions took place, and the inhabitants drank an extremely large quantity of *chianti* and talked enthusiastically of *libertà* and *la patria* for a couple of days ; and then things settled down into their former groove.   On one occasion, Tennyson's friend, Edward Lear, was staying in a Sicilian town, painting.   He left the town for some weeks, and locked up his pictures and other things in a room, leaving the key with the hotel-keeper.   A revolution had just broken out when he returned, and he found the waiters full of *chianti* and of patriotic fervour.   He ventured to ask one of them for the *chiave* of his *camera*, that he might find his *roba*.   The waiter refused entirely to be led down from his dreams of a golden age and of the reign of freedom to such details of daily life. "O che chiave!" he exclaimed, "O che roba! O che camera!   Non c'e piu chiave!   Non c'e piu roba!

Non c'e piu camera! Non c'e piu niente. Tutto e amore e libertà. O che bella rivoluzione!"

His companion mentioned a friend who had lately become a vegetarian. This brought back to him an experience of his own: "Once, in imitation of my friend Fitzgerald, the translator of 'Omar Khayyam,' for ten weeks I ate only vegetables. At first it gave great lucidity of mind. At the end of that time I felt light, and almost foolish. I ate one chop; and a more genial glow came over me than if I had drunk brandy." This led naturally to the dedication of "Tiresias," and he recited the lines:—

> "And once, for ten long weeks, I tried
>   Your table of Pythagoras,
> And seemed at first 'a thing enskied'
>   (As Shakespeare has it), airy light,
> To float above the ways of man,
> Then fell from that half-spiritual height,
> Chilled till I tasted flesh again,
> One night when earth was winter-black,
> And all the heavens flashed in frost;
> And on me, half asleep, came back
> That wholesome heat the blood had lost."

"'Belle comme la prose,'" he said, "is the French expression for that kind of poetry, and a very good one. It applies also to my lines of invitation to F. D. Maurice. Browning's obscurity of style makes this impossible to him. The great aim in such poems is to say what you have to say with melody, but with perfect simplicity. When I felt that I had done this in the dedication of 'Tiresias,' the fools in *The Edinburgh Review* condemned it as 'prose in rhyme.'"

Then the subject of a forthcoming poem of his own might be broached, and its plan discussed with that absolute simplicity in which he had, I think, no

rival in private conversation, although the presence of
numbers occasionally brought with it an element of
self-consciousness.   And here I may remark that this
truly great simplicity led him invariably to accept
criticism which he felt to be honest and just.   " Quon-
doque bonus dormitat Homerus ; " and Tennyson, too,
would at times overlook an obviously unsatisfactory
line in his first draft.   I recall his reading to me and
to another friend (the late Mr. Locker Lampson)
"Vastness" before he published it in *Macmillan's
Magazine.*   The stately couplets—each descriptive of
some phase of the universe or of human existence—
were given with grand effect until he read this one—

> " Love for the maiden crowned with marriage,
>   No regret for aught that has been.
>   Debtless competence, comely children,
>   Happy household, sober and clean."

His hearers smiled very visibly at the last words.
Tennyson looked up.

" Why are you laughing ? " he asked.

" If we laughed perhaps others might laugh," I
ventured.

" True," he said, and closed his book.   Next day
he called us, and read as follows :—

> " Love for the maiden crowned with marriage,
>   No regrets for aught that has been.
>   Household happiness, gracious children,
>   Debtless competence, golden mean."

I think I am right in saying that the great
problems of Metaphysics and of man's destiny and
origin occupied a larger share of his thoughts than
heretofore, during the last ten or twelve years of his
life.   But indications of the trains of thought which

he afterwards matured are to be found comparatively
early. I asked him which was the earliest poem in
which he had begun seriously to consider these problems, and he said " The Two Voices." Two couplets
therein express his method in nearly all his great
metaphysical poems :—

> " As far as might be, to carve out
> Free space for every human doubt,
> That the whole mind might orb about.
>
> " To search thro' all I felt or saw
> The springs of life, the depths of awe,
> And reach the law within the law."

It was by allowing the most free and explicit voice to
doubt that he gradually worked further and further
towards the solution of the mysteries of life and of
the world. He was a thoroughgoing idealist; and his
conclusions recall in some respects portions of the
writings of three great thinkers—Kant, Berkeley, and
Father Malebranche.

His method consisted in the presentation of two
opposing veins of thought—of questioning and doubt
on the one hand, and of instinctive assurance on the
other. Each line of thought is given its weight.
The instinctive assurance is not set aside in consequence of the speculative doubt; nor is it allowed
to check the doubt in its critical function. Doubt
and questioning may lead to the discovery that some
instinctive beliefs are based on mere prejudice. Yet
there are instincts which bear in them signs of
authority—as the inner voice appealed to in the
" Ancient Sage ; " and the fact is recognised that doubt
and questioning may be morbid, and a consequence
of intellectual defect. In " The Two Voices " these

two elements are formally expressed. In the "In Memoriam" they are indicated by the expression of moods of doubt, which are not represented as the final conclusions of the poet, and which are sometimes dismissed as avowedly unsatisfying. "We do him wrong to sing so wildly." In the "De Profundis" the first greeting gives the materialist view of life which is counterpoised by the spiritual view of the later lines. In "Vastness," which had, as he first read it to me, two distinct voices—the last line being placed in the mouth of a separate speaker who answers the rest of the poem,—is still preserved the intimation of two veins of thought, the last line indicating the underlying conviction adhered to in the face of insoluble mystery. In the "Ancient Sage," again—and more dramatically than in the others—we have two voices and two distinct characters. Even where this is not so, the dramatic form is often kept, as in "Despair"—showing that a mood of thought is expressed rather than the convictions of the poet. And the dramatic form of even his greatest solutions of Metaphysical problems reminds us that the poet was rather indicating broad outlines of a philosophical position which became year by year more closely defined, than professing to put in unalterable and final shape the analysis of his convictions.

Bacon has grandly described that attitude of humility and sensitiveness to all facts which is indispensable to the student of nature. Tennyson had this humility pre-eminently in Metaphysics. Bacon's bugbears, the *intellectus sibi permissus*, mere speculation, mere prejudice, which lead to the ignoring of facts which do not square with preconceived theories, have their counterpart in the upholders of dogmatic Metaphysical systems. Tennyson, on the contrary, showed a passionate yearning simply to learn facts as they are. There was no pride, no dogmatism, but the simplicity of a child—of "an infant crying for the light"—alongside of the penetrating and sensitive intellectual nature. To the very end he had the teachableness of true greatness, and his views seemed to grow more accurate and mature to his last year.

And here we have, I think, the quality which made his conversation on these subjects so peculiarly impressive. One felt its intense candour and truthfulness. I use the word "intense" advisedly. With many a man one knows that on such subjects there is no lack of ability or sincerity. But he is ready to theorise and to develop a theory with ingenuity; and what began as a candid attempt to solve the mysteries of the universe soon becomes untrue to fact. Tennyson, on the other hand, tested every step; questioned and questioned again his own conclusions; detected and allowed for the least shadow of prejudice or prepossession; re-examined his own old statements in the light of further experience. He seemed to be ever looking upward at the mysteries of the world behind the phenomena of sense, intently eager to miss no flash of light, however momentary, which might break through the clouds and reveal the heavens beyond. He carried into metaphysics the extraordinary accuracy of perception which he showed with physical nature, and indeed with all the facts of life. That this habit was lifelong in the case of physical nature we are reminded by such a poem as the "Progress of Spring," first written in youth. Such lines as, "The starling claps her tiny castanets," and the description (elsewhere) of the sun-flower which "rays round with flames her disc of seed," are specimens given only to indicate the habit to which I refer, instances of which are too abundant to need further specification. The "thing as it was," instead of being confused by imagination or associations, made an indelible impression on him.

His accuracy as to quite trivial matters was even scrupulous. If a story were told with the slightest inaccuracies of detail he would spoil it by repeated interruptions, rather than let them pass. He was equally severe with himself if memory tripped in the smallest degree. In his "All along the Valley," the opening lines run thus :—

> "All along the valley, stream that flashest white,
> Deepening thy voice with the deepening of the night,
> All along the valley, where the waters flow,
> I walk'd with one I loved two-and-thirty years ago."

One day he discovered that he was wrong by one year—that only thirty-one years had passed when he wrote the poem. He was much vexed, and talked seriously of changing the line. So, too, in speaking of historical or social facts, dates and numbers were always prominent and always accurate. Talking of Buddhism and its later division into so many sects, he gave at once, with perfect exactness, their number and the dates and circumstances of the chief schisms. And above all, he remembered and delighted in the facts of astronomy. Such a book as Ball's "Astronomy" filled his imagination. He would point to a fixed star and tell one the exact pace at which it was moving, and give the distance from us of each planet, and calculate the time the sun's light takes to reach us, and make his figures still more vivid by comparing them with the speed of things familiar to us on our own earth.

This habitual accuracy of memory and perception, and knowledge of detail, instead of being confused when his imagination became most vivid, came out all the more clearly. Ruskin, in " Modern Painters," names three kinds of imagination :—" The man who perceives rightly because he does not feel, and to whom the primrose is very accurately the primrose because he does not love it ; secondly, the man who perceives wrongly because he feels, and to whom the primrose is anything else than a primrose—a star or a sun or a fairy's shield or a forsaken maiden. And then there is lastly the man who perceives rightly in spite of his feelings, and to whom the primrose is for ever nothing else than itself—a little flower apprehended in the very plain and leafy fact of it, whatever and how many soever the associations and passions may be that exist around it." Tennyson's imagination was eminently of the third kind. The vividness it gave was not a halo which may blur or obscure the true features it surrounds, but a strong limelight which shows the minutest details accurately. The new light was never confused or dazzling ; and it was always focussed precisely.

It was then, I think, partly this close truthfulness in his perception and memory of all he spoke of, which gave one such a strong sense of the reality of his Metaphysical thought. He was no theoriser to spin a web of fancy on such questions. One felt that his was peculiarly a mind which could not be constantly brooding on the subject (as it was), and constantly revising and retouching his analysis of its problems, if those problems and his solutions were not very real indeed. Some characteristics which often mar philosophical speculation were entirely absent from him. He was incapable of confounding mistiness with mystery, incapable of occupying his mind with anything which it did not definitely *ap*prehend, although he recognised as much as any one how large is the sphere of mystery which no man can *com*prehend. On the other hand, his clearness never led to the unreal completeness of lovers of system. One felt confidence in his glimpses all the more from the frankness with which he recognised that they were but a partial insight into truths beyond us. What he said won assent not from any logical completeness, but from absolute truth to fact; though it often had the characteristics ascribed by George Eliot to truth under the limitations of our present condition—of being "complex" and "fragmentary." On such subjects this was an additional sign of its exactness.

The problems of the physical Universe and of man's physical life alternated as a theme of conversation with Metaphysics themselves, and thus claim their share in my notes. Nearly all the sayings I have set down belong to the years 1885–1887. He spoke of the mysteries of Metaphysics. "After religion," he said, "Metaphysics are the great hope for mankind. They must stem the tide of materialism. They show materialists that you can't escape from mystery by escaping from religion." A subject which especially exercised him in this connexion was the mystery attaching to space and to extended matter, indications of which are in "Vastness," the second "Locksley Hall," the "Ancient Sage," and "De Profundis." We were passing one day through a ploughed field, and, pointing to the clods, he remarked that to a woodlouse they might look as grand as the Swiss Alps to us. "All greatness is relative," he said. "What are the Swiss mountains themselves when you know their proportion to the earth; and the earth itself when you know its proportion to the Universe?" A little later on I returned to this subject, and instead of "woodlouse" said a "flea." He stopped me at once. "Not a flea: it could jump to the top in a moment, and that would prevent the idea of such greatness." [1] On my saying, then, that it was painful to look on one's impression of the beauty of Swiss mountains as only a subjective feeling, without corresponding objective reality, he said he did not mean this. The *size* is relative; but the *beauty* may be real. The clods in the ploughed field may be really beautiful, but one needs to be as small as a tiny insect to appreciate the beauty. "Then, too, what mystery there is in a grain of sand! Divide and divide it as you will, you never come to an end of it. All that has magnitude is divisible; two atoms without magnitude cannot make one with magnitude. So you can always divide." He passed, then, from the consideration of infinite littleness in matter to that of infinite greatness: "Think of the proportion of one human eye to our earth; of our earth to the sun; of the sun to the solar system; of that to the Universe; and then think that one human eye can in some sense be in contact with the stars of the Milky Way."

Another saying of his connected with this subject

---

[1] On another occasion, remembering the objection to the flea, I spoke of the insect as an "ant." "Just as bad as your flea," he said. "An ant runs so fast that he would be at the top of the clods in a few seconds."

is all the more interesting, because he immediately afterwards embodied it in eight lines of great beauty. Walking one day on the down which stretches from Freshwater Bay to the Freshwater Beacon, his conversation was chiefly of two subjects. One was the mad lawlessness of the Celtic character, which he illustrated by items of news from Ireland — fresh instances of maiming cattle, and of murder and outrage, and the other all the mass of confusion and crime which a great town brought together. Paris was worse than London, he said, because of the Celtic element in the French character. About half-way between Freshwater Bay and the Beacon, he suddenly stopped and pointed with his stick to a star, quite visible, though it was almost daylight. " Do you see that star ? " he asked, in his abrupt way. " It is the evening star. Do you know that if we lived there this earth would look to us exactly like that. Fancy the vice and confusion of London or Paris in that peaceful star." He looked again at the star with an expression half of horror, half of grim humour. We walked on. I did not know at the time that he was writing the second " Locksley Hall ; " and it was with a curious sensation that one read afterwards the exquisite lines which that walk had (apparently) suggested. His few words on the subject proved to have been, what his talk so often was, condensed prose notes of coming poetry :—

" Hesper, whom the poet called the bringer home of all good things,
  All good things may move in Hesper, perfect peoples, perfect
    kings.

" Hesper, Venus, were we native to that splendour, or in Mars,
  We should see the globe we groan in, fairest of our evening stars.

"Could we dream of wars and carnage, craft and madness, lust and
    spite,
Roaring London, raving Paris, in that point of peaceful light?

"Might we not in glancing heavenward on a star so silver fair,
    Yearn and clasp the hands and murmur, 'Would to God that we
    were there!'"

He insisted strongly on misuses of the word
"God," and often condemned the immorality of extreme Calvinism. One could not but trace to the
memories of the Calvinistic surroundings of his boyhood the deep feeling evident in such poems as
"Despair" and "Demeter" against the conception of
a vindictive Deity. "I remember one woman who
used to weep for hours because God was so infinitely
good. He had predestined (she said) most of her
friends to damnation, and herself, who was no better
than they, to salvation. She shook her head at me
sadly, and said, 'Alfred, Alfred, whenever I look at
you I think of the words of Scripture, "Depart from
me, ye cursed, into everlasting fire."' The Calvinist
minister, who was spiritual guide to the neighbourhood,
had typhoid fever. To the horror of his congregation,
on recovering he became a Universalist, and ceased
to believe in hell." He told me of another Calvinist
minister who argued with a clergyman of more liberal
views on the ways of Providence. "Wait a moment,"
interrupted the latter, "we have not defined our terms.
We are using them in different senses. Your God is
my devil."

This vindictive idea of God was perhaps his
greatest trial in popular religion. Another was the
anthropomorphism which regarded the Supreme Being
as a sort of "magnified clergyman." But he admitted

that this was almost inevitable with some of the un-educated. "These misuses of the word 'God' make me prefer another name," he said. "I prefer to say the Highest or the Supreme Being. In the 'Ancient Sage' I have called God 'the Nameless.' I have sometimes demurred to the phrase 'personal' as applied to God, for that same reason. It has been used as though personality were quite similar in God and in man. But I only mean that His personality is higher than ours. Lotze says the lack of personality is in us. God is unknowable as he is in Himself, but He touches us at one point. That point is the con-science. If the conscience could be further developed, we might in some sense see God." And again: "The conception in us of a perfect being realising our highest ideals is some proof of God's existence, though not a conclusive proof. Why should we conceive of such a being unless it were put into us to do so?"

"Lushington [1] used to say to me," he continued, "that if there were no other world, this world would be all the more valuable. I, on the contrary, feel that it is only the light shed on our earth from another world which gives it any value. The thought of working for the human race is not incentive enough to virtue if man is not immortal. The whole race will be extinct, probably, in a few thousand years. All the greatest aspirations are without meaning if man be not immortal. Religious belief is necessary to give life any meaning or value. A man without religious aspirations is only half a man." [2]

Speaking of free will, he said: "Man is free, but

[1] Edmund Lushington, his brother-in-law.
[2] "A gelded man" was his phrase.

only free in certain narrow limits. His character and his acquired habits limit his freedom. They are like the cage of a bird. The bird can hop at will from one perch to another, and to the floor of the cage, but not beyond its bars." And of the Buddhist Nirvana : "Place a cork at the bottom of a jar of water. Its tendency will be to work its way upwards, whatever obstacles you may place in the way. At last it reaches the top and is at rest. That is my conception of Nirvana."

Evolution was a very favourite topic with him. He had made a close study of it, and Huxley once said to me that Tennyson's grasp of the principles of physical science was equal to that of the greatest experts. Wallace's book on Darwinism was not published until 1889, but long before that time Tennyson often spoke of his genius, and was disposed to think his conclusions more exact in some respects than Darwin's : "Wallace pointed out that man has a prospective brain—that he has faculties in excess of his physical needs. This would show that you can't account for his higher faculties by natural selection." Again : "The descent of man's body from lower animals," he once said, "if it is true, helps to solve the mystery of man's dual nature. We naturally inherit a great deal from our brute ancestors. The spiritual nature is something superadded, but the brute nature is there, and remains side by side with the other."

I may conclude these recollections with some account of a conversation in which he explained to me his "De Profundis," one of the two later poems to which as mature expressions of his Metaphysical thought he attached the greatest value—the other

being "The Ancient Sage." [1]   He had often said he
would go through the "De Profundis" with me line
by line, and he did so late in January or early in
February, 1889, when I was staying at Farringford.
He was still very ill, having had rheumatic fever in
the previous year; and neither he nor his friends expected that he would recover after his many relapses.
He could scarcely move his limbs, and his fingers
were tied with bandages.   We moved him from bed
to sofa, but he could not sit up.   His mind, however,
was quite clear.   He read through the "De Profundis,"
and gave the substance of the explanation I have
written down.   He began languidly, but soon got
deeply interested.   When he reached the prayer at
the end, he said: "A B" (naming a well-known
Positivist thinker) "exclaimed, when I read it to
him, 'Do leave that prayer out; I like all the rest
of it.'"

I proceed to set down the account of the poem
written (in substance) immediately after his explanation of it.   The mystery of life as a whole which so
constantly exercised him is here most fully dealt with.
He supposes a child just born, and considers the
problems of human existence as presented by the
thought of the child's birth, and the child's future life
with all its possibilities.   The poem takes the form
of two greetings to the new-born child.   In the first
greeting life is viewed as we see it in the world, and
as we know it by physical science, as a phenomenon;
as the materialist might view it; not indeed coarsely,
but as an outcome of all the physical forces of the

I do not mention "Akbar," to which he also attached great importance, as it was not then written.   Moreover, "Akbar," though a full
expression of his religious attitude, is not directly metaphysical.

universe, which have ever contained in themselves the potentiality of all that was to come—"all that was to be in all that was." These vast and wondrous forces have now issued in this newly given life—this child born into the world. There is the sense of mystery in our greeting to it; but it is of the mysteries of the physical Universe and nothing beyond; the sense of awe fitting to finite man at the thought of infinite Time, of the countless years before human life was at all, during which the fixed laws of Nature were ruling and framing the earth as we know it, of the countless years earlier still, during which, on the nebular hypothesis, Nature's laws were working before our planet was separated off from the mass of the sun's light, and before the similar differentiation took place in the rest of the " vast waste dawn of multitudinous eddying light." Again, there is awe in contemplating the vastness of space; in the thoughts which in ascending scale rise from the new-born infant to the great globe of which he is so small a part, from that to the whole solar system, from that again to the myriad similar systems "glimmering up the heights beyond" us which we partly see in the Milky Way; from that to those others which human sight can never descry. Forces in Time and Space as nearly infinite as our imagination can conceive, have been leading up to this one birth, with the short life of a single man before it. May that life be happy and noble! Viewing it still as the course determined by Nature's laws—a course unknown to us and yet unalterably fixed—we sigh forth the hope that our child may pass unscathed through youth, may have a full and prosperous time on earth, blessed by man for good done to man, and may pass peacefully at last to rest.   Such is the first greeting—full of the poetry of life, of its wondrous causes, of the overwhelming greatness of the Universe of which this new-given baby is the child, cared for, preserved hitherto unscathed amid these awful powers, all in all to its parents, inspiring the hope which new-given joy makes sanguine, that fortune may be kind to it, that happiness may be as great, sorrow and pain as little, as the chances of the world allow.

After his explanation, he read the first greeting to the child—

> " Out of the deep, my child, out of the deep,
>   Where all that was to be, in all that was,
>   Whirl'd for a million æons through the vast
>   Waste dawn of multitudinous eddying light—
>   Out of the deep, my child, out of the deep,
>   Thro' all this changing world of changeless law,
>   And every phase of ever-heightening life,
>   And nine long months of antenatal gloom,
>   With this last moon, this crescent—her dark orb
>   Touch'd with earth's light—thou comest, darling boy ;
>   Our own ; a babe in lineament and limb
>   Perfect, and prophet of the perfect man ;
>   Whose face and form are hers and mine in one,
>   Indissolubly married like our love ;
>   Live and be happy in thyself, and serve
>   This mortal race thy kin so well, that men
>   May bless thee as we bless thee, O young life,
>   Breaking with laughter from the dark ; and may
>   The fated channel where thy motion lives
>   Be prosperously shaped, and sway thy course
>   Along the years of haste and random youth
>   Unshatter'd ; then full-current thro' full man ;
>   And last, in kindly curves, with gentlest fall,
>   By quiet fields, a slowly-dying power
>   To that last deep where we and thou art still."

And then comes the second greeting. A deeper chord is struck. The listener, who has, perhaps, felt

as if the first greeting contained all,—all the mystery
of birth, of life, of death, hears a sound unknown,
unimagined before. A new range of ideas is opened
to us. The starry firmament disappears for the
moment. The "deep" of infinite time and space is
forgotten. A fresh sense is awakened, a deeper depth
disclosed. We leave this wondrous world of appearances. We gaze into that other deep—the world of
spirit, the world of realities; we see the new-born
babe coming to us from that true world, with all the
"abysmal depths of personality," no longer a mere
link in the chain of causes, with a fated course through
the events of life, but a moral being, with the awful
power of making or marring its own destiny and that
of others. The proportions are abruptly reversed.
The child is no longer the minute outcome of natural
forces so much greater than itself. It is the "spirit,"
the moral being, a reality which impinges on the
world of appearances. Never can I forget the change
of voice, the change of manner, as Lord Tennyson
passed from the first greeting, with its purely human
thoughts, to the second, so full of awe at the conception of the world behind the veil and the moral nature
of man; an awe which seemed to culminate when he
paused before the word "Spirit" in the seventh line,
and then gave it in deeper and more piercing tones:
"Out of the deep—*Spirit*,—out of the deep." This
second greeting is in two parts—

I.

" Out of the deep, my child, out of the deep,
From that great deep, before our world begins,
Whereon the Spirit of God moves as He will—
Out of the deep, my child, out of the deep,

From that true world within the world we see,
Whereof our world is but the bounding shore—
Out of the deep, Spirit, out of the deep,
With this ninth moon, that sends the hidden sun,
Down yon dark sea, thou comest, darling boy.

II.

" For in the world, which is not ours, they said,
' Let us make man,' and that which should be man,
From that one light no man can look upon,
Drew to this shore, lit by the suns and moons
And all the shadows.   O dear Spirit, half-lost
In thine own shadow and this fleshly sign
That thou art thou—who wailest being born
And banish'd into mystery, and the pain
Of this divisible-indivisible world
Among the numerable-innumerable
Sun, sun, and sun, thro' finite-infinite space,
In finite-infinite Time—our mortal veil
And shatter'd phantom of that infinite One,
Who made thee unconceivably Thyself
Out of His whole World-self, and all in all—
Live thou, and of the grain and husk, the grape
And ivyberry, choose ; and still depart
From death to death thro' life and life, and find
Nearer and ever nearer Him, who wrought
Not matter, not the finite-infinite,
But this main-miracle, that thou art thou,
With power on thine own act and on the world."

Note that the second greeting considers the reality
of the child's life and its meaning, the first only its
appearance. The great deep of the spiritual world
is "that true world within the world we see, Whereof
our world is but the bounding shore."   And this indication that the second greeting gives the deeper and
truer view, is preserved in some of the side touches
of description.   In the first greeting, for example, the
moon is spoken of as "touch'd with earth's light;" in
the second the truer and less obvious fact is suggested.

It "sends the hidden sun down yon dark sea." The material view again looks at bright and hopeful appearances in life, and it notes the new-born babe "breaking with laughter from the dark." The spiritual view foresees the woes which, if Byron is right in calling melancholy the "telescope of truth," are truer than the joys. It notes no longer the child's laughter, but rather its tears, "Thou wailest being born and banished into mystery." Life, in the spiritual view, is in part a veiling and obscuring of the true self as it is, in a world of appearances. The soul is "half lost" in the body which is part of the phenomenal world, "in thine own shadow and in this fleshly sign that thou art thou." The suns and moons, too, are but shadows, as the body of the child itself is but a shadow—shadows of the spirit-world and of God Himself. The physical life is before the child; but not as a fatally determined course. Choice of the good is to lead the spirit ever nearer God. The wonders of the material Universe are still recognised: "Sun, sun, and sun, thro' finite-infinite space, in finite-infinite Time;" but they vanish into insignificance when compared to the two great facts of the spirit-world which consciousness tells us unmistakably—the facts of personality and of a responsible will. The great mystery is "Not Matter, nor the finite-infinite," but "this main-miracle, that thou art thou, with power on thyself and on the world."

"Out of the deep"—in this conception of the true "deep" of the world behind the veil we have the thought which recurs so often, as in the "Passing of Arthur" and in "Crossing the Bar"[1]—of birth and death

---

[1] "From the great deep to the great deep he goes;" and "when that which drew from out the boundless deep turns again home."

as the coming from and returning to the spirit-world and God Himself. Birth[1] is the coming to land from that deep; "of which our world is but the bounding shore;" death the re-embarking on the same infinite sea, for the home of truth and light.

He seemed so much better when he had finished his explanation that I asked him to read the poem through again. This he did, more beautifully than I ever heard him read. I felt as though his long illness and his expectation of death gave more intensity and force to his rendering of this wonderful poem on the mystery of life. He began quietly, and read the concluding lines of the first "greeting," the brief description of a peaceful old age and death, from the human standpoint, with a very tender pathos :—

> " And last, in kindly curves, with gentlest fall
> By quiet fields, a slowly-dying power,
> To that last deep where we and thou are still."

Then he gathered force, and his voice deepened as the greeting to the immortal soul of the man was read. He raised his eyes from the book at the seventh line and looked for a moment at his hearer with an indescribable expression of awe before he uttered the word "spirit": "Out of the deep— Spirit,—out of the deep." When he had finished the second greeting he was trembling much. Then he read the prayer—a prayer, he had told me, of self-prostration before the Infinite. I think he intended

---

[1] " For in the world which is not ours, they said,
'Let us make man,' and that which should be man,
From that one light no man can look upon,
Drew to this shore, lit by the suns and moons
And all the shadows."

it as a contrast to the analytical and reflective
character of the rest. It is an outpouring of the
simplest and most intense self-abandonment to the
Creator, an acknowledgment, when all has been
thought and said with such insight and beauty, that
our best thoughts and words are as nothing in the
Great Presence—in a sense parallel to the breaking
off in the Ode to the Duke of Wellington :—

> "Speak no more of his renown,
> Lay your earthly fancies down."

He began to chaunt in a loud clear voice—

> " Hallowed be Thy Name—Halleluiah."

His voice was growing tremulous as he reached the
second part—

> " We feel that we are nothing—for all is Thou and in Thee ;
> We feel that we are something—that also has come from Thee."

And he broke down, and sobbed aloud as he finished
the prayer—

> " We know we are nothing—but Thou wilt help us to be.
> Hallowed be Thy Name—Halleluiah."

VII.

THOMAS HENRY HUXLEY.

A Reminiscence.[1]

The "personal equation" is often an element very necessary to the true interpretation of a great writer's words. Of the many thousands in England and America who have eagerly read their "Huxley," few have known the man. They are familiar, perhaps, with his essays on the "Gadarene pig affair" and the "Noachian deluge;" and they have in all probability—as the present writer once had—a one-sided impression of the intention and *animus* of such sallies. And a similar difference between the writer and the man extends to many other subjects. If this be so, it may be worth while for those who knew Mr. Huxley in later life to record personal traits which have interpreted for them much of his writing. Doubtless such sketches are necessarily themselves made from a special point of view. But what Huxley was to all his acquaintance can only be learnt by knowing what he was to each. And conscious though I am how imperfectly I shall express recollections which are very vivid, I make the attempt with the

---

[1] I am indebted to the kindness of Mrs. Huxley and Mr. Leonard Huxley for permission to print the letters from the late Professor Huxley which appear in the present Essay.

less scruple, as it was suggested to me by one whose wishes in the matter should be paramount.

My first direct intercourse with Mr. Huxley was accidentally such as to confirm my original impression of him as a somewhat uncompromising and unapproachable man of war. I was collecting materials about the year 1885 for some account of the old Metaphysical Society, to be published in the biography of my father, W. G. Ward, who was at one time its chairman. I wrote to several prominent members of the society, and received kind answers and contributions from all of them except Mr. Huxley, who did not reply to my letter at all. I remember thinking that I had made a mistake in writing to him, and that probably his antagonism to my father in the debates made him unwilling to say anything on the subject.

I was therefore the more pleasantly surprised when, in the year 1890, a common friend of mine and Mr. Huxley's (Sir M. E. Grant Duff) brought me a friendly message, expressing great contrition in the matter of the unanswered letter, explaining that it had arrived at a time of total prostration through ill health, and offering to write for my book an account of my father's share in the debates of the society. I gladly accepted the offer ; and the paper came, which, though brief, was very characteristic of Mr. Huxley himself, both in its matter and its manner. As, moreever, the account it gives will serve to show that side of Huxley which made him and myself afterwards, to use his own phrase, " the friendliest of foes," I here insert it.

" It was at one of the early meetings of the Metaphysical Society that I first saw Dr. Ward.[1] I forget whether he or I

---

[1] My father was known in the Society as " Dr." Ward, from his papal degree of Doctor in Philosophy.

was the late comer ; at any rate we were not introduced. I
well recollect wondering what chance had led the unknown
member, who looked so like a jovial country squire, to embark
in our galley—that singular rudderless ship, the stalwart oarsmen of which were mostly engaged in pulling as hard as they
could against one another, and which consequently performed
only circular voyages all the years it was in commission.

"But when a few remarks on the subject under discussion
fell from the lips of that beaming countenance, it dawned
upon my mind that a physiognomy quite as gentle of aspect
as that of Thomas Aquinas (if the bust on the Pincian Hill
is any authority) might possibly be the *façade* of a head of
like quality. As time went on, and Dr. Ward took a leading
part in our deliberations, my suspicions were fully confirmed.
As a quick-witted dialectician, thoroughly acquainted with
all the weak points of his antagonist's case, I have not met
with Dr. Ward's match.   And it all seemed to come so easily
to him ; searching questions, incisive, not to say pungent,
replies, and trains of subtle argumentation were poured forth,
which, while sometimes passing into earnest and serious
exposition, would also—when lighter topics came to the front
—be accompanied by an air of genial good humour, as if the
whole business were rather a good joke. But it was no joke
to reply efficiently.

"Although my personal intercourse with Dr. Ward was as
limited as it might be expected to be between two men
who were poles asunder, not only in their occupations and
circumstances, but in their ways of regarding life and the
proper ends of action, yet I am glad to remember that we
soon became the friendliest of foes. It was not long after we
had reached this stage that in the course of some truce in
our internecine dialectic warfare (I think at the end of one of
the meetings of the Metaphysical Society) Dr. Ward took
me aside and opened his mind thus : 'You and I are on such
friendly terms that I do not think it is right to let you
remain ignorant of something I wish to tell you.' Rather
alarmed at what this might portend, I begged him to say on.
'Well, we Catholics hold that So-and-so and So-and-so
[naming certain of our colleagues whose heresies were of a

less deep hue than mine] are not guilty of absolutely un-pardonable error ; but your case is different, and I feel it is unfair not to tell you so.' Greatly relieved, I replied, with-out a moment's delay, perhaps too impulsively, 'My dear Dr. Ward, if you don't mind, I don't ;' whereupon we parted with a hearty hand-shake, and intermitted neither friendship nor fighting thenceforth.

"I have often told the story, and not unfrequently I have regretted to observe that my hearer conceived the point of it to lie in my answer. But to my mind the worth of the anecdote consists in the evidence it affords of the character of Dr. Ward. He was before all things a chivalrous English gentleman—I would say a philosophical and theological Quixote, if it were not that our associations with the name of the Knight of La Mancha are mainly derived from his adventures, and not from the noble directness and simplicity of mind which led to those misfortunes."

Not very long after I received this graphic word-picture, I became a neighbour of Mr. Huxley's at Eastbourne. We exchanged visits, and afterwards had many a talk, on nearly every conceivable subject, —talks which were among the most intellectually stimulating that I have ever known.

I shall best describe the impression Huxley made on me by contrasting it with the general idea which I, in common no doubt with many another, had formed of him. He always wrote, as Darwin has said, with his pen dipped in aqua fortis, and one naturally con-ceived of him as a combative and even an aggressive man. Moreover, the layman's idea of the professional man of science generally includes something of the pedantic. One anticipates that his conversation, how-ever instructive, will deal largely with very technical subjects in very technical language. Again, the tone of some of the essays to which I have referred was unquestionably Voltairian.

All the greater was my surprise to find the three elements of pugilist, pedant, and scoffer not only not prominent, but conspicuous by their absence. In their place was a personality of singular charm. External gifts of manner and presence, and powers of general conversation which would have ensured popularity to any mere man of the world, were combined with those higher endowments—including great breadth of culture as well as the acquirements of a distinguished specialist—to which no mere man of the world could aspire. I must add that I believe the elements of gentleness and sympathy which gave so much additional charm to his singular brilliancy had become more noticeable in later life; and I have not always found my own impression of a kindliness which suggested great tenderness of feeling shared by those whose acquaintance with him belonged to a much earlier date. But these things were conspicuous at the time I speak of; and while I gradually learnt how to explain their consistency with the polemical style which he preserved to the end in his writing, my first impression was that the man and the writer were very dissimilar people.

His appearance is well known. He was above the middle height, the white hair without parting was brushed straight back, the lips firm and slightly compressed; he had a very mobile expression; and I would add (what the current photographs do not represent) that the eyes, full of fire, were rather deep-set beneath bushy eyebrows, with a look of keenest interest in all around him, often of great wistfulness. In his manner and in his appearance there were marked distinction and dignity. The general impression left by his face was one of intellectual force and activity rather than of scorn.

His conversation was singularly finished and (if I may so express it) clean-cut; never long-winded or prosy; enlivened by vivid illustrations. He was an excellent *raconteur*, and his stories had a stamp of their own which would have made them always and everywhere acceptable. His sense of humour and economy of words would have made it impossible, had he lived to ninety, that they should ever have been disparaged as symptoms of what has been called "anecdotage." I was naturally led to compare his conversation with that of two remarkable men whom I had recently been seeing when first I met Huxley. There was the same contrast between his conversation and that of Tennyson or of Cardinal Newman as there was between their views. Tennyson and Newman alike always suggested more than they said. There was an unspoken residuum behind their speech, which, as Wordsworth once said of the peak of a Swiss mountain hidden behind the low clouds, you felt to be there, though you could not see it. Huxley, on the contrary, finished his thoughts completely, and expressed them with the utmost precision. There were not the ruggedness and the gaps which marked Tennyson's speech, nor the pauses, the reserve, the obvious consciousness of suggestion on subjects too wide and intricate for full expression which one felt with Newman. The symmetry and finish of Huxley's utterances were so great that one could not bring one's self to interrupt him, even when this completeness of form seemed to be possible only through ignoring for the moment much that should not be ignored. No doubt the deafness, which increased in later years, made his friends yet more ready rather to listen than to talk; but the quickness of his perceptions was so

great that dialogue was in its place a matter of no
great difficulty. If he heard even a word or two he
had the clue to the rest, and seldom failed to follow it
successfully.

He seemed to me to be almost the ideal of a
converser. He was never frivolous and yet never
dull. He did not plunge abruptly into deep subjects,
but exchanged the ordinary remarks and greetings
with naturalness and simplicity, and then talked
according to his company. If one cared for the
problems of the mind and of human life, one came
to them quickly enough. But he was perfectly happy
and at home talking about politics or persons, about
his garden, or even about the weather, if his hearers
preferred it. And there was nothing which he did
not contrive to make interesting.

No doubt such exceptional charm followed the
law by which natural gifts keep a certain measure
of equality in different persons. It was purchased
at some cost. Incisiveness and brilliancy went with
over-positiveness. Intolerance and one-sidedness
appeared at a certain stage. And although to
know him was to reject for ever the idea that he
was a mere scoffer, he treated the conclusions of
the scientific leaders, even outside the sphere of
science, somewhat as the Grand Inquisitor treated
the definitions of the Church. Those who called
them in question were regarded as being "outside
the pale." It will seem inevitable that one who
differed so widely from him should think him (as I
did) more ready to see the weaker side of theological
or philosophical positions far apart from his own, than
to enter into their real strength. I except, however,
from this remark the works of Bishop Butler and

Sir William Hamilton, with whose methods he had much in common, though he rejected many of their conclusions.

The form of his conversation was dialectical rather than suggestive or meditative. One was often reminded that he was, in some matters, the professed advocate of a cause, and even of a party. It was easy to accept his own statement in his autobiography that his temper was not naturally an even one. One could readily conceive that in word as well as in writing he would be, on provocation, a thoroughly good fighter ; and one could picture him driven to bay, with his back to the wall, and dealing out destruction against great odds. I never felt in his discussions the full measure of philosophic calm. Opposite considerations to those which determined his own conclusions were indeed often seen and expressed with great lucidity, but less in the spirit of philosophic inquiry than in that of a clear-headed but convinced advocate, whose ultimate positions are absolutely predetermined. Doubtless one felt at the same time that there had been a more judicial sifting of considerations on all sides before his conclusions had been reached, and that the advocacy was not special pleading to order, but the outcome of deep conviction. But none the less his method was distinctly that of the able and lucid exponent of one side. " That is my case, my lord," would have come naturally at the end. His exposition was not that of the thinker who sees horizons on every side, too wide-reaching to be fully described, and yet too unmistakable to be ignored. There were no half-lights or hesitations. All that was contemplated was very distinct ; the results arrived at were very definite, and their drift consciously told for the defence of the clear system he had elaborated.

Yet so far as my own experience went, the intellectual pleasure he seemed to find in letting each side say its say and do its best, prevented these characteristics of the partisan from marring intercourse; although, in weighing the value of his own views of things, they must be taken into account. In conversation, I nearly always found him, up to the point beyond which we tacitly agreed not to carry our debates, tolerant as a listener, though always more brilliant, forcible, and definite, than convincing, suggestive, or entirely comprehensive in his replies. His love of the free play of dialectics, irrespective of the side on which they were exercised, was exemplified in his enjoyment of the " Summa " of St. Thomas Aquinas. I have on several occasions found him (as he told me at the time) in the act of perusing its pages. " Aquinas' bust on the Pincian Hill," he once said, " shows a combination of a singularly simple and devout heart, with a head of very remarkable capacity. He got his premises from his heart, and reached his conclusions through the admirable logical force of his intellect." " His marvellous grasp and subtlety of intellect seem to me to be almost without a parallel," is the tribute which Mr. Huxley has paid in print to the " Angelic Doctor." [1]

The same appreciation of the intellectual drill of the Schoolman is visible in his account (in the " Lay Sermons ") of a visit he paid some thirty years ago to a Catholic College—which, after the lapse of time, I may mention to have been Maynooth :—

" It was my fortune some time ago," he writes, " to pay a visit to one of the most important institutions in which the

---

[1] See " Science and Morals," p. 142.

clergy of the Roman Catholic Church are trained in these islands, and it seemed to me that the difference between these men and the comfortable champions of Anglicanism and Dissent was comparable to the difference between our gallant volunteers and the trained veterans of Napoleon's Old Guard.

"The Catholic priest is trained to know his business and do it effectually. The professors of the college in question— learned, zealous, and determined men—permitted me to speak frankly with them. We talked like outposts of opposed armies during a truce—as friendly enemies."

And after recording the confidence with which the professors prophesied that a Church which had survived so many storms would survive the existing infidel movement; and describing the systematic training given to the divinity students, with a view to refuting contemporary attacks on Christianity, he adds—

"I heartily respect an organisation which meets its enemies in this way, and I wish that all ecclesiastical organisations were in as effective a condition. I think it would be better not only for them but for us. The army of liberal thought is at present in very loose order; and many a modern free-thinker makes use of his freedom mainly to vent nonsense. We should be the better for a vigorous and watchful enemy to hammer us into cohesion and discipline; and I for one lament that the bench of Bishops cannot show a man of the calibre of Bishop Butler of the 'Analogy,' who, if he were alive, would make short work of the current *à priori* infidelity."

My first talk with Huxley naturally enough turned on the meetings of the old Metaphysical Society at which he had known my father. The society, which was originated at the suggestion of Mr. James Knowles, included most of the prominent thinkers on the philosophy of Religion, amateurs as well as professionals. Mr. Gladstone, Dr. Martineau, Cardinal Manning, the Duke of Argyll, Tennyson, and Ruskin were among the more distinguished members. Huxley was very graphic and amusing in his remarks on this subject. "They were afraid of asking me to join at first," he said; "they thought I should be such a firebrand."

Eventually, however, Huxley did join, and the most friendly relations subsisted between him and (curiously enough) the Catholic members of the society, Father Dalgairns, Cardinal Manning, and my father. But, indeed, members of all schools of thought rapidly became friendly and sympathetic. "This was a great surprise," said Huxley. "We thought at first that it would be a case of Kilkenny cats. Hats and coats would be left in the hall before the meeting, but there would be no wearers left, after it was over, to put them on again. Instead of this we came to love each other like brothers. We all expended so much charity, that, had it been money, we should have been bankrupt." The work of the society was principally one of mutual understanding. Once each member thoroughly understood the position of his opponents, it was seen to involve a divergence in first principles which no argument could affect. Friendliness became the order of the day, and debate grew less useful. "The society died of too much love," added Mr. Huxley.

I used, rightly or wrongly, to trace to the influence of the Metaphysical Society a very curious mixture of feelings in Mr. Huxley in respect of his theological opponents. No doubt his polemic against the theologians had been, as he said, suggestive of the "firebrand." Yet nothing could be more kindly than the two accounts I have cited of the Maynooth priests and of the Catholic theologian. And I believe it was the Metaphysical Society which fashioned this somewhat remarkable blend.

The society was founded in 1869. The years immediately preceding its formation had probably stamped deep on his mind a sense of unjust treatment at the hands of professional ecclesiastics. The advocates of Darwinism and of the "higher" criticism of the Scriptures—and Huxley was in both ranks— had been for years treated simply as the enemies of religion. The distinctions familiar to all of us now, the admission on all sides of a measure of truth in both these phases of speculation, were little thought of in the sixties. The "Origin of Species" had appeared in 1859, and Colenso had raised the Scripture question at about the same time. 1859 to 1869 had been for Huxley years of war; and with his very direct and practical mind, he saw in the theological protests of the hour nothing but a thoroughly unjust persecution of himself and his friends for researches undertaken in the interests of truth. The ecclesiastical "obstructives" who condemned him without attending to his arguments remained in his mind for a long time as absolute types of bigotry. Their line of action appeared to him to set a *premium* on hypocrisy. The men who had the courage of their convictions were ostracised; and the time-servers among men of science who refused to brave the ignorant clamour of the multitude enjoyed an unenviable popularity. Huxley's moral sense appeared to be simply revolted by this. Some will think that he failed to do justice to the element of instinctive caution which blended with the real bigotry of those critics who took up the narrowest attitude—the element explained by Cardinal Newman in his defence of the condemnation of Galileo. The principle of economy for the protection of weak minds was not at all congenial to Mr. Huxley, although he did in some degree recognise it. His ruling passion was the advance of scientific truth, and this was being impeded, and a noble sincerity of conviction treated as a crime (he thought) by men, some of whom at least did not seem to him even deeply sincere. It was officialism *versus* true genius.

He was not insensible to the element of moral reprobation among the opponents of evolution, which made them mark him out as a dangerous man, and which struck, as he has humorously said, at his "respectability." And I have always supposed that it was in these earlier years of the struggle that he acquired the deep and genuine sense of ecclesiastical injustice, and of anger at what he considered pre-posterous superstition, which frequently reappeared, to the very end, in his writing.

On the other hand, in the Metaphysical Society the conditions were so different that he inevitably met theological foes on far pleasanter terms. Intercourse was personal, and candid debate was the order of the day. Notably in the case of the Catholic members of the society, he could have no feeling of the substitution of a sanctimonious moral reprobation for frank dis-cussion. The great friendliness which arose between the extreme parties in the society introduced a new element of kindly divergence, and apparently gave birth to a real intellectual respect in Huxley for some of the detested theologians. His two sentiments were perhaps not entirely consistent, for men of intellectual force are not likely to defend absurd superstitions; but both remained. And they occasionally led, in conversation, to a playful combination of language recalling the severest theological condemnation of his views, with the humour and friendly feeling which in almost all cases subsisted in his personal intercourse with opponents. "We wicked people," he would often say, in speaking of himself and his allies. A friendly meeting with priest or clergyman was enjoyed, perhaps as a sign that to some extent bygones were bygones; while enough remembrance of opposition remained to give piquancy to the *rencontre.*

I have a good many notes illustrative of some of these phases of his thought. I think it was in 1892 that I saw him just after he had been to a meeting of the Trustees of the British Museum. "After the meeting," he told me, "Archbishop Benson helped me on with my great-coat. I was *quite overcome* by this species of spiritual investiture. 'Thank you, Archbishop,' I said; 'I feel as if I were receiving the *pallium.*'" A little later he met at Maloja a Catholic professor of Freiburg University, Dr. Steffens, and had many a story to tell of their frequent conversations, and of the pleasure he derived from the priest's company, which he had evidently cultivated.

On another occasion he was at a meeting of the British Association in York, and he and Mrs. Huxley went to visit the Minster. He greatly enjoyed the remark of Henry Smith (of Oxford celebrity), who met them there. "You did not expect to see us here?" asked Huxley. "Yes, I did," replied Smith, "but *on the pinnacle.*"

Something of the same humour, coupled with a remembrance of the days when his championship of evolution was most widely reprobated, appears in a letter which he wrote me from Gloucester in September, 1892, in reply to my congratulations on his being made a Privy Councillor—

"Very many thanks," he wrote, "for your kind congratulations. Morris has a poem somewhere about the man who was born to be a king, and became one in spite of probability. It is evident to me now that I was born to be respectable. I have done my level best to avoid that honour, but behold me indelibly stamped.

"We are staying here with one of our daughters and enjoying the festival. . . . We hope to be back in Eastbourne next week, but we shall have to go to the Grand Hotel, as seven devils in the shape of workmen must be driven out of our house.

"See what an opening I have given you for a conclusion to that sentence."

He often resented being identified with simple destruction in matters of religious faith, and disclaimed all sympathy with the scoffing spirit. His opposition to theology had not meant, he said, opposition to religion. I remember his showing me Boehm's bust of himself, and expressing strongly his dislike of its expression. "It is almost Voltairian," he said. "You should not destroy until you are in a position to build up something to replace what you have destroyed," was another saying of his : "Descartes saw that, and advocated a *morale par provision*, a system to act upon (pending the conclusion of his philosophical inquiries)—a system which included adhering to the religion in which he had been brought up." Huxley's application of this principle was very intelligible in his protests against dogmatic infidelity.[1] But it used to

[1] "Physical science is as little atheistic as it is materialistic" ("Science and Morals," p. 140. Cf. "Life of Hume.")

seem to me, as I once told him, to be forgotten in his extremely polemical tone, which unquestionably did often lead others to abandon even a provisional adherence to any religious system. But I believe his failure to take this into consideration to have been partly due to the exclusively scientific cast of his mind. The cause of scientific discovery was paramount to all else; and whatever even appeared to impede it he assailed ruthlessly. Moreover, he wrote primarily for experts, or at least for careful students. In point of fact, his readers included the impressionable and unintellectual as well as the intellectual; and his anti-Christian rhetoric was calculated, for such readers, to destroy religious belief wholesale, including positions which the writer himself, to say the least, considered quite tenable. He said to me once, in 1894, "Faulty and incorrect as is the Christian definition of Theism, it is nearer the truth than the creed of some agnostics who conceive of no unifying principle in the world." He proceeded to defend eloquently the argument from design, referring me to his volume of "Darwiniana," to show that he had admitted in print that it could not be disproved by the evolution theory.[1] This position, which entirely tallies with his statement that only a "very great fool" would deny in his heart a God conceived as Spinoza conceives Him,[2] was distinctly short of the degree of agnosticism currently attributed to him by those who read him hastily and blended their own logic with his rhetoric. Such an attitude towards destructive thought, coupled with Descartes' maxim, was perhaps the explanation of his recognising a value and real sacredness in current religious forms

---

[1] See "Darwiniana," p. 109.
[2] See Essay on "Science and Morals," p. 140.

which the aggressive irreligionists of France osten-
tatiously despise.

Nevertheless, he claimed (half humorously) the
sanction of Descartes, who lived and died a Catholic,
for pressing his speculative doubts to their utmost
limit. He once told me that he thought his own
Lecture on Descartes the best exhibition of his
religious attitude as a whole. And it was impossible
not to recognise the strenuous honesty which led him
to look frankly in the face problems for which he
could find no speculative solution. Regarded as a
contribution to philosophy, such a method has com-
mended itself to thinkers whose ultimate positions
were various—Catholics like Descartes and Pascal,
Theists like Kant, as well as negative thinkers. But
Descartes did not abandon his religious convictions
when he instituted his "methodic doubt," which was
to be the instrument of their theoretic justification.
It was Huxley's treatment of what is really only a
step towards the analysis of the foundations of belief
as though it were the guide to practical conviction,
which marks the difference between him and Descartes.
Apart from this, one felt the value to the cause of
truth of Huxley's lucid and candid exhibition of the
"case" of the negative thinker; and one could not
but respect his enthusiasm for the man who gives
forth his deepest convictions in the face of obloquy,
even while one felt that in point of fact consideration
for its effect on society might show what was in
intention a protest against insincerity, to have been
in effect rash and misleading. To Huxley this
thought was not, I think, of weight. To speak
out each fresh fragment of truth which he supposed
himself to have discerned was to him a duty, and not

a complex one. He who thus spoke was confessor or martyr. Huxley did not, I think, realise how often the truest he could see at the moment in science might mislead from the crudity and inaccuracy of its first statement, and from its apparent conflict with true convictions of society in other departments. He tended to identify outspoken candour with love of truth, and prudent reserve or patient suspense of judgment with insincerity.

This feeling came out in the course of a talk with him in 1894. He was speaking of Dean Stanley, whose brother Owen he had known in early life, and who had died out at sea in Huxley's arms. "Arthur Stanley was before all things a sincere man," he said. "Men of ability are common enough, but men of character and conviction are very rare. It is the grandest thing conceivable to see a man speaking out and acting out his convictions in the face of unpopularity. What a grand man was your Gregory the Seventh! though I should not have been pleased for his views to have prevailed. But he was a man of strength and conviction."

He also talked of Kant. "It is remarkable," he said, "that Kant is a very clear writer on Physics, though obscure on Metaphysics." I said that this seemed a testimony to his depth; it showed the obscurity not to be due to Kant's own want of perspicuity, but to the difficulty of the subject. Huxley, to whom things were always either evident or unknowable, demurred. "No," he replied, "it was because he did not want too many people to understand him. *He would have been persecuted for his scepticism.*"

The Romanes Lecture of 1893 has been much

commented on as a recantation of his most aggressive theological views, and Huxley resented this account of it. He pointed out most truly that the position taken up in it had been long ago indicated by him. But many will continue to look on it as an example of his insistance in later years on the more religious admissions of his own public teaching. If the logic was that of his other writings, the rhetoric was not; and it was natural that average readers who had ascribed to him an irreligious attitude, much of which was really due to the rhetoric rather than the logic of his earlier works, should now in turn note the change from the hostile tone which they had observed, rather than the identity of his logical position which they had never mastered. I saw him more than once before he went to deliver the lecture, and he was suffering both from weakness and from loss of voice— so much so, that he doubted his being able to deliver it at all.

In the end he went to Oxford, and was most cordially received. The lecture was a remarkable one. He shows in it with great force how entirely the struggle for existence and survival of the fittest, as represented in the "cosmic process" antecedent to human civilisation, fails to account for the ethical element in man. The cosmic process is destructive, and survival in its course is due to the selfish and self-assertive elements in sentient nature. These elements—which in man are the "original sin" of the theologians—remain in the race, and have to be counteracted, if social life is to be possible, by the more or less artificial cultivation of the sympathetic and conscientious elements. He sent me a copy of the lecture, and I wrote expressing my strong assent

to some of its main propositions, although I added
that he would no doubt not accept the "transcendental"
conclusion which I should draw from his arguments.

"The Oxford business," he wrote to me in reply, "lecture,
dinner, and all, was too much for me; and even after three
or four days' rest in a quiet country house I collapsed on our
way to another, and had to come straight home. Since my
return I have been almost living in the garden, and otherwise most diligently idle. I read [your] chapter on the
Metaphysical,[1] though, and was delighted with the saying
that it died of too much love, attributed to me by such a
competent witness that I am not going to dispute the fact,
though I had utterly forgotten it.

"I was quite sure you would agree with my main thesis (in
the Romanes Lecture), for it is only the doctrine that Satan
is the Prince of this world—from the scientific side.

"Why should not materialists be transcendentalists?
What possible difference can it make whether the hyposta-
tised negative 'substance' is the same for mind and matter
or different?

"I am very sorry my cigar man served you so badly. I
cannot make it out, as he invariably sends me the same
quality. That confounded 'cosmic process' has got hold
of him.

"Ever yours very faithfully,

"T. H. HUXLEY."

I have said that his conversation had the widest
range. Point and humour were always there. If he
spoke of persons or scenes, you carried away some
definite feature of the personality or events in
question.

I well remember his description—given with true
Yankee twang—of a lecture he had to deliver at New
York, where he was received with great enthusiasm.

[1] In "W. G. Ward and the Catholic Revival" (Macmillan).

The reporters of the Baltimore paper called on him, and said they must have the lecture for publication on the day of its delivery. Huxley explained that the lecture existed as yet only in his own head. Still they pressed for it, and he complied with their demand, stipulating that if he rehearsed it for them they must give him a copy, lest they should publish one lecture and he should give another. The rehearsal was made, and the copy sent; but when he opened it—in the very lecture hall itself—it proved to be a wholly illegible transcript on tissue paper. To make the story perfect he ought to have delivered an entirely different lecture from the one reported; but his excellent memory served him, and the reports of the actual lecture and of the rehearsal, although somewhat different, were not sufficiently so to betray what had occurred.

I felt my impression of Carlyle's dogged unsympathetic persistency, in measuring everything by his own ideas, sensibly deepened by a story which Huxley told me of their mutual relations. Carlyle and he were for long good friends, but had a serious difference on the evolution question in the early stages of the controversy. Their personal intercourse ceased in consequence. After an interval of many years Huxley happened to see the Scotchman crossing the street in London, and thinking that bygones might be bygones, went up to him and spoke to him. Carlyle did not at first recognise Huxley, but when he succeeded in identifying him, he at once said, with his Scotch twang, as though he were continuing the last conversation of years ago, "You're Huxley, are you? You're the man that's trying to persuade us all that we're the children of apes; while *I* am saying that the great thing we've really got to do is to make ourselves as much unlike apes as possible." Huxley, who had hoped that the weather or politics might have been admitted for the sake of peace, soon found that the best thing he could do was to retreat, and return to their tacit agreement to differ.

So, too, Stanley's impressionable and imaginative nature was brought out by him in an anecdote. Stanley, keenly alive to the newest thought of the hour, liberal by family and school tradition, had sympathised in some degree with Colenso's treatment of the Bible; yet his historical impressionableness told the other way. Huxley explained his position thus—

"Stanley could believe in anything of which he had seen the supposed site, but was sceptical where he had not seen. At a breakfast at Monckton Milnes's, just at the time of the Colenso row, Milnes asked me my views on the Pentateuch, and I gave them. Stanley differed from me. The account of creation in Genesis he dismissed at once as unhistorical; but the call of Abraham and the historical narrative of the Pentateuch he accepted. This was because he had seen Palestine—but he wasn't present at the Creation."

He gave me a description of his dining one day at Archbishop's House with Cardinal Manning, which was very amusing and characteristic of both men. "Manning asked me to dine, and I expected a mixed party. But I found that I was the only heretic present. All the others were Bishops and Monsignori and their clerical myrmidons. Manning was very kind, but I could not help feeling that I was arraigned before the Inquisition. And he himself

looked every inch the dignified and ascetic Grand
Inquisitor. After dinner we had a discussion on the
education question, and I defended the School Board
system. Manning declared that Catholics could not
accept it, and that, on the principle of fair play to all,
the Catholic schools should receive as much State aid
as the Board schools. Manning, I am bound to say,
put his case very well, but I felt that he had an unfair
advantage. A faint murmur of applause from his
satellites, sitting round the table, followed each of his
sentences, and no one took the slightest pains to
attend to my replies. I got rather nettled, and determined to take the first opportunity of hitting really hard.
Manning was beginning to summarise his argument
for the benefit of his triumphant admirers, who seemed
almost sorry for the utterly routed infidel. Gazing
at me with piercing eye, his finger uplifted, he said in
measured tones, ' I will now recapitulate my arguments.
I will enumerate three heads under which your proposed actions, Mr. Huxley, would belie your words
and your policy stand in manifest contradiction to
the principles you profess. In the first place, you
profess to advocate the principle of liberty and equal
treatment for all. Yet the policy you are supporting
would place Catholics at a serious disadvantage on
the sole ground of their religion.' At this point I felt
that the most effective strategy was to break in, to hit
hard, and to get away. ' You misunderstand me,
Archbishop,' I interrupted. ' My attachment to
liberal principles is great, but it is nothing to my
desire for your extermination.' This abruptly ended
the debate."

Of another eminent person whose great subtlety of
mind was being discussed, Huxley said that the constant

over-refinement of distinctions in his case destroyed all distinctness. Anything could be explained away, and so a thing came to mean the same as its opposite. Some one asked, " Do you mean that he is untruthful?" " No," replied Huxley, " *he is not clear-headed enough to tell a lie.*"

One of the subjects of his enthusiasm was John Bright—his transparent sincerity, his natural distinction, his oratorical power. " If you saw him and A B " (naming a well-known nobleman) " together," he said, " you would have set down Bright as the aristocrat, and the other as the plebeian. His was the only oratory which ever really held me. His speeches were masterpieces. There was the sense of conviction in them, great dignity, and the purest English."

Tennyson he considered the greatest English master of melody except Spenser and Keats. I told him of Tennyson's insensibility to music, and he replied that it was curious that scientific men as a rule had more appreciation of music than poets or men of letters. He told me of one long talk he had had with Tennyson, and added that immortality was the one dogma to which Tennyson was passionately devoted.

Of Browning, Huxley said : " He really has music in him. Read his poem, ' The Thrush,' and you will see it. Tennyson said to me," he added, " that Browning had plenty of music *in* him, but he could not get it *out.*"

A few more detached remarks illustrate the character and tastes of the man. He expressed once his delight in Switzerland and in the beauty of Monte Generoso. " There is nothing like Switzerland," he said. " But I also delight in the simplest rural

English scenery. A country field has before now *entranced* me." "One thing," he added, "which weighs with me against pessimism, and tells for a benevolent Author of the universe, is my enjoyment of scenery and music. I do not see how they can have helped in the struggle for existence. They are gratuitous gifts."

He enjoyed greatly the views within his reach at Eastbourne, and his enjoyment was stimulated by the constitutional walk which took him frequently up the downs. "The incubus of thought is got rid of," he said, "if you walk up a hill and walk fast." He was eloquent on the beauty of Beachy Head. "Building at Eastbourne is one of the few prudent things I ever did. It contradicts the proverb, ' Fools build houses for wise men to live in.'"

He spoke of the Royal Commission on Vivisection. "The general feeling was at first strongly for vivisection," he said, "but one German changed the current of opinion by remarking, 'I chloroform a cat because it scratches, but not a dog.'" This at once suggested possibilities of cruelty, and (as I understood) was the cause of the amount of restriction ultimately placed on the practice. *Apropos* of vivisection, he spoke strongly of the absurdity of the outcry against it, as long as such things as pigeon-shooting were tolerated for mere amusement.

Speaking of two men of letters, with neither of whom he sympathised, he once said, "Don't mistake me ; I don't class them together. One is a thinker and man of letters, the other is only a literary man. Erasmus was a man of letters, Gigadibs a literary man. A B is the incarnation of Gigadibs. I should call him *Gigadibsius optimus maximus*. When I showed him the various accounts of the Metaphysical Society which had been sent to me, and which revealed certain discrepancies, he said, " Don't get any more, or the German critics will prove conclusively that it never existed." Characteristic, too, was his genial pleasure in telling us how his little granddaughter looked at him, and then said emphatically, " Well, you're the curiousest old man I ever saw."

My talks with him during the last years of his life were almost entirely connected with the philosophy of religious Faith. In 1894 I introduced to him a young friend of mine, an Oxford man, who lived in Eastbourne. On this occasion he was very eloquent in Bishop Butler's praise, and on the conclusiveness of his argument in the " Analogy " as far as it went. " But Butler was really one of *us*," he added. " That halting style, that hesitancy in expression, show that he was looking for a conclusion—something which he had not yet found." My friend remarked that Newman thought that that something was Catholicism, and that Newman had developed Butler in a Catholic sense. " A most ingenious developer," replied Huxley, with amused emphasis.

He went up to Oxford for the meeting of the British Association, and I saw him shortly after his return. The whole thing had tired him very much, but the enthusiastic reception he had met with evidently gratified him. He criticised Lord Salisbury's address, in which he had spoken of the argument from design, and had attacked Weismann for ruling it out of court.

" After all," Huxley continued, " my predominant feeling was one of triumph. I recalled the last meeting of the British Association at Oxford in the

sixties, when it was supposed to be downright
atheism to accept evolution at all, and when Bishop
Wilberforce turned to me in public and said, ' Was it
your grandfather or your grandmother, Mr. Huxley,
who was an ape ? '   And now Lord Salisbury, though
he ventured to attack us, did not venture to question
the doctrine of evolution—the thing for which we had
really been struggling."

He was highly pleased with an article on him
which appeared in January, 1895, in the *Quarterly*.
" It made me feel quite young again," he said.   " It
is a strong attack, of course, but very well written.   I
know a good bit of work when I see it."   He recurred
several times to this article, and the significance of
his pleasure struck me when I came to read it.   For,
like the Romanes Lecture, the article emphasised that
side of Huxley's teaching which was consistent with
the Theistic view of life—a side so often ignored by
his critics.   " I have been attacked all my life," he
added, "but so are many better men than I.   Those
whose views ultimately triumph often go through the
most obloquy in their own time."

There is a sad interest in the closing scenes of the
life of a man of genius which will be sufficient excuse
for describing in some detail the last long conversation which I had with Mr. Huxley.   Some one had
sent me Mr. A. J. Balfour's book on " The Foundations
of Belief " early in February, 1895.   We were very full
of it, and it was the theme of discussion on the 17th
of February, when two friends were lunching with us.
Not long after luncheon Huxley came in, and seemed
to be in extraordinary spirits.   He began talking of
Erasmus and Luther, expressing a great preference
for Erasmus, who would, he said, have impregnated

the Church with culture and brought it abreast of the
thought of the times, while Luther concentrated attention on individual mystical doctrines. " It was very
trying for Erasmus to be identified with Luther, from
whom he differed absolutely. A man ought to be
ready to endure persecution for what he does hold ;
but it is hard to be persecuted for what you don't
hold." I said that I thought his estimate of Erasmus's
attitude towards the Papacy coincided with Professor
R. C. Jebb's. He asked if I could lend him Jebb's
Rede Lecture on the subject. I said that I had not
got it at hand, but I added, " I can lend you another
book which I think you ought to read—Balfour's
'Foundations of Belief.' "

He at once became extremely animated, and spoke
of it as those who have read his criticisms, published
in the following month, would expect. " You need
not lend me that. I have exercised my mind with it
a good deal already. Mr. Balfour ought to have
acquainted himself with the opinions of those he
attacks. One has no objection to being abused for
what one *does* hold, as I said of Erasmus—at least,
one is prepared to put up with it. An attack on us
by some one who understood our position would do all
of us good—myself included. But Mr. Balfour has
acted like the French in 1870—he has gone to war
without any ordnance maps, and without having surveyed the scene of the campaign. No human being
holds the opinions he speaks of as 'naturalism.' He
is a good debater. He knows the value of a word.
The word 'naturalism' has a bad sound and unpleasant associations. It would tell against us in the
House of Commons, and so it will with his readers.
'Naturalism' contrasts with 'supernaturalism.' He

has not only attacked us for what we don't hold, but he has been good enough to draw out a catechism for 'us wicked people' to teach us what we *must* hold."

It was rather difficult to get him to particulars, but we did so by degrees. He said, " Balfour uses the word *phenomena* as applying simply to the outer world and not to the inner world. The only people whom his attack would hold good of would be the Comtists, who deny that psychology is a science. They may be left out of account. They advocate the crudest eighteenth-century materialism. All the empiricists, from Locke onwards, make the observation of the phenomena of the mind itself quite separate from the study of mere sensation. No man in his senses supposes that the sense of beauty, or the religious feelings [this with a courteous bow to a priest who was present], or the sense of moral obligation, are to be accounted for in terms of sensation, or come to us through sensation." I said that, as I understood it, I did not think Mr. Balfour supposed they would acknowledge the position he ascribed to them, and that one of his complaints was that they did not work out their premises to their logical conclusions. I added that so far as one of Mr. Balfour's chief points was concerned—the existence of the external world—Mill was almost the only man on their side in this century who had faced the problem frankly, and he had been driven to say that all men can know is that there are " permanent possibilities of sensation." He did not seem inclined to pursue the question of an external world, but said that though Mill's "logic" was very good, empiricists were not bound by all his theories.

He characterised Balfour's book as a very good and even brilliant piece of work from a literary point of view; but as a helpful contribution to the great controversy, the most disappointing he had ever read. I said: "There has been no adverse criticism of it yet." He answered with emphasis: "No! *but there soon will be.*" "From you?" I asked. "I let out no secrets," was the reply.

He then talked with great admiration and affection of Mr. Balfour's brother, Francis. His early death and W. K. Clifford's, Huxley said, had been the greatest loss to science—not only in England but in the world—in our time. "Half a dozen of us old fogies could have been better spared." He remembered Frank Balfour as a boy at Eton, and saw his unusual talent there. "Then my friend Michael Forster, took him up at Cambridge, and found out that he had real genius for biology. I used to say there was science in the blood, but this new book of his brother's," he added, smiling, "shows I was wrong."

Apropos to his remark about the Comtists, one of the company pointed out that in later life Comte recognised a science of "the individual," equivalent to what Huxley meant by psychology. "That," he replied, "was due to the influence of Clotilde de Vaux. You see," he added, with a kind of Sir Charles Grandison bow to my wife, "what power your sex may have." As Huxley was going out of the house I said to him that Father A B (the priest who had been present) had not expected to find himself in his company. "No! I trust he had plenty of holy water with him," was the reply.

Before he left we had an amusing instance of his positiveness. I reminded him that I had met him a month earlier in embarrassing circumstances. My hat had fallen into a pond, and I had asked him whether I ought to walk home hatless or in the wet hat. "I took your advice," I said, "as the most learned man in England on such subjects. I put on the hat, and I have had a frightful cold in the head ever since." He replied promptly and quite seriously, "You would have had pneumonia if you had kept it off."

After he had gone we were all agreed as to the extraordinary vigour and brilliancy he had shown. Some one said : "He is like a man who is what the Scotch call 'fey.'" We laughed at the idea ; but we naturally recalled the remark later on.

Shortly afterwards I was anxious to get Huxley's advice as to an illustration I proposed to use in a review of the "Foundations of Belief," connected with the gradual growth of sensitiveness to light in sentient beings. Being away from Eastbourne, I wrote to him. His reply, written on the 27th of February—just before the commencement of his last illness—has a melancholy interest now.

"I am not sure," he wrote, "that any information of the kind you need is extant. Among the lowest forms of life ' sensitiveness to light ' is measured only by the way in which they group themselves towards or away from light, and it may signify nothing but a physical operation with which sensitiveness in the ordinary sense has nothing to do. The only clue here is in the state of the visual organ, where such exists. It can be traced down from the highest form of eyes step by step to the end of a single nerve-filament surrounded by dark pigment and covered by the transparent outer skin. But whether in the last case the nerve-ending is as much affected by the light (*i.e.* ether waves) as the nerve-endings in the higher eyes are, and whether the affection of the nerve-substance gives rise to a state of consciousness like that produced in us by light-waves, are quite insoluble questions.

"The most comprehensive discussion of the subject I can

call to mind is in tom. xii. of Milne Edwards's 'Leçons sur la Physiologie.' I can lend you the volume, and if you are back here before you want to use your information, I can supply you with oral commentary and diagrams *ad libitum.* There is not much water in the well, but you shall pump it dry with pleasure.

"The first instalment of my discussion of the 'Foundations of Belief' will be out in a day *or* two. I am sorry to say that my opinion of the book as anything more than a mere bit of clever polemic sinks steadily.

"My wife is much better, and I have contrived to escape the pestilence yet. If I could compound for a day or two's neuralgia, I would not mind, but I abhor that long incapacity and convalescence.

" Ever yours very faithfully,
"T. H. HUXLEY."

The very next day he was taken ill, and after four months, in which that vigorous mind and frame struggled with illness and exhaustion, he passed away.

So ended the life of one of whom Englishmen are justly proud for the extraordinary lucidity and brilliancy with which he impressed on his generation the characteristic scientific creed of his time, as well as for much else which specialists will measure with greater accuracy than the general reader.

In the problems of ethics and of religion, to which he gave so much attention, I have attempted to convey my own impression, which will not be shared by those who fix their attention wholly on the destructive side of his teaching, that he united two divergent tendencies. Descartes combined the philosophy of " methodic doubt " with the faith of a Catholic. The same certainly cannot be said of Huxley. But that an antithesis between certain of his theoretical conclusions and his practical attitude did impress some of those interested in his remarkable mind, the foregoing pages have shown. I concur with those who believe that his rooted faith in ethical ideals, which he confessed himself unable to account for by the known laws of evolution,[1] implied a latent recognition of the claims of religious mystery as more imperative and important than he could explicitly admit on his own agnostic principles. Careful students of his writings are aware how far more he left standing of Christian faith, even in his explicit theories, than was popularly supposed ; and this knowledge appeared more and not less significant to some of those who conversed with him on these questions.

One thing, at all events, was beyond question— that his occasional flippancy in controversy represented no levity in his way of regarding serious and sacred subjects as a whole. It was in some cases provoked by real narrowness in good people, and in others by what I could not but consider his own narrowness, which failed to view minor details of popular Christianity in their true proportion ; and sometimes by the temptation to take controversial advantage of positions current among the orthodox which theologians themselves are likely eventually to abandon. Had he lived in the early seventeenth century he would have represented Christianity as standing or falling with the truth of the Ptolemaic system, and have depicted the theologians, who would not at once break with the Ptolemaic interpretation of Josue, as the most vivid caricatures of unreason.

Such considerations made it seem to many of

---

[1] " Cosmic evolution may teach us how the good and the evil tendencies of man may have come about ; but, in itself, it is incompetent to furnish any better reason why what we call 'good' is preferable to what we call 'evil' than we had before."

those who met him more philosophical, as it certainly was more natural, not to attach the weight currently given to his attacks on incidental features of a system whose laws of organic growth he never comprehended.

Apart from matters theological, one could not but learn much from conversation with him, even amid great divergence, and feel that divergence itself became less by mutual explanation. Had he found a logical place in his theory of knowledge for the great ethical ideals he so much reverenced in word and in practice, I cannot but think that a far greater change in his philosophy would have taken place than he ever contemplated. At all events, he had the power of intercourse, largely sympathetic, with those who could have had little in common with him, had the man been simply identical with his speculative agnosticism.

VIII.

TWO MOTTOES OF CARDINAL NEWMAN.

IT was the fate of Cardinal Newman to be an occasional writer. Sermons for the occasion, tracts for the times, letters to the newspapers on topics of the hour, articles for reviews, lectures on some pressing but ephemeral controversy—eliminate these from the thirty volumes which contain his works, and what remains? The "Arians," the "Grammar of Assent," the two brief tales "Callista" and "Loss and Gain," the "Dream of Gerontius"—little else. The "Essay on Development" is only an expanded pamphlet, distinctly controversial in its occasion and in its form. The "Apologia" was an extempore reply to a pamphlet by Kingsley. The "Idea of a University" consists of lectures undertaken under stress of circumstances to meet a need of the hour, though they have not the pre-eminently controversial character of the Birmingham lectures of 1851 on the "Present Position of Catholics," or of the "Difficulties of Anglicans," written two years earlier. The admirable and picturesque account, now printed among the "Historical Sketches" as a separate volume, of the various exhibitions in history of university education, is made up of a series of articles, obviously prompted by circumstances of the moment, which appeared originally in the *Catholic University Gazette.*

The bulk of Newman's writings are in form more or less controversial because they were occasional. He has told us that controversy was ever distasteful to him.[1] It was forced upon him by circumstances. He naturally loved the reflective form of thought, and not the argumentative. St. Ambrose's "non in dialectica" was one of his favourite sayings.[2] The accumulation of facts and collection of parallel passages, or the calm philosophic study of life in its various aspects,—these were the occupations to his taste. Yet no single work of his mature life can be named in which that taste was entirely gratified. The work on the "Arians" and the "Lectures on Justification" were written before his genius was fully ripe. The "Grammar of Assent," the work which in intention most nearly fulfils his ideal, presents but one aspect of his philosophy, and had to be written, owing to intellectual conditions among Catholics at the time, with so much of consideration for readers whose philosophical traditions were other than his own, that unity of thought and of treatment is seriously damaged.

On the other hand, in some of the works ostensibly argumentative and really "occasional" is to be found a veritable treasure-trove of pregnant thought. Controversial in form, they are really philosophical. The "Essay on Development" professes to be a contribution to the old controversy on "Romish" corruptions *versus* the Anglican claim to preserve primitive doctrine. And such it is in form,

---

[1] Cf. "Idea of a University," p. 3.
[2] Cf. "Apologia," p. 169.

as I have already said. But it contains material for a philosophical work incomparably wider in sweep than the "Grammar of Assent," of which, indeed, the "Grammar of Assent" would form but one chapter. Tract 85 is only one of the series identified with the conventional writing and very limited outlook of the Tractarians; but it affected the intellectual lives of men, whose horizon was far wider, whose minds were concentrated on the very foundations of religious knowledge. And if we look for the fullest indication of his views on the philosophy of Theism, and on the reality of that mysterious world with which religion brings us into relation, we should go not to the " Grammar of Assent "—the one formal treatise—but to the sermons preached as occasion required them, in his own turn as select preacher or in the turns of others, sometimes at short notice, before the University of Oxford.

Take, again, his historical research : it is represented in no one book written later than the "Arians" (which belongs to his youth). We know what such specialists as Döllinger and Duchesne have thought of his unique and exhaustive knowledge of the history of Christianity in the early centuries. Yet the evidence for it is not to be sought in any professedly historical *magnum opus*. It is scattered up and down in articles which appeared in the *Rambler*, the *Atlantis*, the *British Critic*, the *Catholic University Gazette* and elsewhere, and is most fully exhibited in the "controversial" " Essay on Development."

Nevertheless, in spite of this lack of formal unity and apparent thoroughness, it may be maintained that the work of very few great writers has been in reality more consistent. His view of history has been consistent, and so has his philosophy. And both are unified in his analysis of the essential genius of the Church as exhibited in the story of her gradual development. If he has not summarised his positions in one or two great treatises, his teaching has had fully as real a coherence as that of those who have. He has left no " Treatise on Human Nature," no " Essay on the Human Understanding." But without maintaining that his treatment of metaphysics proper has been fully elaborated, I venture to say that he has left some contributions which are simply indispensable to any satisfactory theory of knowledge.

What, then, is Newman's philosophical teaching? What his distinctive discovery or doctrine? What great thought, what point of view, has he been the first to present—or seen with a new vividness? What is there in his philosophy which corresponds to Idealism in Berkeley, to Empiricism in Locke, to the philosophy of "common sense" in Reid?

Various inadequate answers suggest themselves. His doctrine of the "illative sense;" his doctrine of " development;" his teaching that there is no rational halting-place between Catholicism and Atheism;—these are obvious suggestions, and they are unsatisfactory. Such doctrines are salient features in his teaching, but they all depend on something more fundamental.

In his last years he chose two mottoes on two occasions. When he received the Cardinal's hat in 1879 he chose the motto, "Cor ad cor loquitur." [1] When he designed his own monument he wrote as the appropriate inscription these words: " Ex umbris et imaginibus in veritatem." [2]   It used to be said of him

[1] " Heart speaketh to heart."
[2] " From shadows and images unto truth."

that a remark in sermon or essay—apparently made *en passant* and quite incidental—often contained what was most important in the whole. And in this case I believe that these mottoes—chosen only incidentally— point the way to the really fundamental elements of his philosophy.

In an unpublished fragment, dated 1876, he wrote some pregnant sentences on the knowledge which one thinking being has of his fellows. "Our experience of each other, or of society," he wrote, "has the two characteristics of conveying to us a knowledge of others, yet bringing home to us our ignorance of them." Referring to the whole visible world, he says: "What is my belief in its reality? What is its existence but an inference or apprehension follow- ing upon impressions made on the retina?" In each case—of spirit and of matter—the *direct analysable knowledge* is but of the shadow; the belief is in the substance—in the Reality behind it.

When we apprehend—through the medium of light- undulations—those changes of facial expression which indicate the joy, the sorrow, the fear, the love, the hatred, of those with whom we hold intercourse; when the waves of sound convey to us their speech; of what interest to us in themselves are the waves of ether which affect our eye or our ear? Of what interest are even the movements of face or the tone of voice, of which the ether-waves make us aware? Of little or none. It is the feelings and thoughts to which we pass, and which we interchange through their instru- mentality, that interest us. What we observe directly is but the shadow. These are the reality. All we *directly know* in this world of appearances is but the shadow and the sign—*umbra et imago*. Complex

though the physical machinery may be, much knowing
though it may take, we mainly value it as an indication of the Reality beyond, to which our mind passes.
" Ex umbris et imaginibus in veritatem."

But, again, when we listen to the voice, and watch
the smile or the frown, we do not perform any long
process of argument from the sign to its meaning,
from the waves of ether to the sensations they produce in ourselves, from those sensations to their
combined effect and significance. The spirit of one
man seems to go straight to that of the other. We
talk of "seeing" the expression, and "hearing" the
words, as if the perception were immediate, and sometimes as if the further inference to the meaning of
words and looks were already contained in it. The
links in the chain of knowledge are not thought of.
Many of them are not known. Mind speaks to mind,
and soul to soul, imperfectly indeed, but by a simple
and seemingly direct process. " Cor ad cor loquitur."
Little, indeed, can one man know of the unseen world
which makes up his neighbour's consciousness. Taken
in its full extent (to use the Cardinal's words), " the
action of the mind of each individual is at once a
reality, yet to all but ourselves a hidden reality. Each
man thinks, hopes, fears, loves, likes, dislikes, has
pleasure and pain, plans and performs, yet in himself,
not to others." Still, the whole of human intercourse
consists in the electric communication from one man
to another, through physical media of which we
scarcely for a moment think, of portions of this unseen
world of individual consciousness, and in the part-
revelation to one another of the individual personality
which is its basis. The Reality as a whole we cannot
know. Portions of it flash upon us, we understand

not fully how, through the knowledge of its shadow—
of the physical signs whereby it expresses itself.   We
see the visible ; we have faith in the invisible.

This simple fact, revealed in personal intercourse
—that our direct experience is of the phenomena ;
that our faith, most confident yet largely inexplicable,
all-important, yet impossible to justify by adequate
analysis, is in what is beyond the phenomena ; that
our knowledge of the thinking Reality is like an
instinct, whereby we pierce through the sensible media
of intercourse, whereby soul attains to communion with
soul—is at the root of Newman's whole philosophy,
and   he   traces   its   counterpart   in   various   fields   of
knowledge.

What   is   the   knowledge   of   God   in   conscience ?
Newman   himself   distinctly   says   it   is   knowledge   of
the   substance   through   the   shadow—*ex umbra et
imagine.*   " Conscience is to me a proof of a God,"
he has written,[1] "as a shadow is a proof of a substance ! "   Yet   so   apparently   direct,   so   vivid   and
piercing,   is   this   knowledge,   in   his   opinion,   that   he
places it on a level with his knowledge of himself.   " I
rested," he writes of his religious life from youth
upwards, " in the thought of two, and two only,
absolute and luminously self-evident beings—myself
and   my   Creator."[2]   The   communion   between   the
two   is   regarded   by   him   almost   as   though   it   were
consciously direct—" Cor ad cor loquitur."

And   his   recognition   of   the   visible   Church—at
first sight so different an object of knowledge—is of
the same nature.   The existence of God and His

---

[1] See letter to W. G. Ward, cited in " W. G. Ward and the Catholic
Revival," p. 217.
[2] "Apologia," p. 4.

relations with man are revealed roughly through conscience. The Divine nature and those relations are
more fully revealed through the Church. Dogmatic
truth is primarily the exposition of the nature of God
in its relations to man. The Church and its *formulæ*
are to the truth, as it is in itself, something like what
the living body, with its organs of expression, is to
the soul whose thoughts it partially reveals. They
"half reveal and half conceal the soul within."

Such is the view which is presupposed throughout
his works, and is most clearly expressed in the last
of the "University Sermons." The Christian soul is
moulded by means of the Church. The rites, the
dogmatic *formulæ*, the external organisation, are
again the *umbra et imago* of the Reality. But through
these God appears to speak directly to the faithful
soul. To him who opens his heart to the influences
the Church supplies, and receives the image of Christ
and the Christian *ethos* stored in its liturgy, its sacred
writings, and its traditions, these media of communication become, for the purpose of intercourse between
earth and heaven, what language is between man
and man. The Spirit of God thus speaks to the
spirit of man. "Cor ad cor loquitur."

And this thought seems really to underlie the
whole of the treatise—at first sight controversial—on
the "Development of Christian Doctrine." Man speaks
to man ; friends converse at intervals through many
years. The personality of each abides; the body
changes. The change of the body makes no difference
to personal intercourse, so long as the same living soul
is behind it. In like manner the genius of Catholicism,
its *ethos*, its soul, are regarded as throughout one and
the same from the coming of Christ onwards, and as a

partial reflection (visible to man) of the Divine nature.
The soul of the Church expresses itself to different
ages (as it were) through bodily organs which necessarily grow and modify with time. "Old principles,"
he writes, in the work on "Development," "reappear
under new forms. [Christianity] changes with them,
in order to remain the same. In a higher world it is
otherwise, but here below to live is to change, and to
be perfect is to have changed often." Through this
changing bodily framework of the Church, the one
God, then, declares the same truth to different ages,
and stamps a similar character on the saints of separate epochs—men who have the culture and character
each of his own time. However different the language,
the thoughts and ideals are the same. Only thus can
the everlasting and changeless God speak to the heart
of short-lived, changing man. Only thus can we
explain the similarity of the distinctly spiritual mould
of an Augustine, an Ignatius, a Père Lacordaire
(amid great differences of natural character)—each of
them taught by a Church whose external framework,
whose intellectual language, was widely different.
The single spirit has been preserved beneath the
growing and changing frame, and has been infused
into each individual saint by *media* adapted to the
requirements of his own age.

The controversies of Newman's early life are
concerned with this one question : Is the Anglican
Church a part of that organism or framework which
was created by God to impress his revelation on man ?
Is it the normal guardian of the *umbra et imago* of the
Reality ? Can we find in the story of the Church
established in England the story of an ever-identical
spiritual *ethos* and essential teaching preserved for

man under the changed forms of expression which advancing time and changing conditions require ? Does it show a law of organic development indicative of a persistent Reality determining the changes ? Or is it, *as an institution*, a merely mechanical combination, with no distinctive Reality or informing character behind it ?

This latter view is what he gradually came to take, in spite of the deep reverence for Christ and the Catholic spirit which he recognised in individual Anglicans.

It was to this view of Anglicanism as such that the whole Monophysite and Donatist controversy led. The *Securus judicat* of St. Augustine gave the clue to the law of organic development in the Church as a whole. The acquiescence of the one *Ecclesia*, federated throughout the world, sealed and ratified the most faithful expression of the Christian doctrine in response to the questions raised by growing and changing secular thought. And this conception enabled Newman to detect the abiding Reality, the unchanging truth, under the progressing and changing framework of the Church. The appeal to antiquity on the part of a *section*, whether Anglican or Monophysite, was a protest against that normal corporate growth, which is the inevitable response of what is living to a changing environment. A stone which has no vital relation to its surroundings remains unchanged and inoperative. A living being preserves its identity and vigour by continual though unessential change. The Monophysite argument was the argument of one limb that it ought not to have grown; its realisation must imply logically separation from the Divine organic system which normally preserved the living spiritual reality. Thus heresy was | in principle agnostic. The variations, then, of the Anglican teaching from Catholic developments were not due, in his judgment, to the Christian spirit animating that teaching—to the life it embodied—but, like all corruptions, to external causes making for death. They tended not towards the preservation of Christian faith in new conditions, but towards its negation.

And in the work of his middle life Newman had once more to apply similar principles in a different sphere. For seven years he devoted himself to university education as Rector of the Catholic University at Dublin. As in the Anglican Church he had endeavoured to create out of his own resources a Church with the type and character of the Catholic Church, so he desired at Dublin to found from his own resources a University with the formative power of Oxford. In the course of the masterly effort which he so persistently made for ten years to graft Catholicism on to Anglicanism, he was forced to recognise that no individual could do the work. Catholicism was an objective reality embodied in an existing system, with its own laws of development. An individual might profoundly affect its development—as St. Augustine did in the fifth century, St. Thomas Aquinas in the thirteenth, St. Ignatius Loyola in the sixteenth. But the condition was to be part of the actually existing organism. Fully to gain the Catholic *ethos* and share in the Catholic life one must be part of the historical Church. Membership was essential, both to inheriting its past and to influencing its future. The objective religion of Catholicism was not commensurate with any system which even Newman's genius could create.

And so, too, the best analysis of some aspects of

the theory of education which has ever been made—
I speak of the lectures on the "Scope and Nature of
University Education"—could not take the place of
the actual *genius loci* of the old Universities, the outcome of the actual historical evolution of the "Idea of
a University." Dublin, *plus* all the genius of Newman
could no more replace Oxford than Anglicanism, *plus*
the genius of Newman, could become Catholicism.
And, just as he ended his Anglican career by
writing the essay on the "Development of Christian
Doctrine," in which he traces from history the law of
the development of Catholicism as an objective fact,
so he supplemented the Dublin lectures by a very
remarkable series of papers, little read now, on the
development of the idea of a University from the days
of Plato at Athens to his own times; from the beginnings of the English Schoolmen to the present Oxford
and Cambridge. We see, throughout these essays,
the theory that a University, like a Church, is a body
with a soul—a framework through which a given *ethos*
impresses itself on individuals. The microcosm reflects
the macrocosm. Just as there is a unity of type in
the Catholic saints, amid all personal differences, so
too the Oxford and Cambridge training is recognisable
more often than not even in the chance comers from
Scotland and Ireland, from Yorkshire and Cornwall,
who live together and meet together at the National
Universities. The Universities have each a quasi-
personality of their own and a formative character
which is separate from, though conveyed through, its
living institutions, and tends to impress its counterpart on their *alumni*. *Its* genius fashions *their* culture,
communicating itself we scarcely know how. "Cor ad
cor loquitur."

Now, it is observable that these instances are *all* resolvable in the last resort into the simple action from which we set out of one personality on another,—into the simplest illustration of the motto, " Cor ad cor loquitur." And they thus help us to understand the immense space assigned by Newman in all his writings to the undefinable action of personality. The development of the Church is the story of the reaction of one mind on another—of the expulsion again and again of the incompatible *ethos* (rationalism in all its disguises), of the fusion of different forms of spiritual genius essentially similar, of the resulting conflux of streams of thought. An Origen, an Augustine, a Chrysostom, a Bonaventure, an Aquinas, each contributes his share to the whole. Their distinctive genius is dominated and checked and guided by the original Divine thought—representing the Divine Personality—revealed by Our Lord Himself. The Christian is being moulded by a social quasi-personality made up of individual personalities all partly sharing the original Divine type which moulded the Apostles themselves, but developing its expression.

And so, too, the intellectual atmosphere of a University—its " psychological climate "—is mainly due to the combined influence of its strong personalities in the past and in the present. In both cases the atmosphere may be greatly affected by an individual who is himself endowed with dominating gifts, though its leading features are too strong and definite to be revolutionised.

Only a spiritual genius could, in the first instance, create the great religious corporations. The founder's character informed the whole, and it could not be radically changed without destroying the corporate

society; but others could, more or less, give a turn
to its development. St. Paul left his mark on biblical
Christianity itself. St. Augustine made an indelible
impression on the theological thought of the Latin
Church: so, too, did Origen. So, again, did St.
Thomas Aquinas at a later period. The Order of
St. Benedict has ever represented the genius of its
founder; yet St. Bernard of Clairvaux grafted his
own character on the monks of Citeaux and their
successors. St. Francis Xavier added something to
the impress of Loyola on the Jesuits, and the whole
of the Dominican spirit cannot be detected in the life
and special genius of St. Dominic. In each case there
is a distinctive *ethos*—the main current, character,
direction, supplied by the founder, with tributary
streams from characters congenial yet not wholly
similar. Behind the institutions and rules of the
order, and giving them life, is this quasi-personality
from a personal source or personal sources.

And how is this corporate quasi-personality preserved—whether it be the Christian *ethos*, or the
distinctive genius of a religious order, or the intellectual
tone of a University? No order or institution is made
up wholly of men of genius. The tributary streams I
have spoken of—the lesser geniuses—must be at best
occasional. How does the personality of the founder
nevertheless continue to animate his order, centuries
after he is gone? The answer is, that as the spirit
was created by individual personalities, so it is communicated to individual personalities. The founder
fashions his disciples, and they in their turn hand
down the tradition. And its faithful preservation is
secured, or at least aided by the external rule or rites.
Christ taught His disciples; the Church preserved

the faith for their successors.   The Christian dogma, ritual, liturgy, and tradition is the machinery whereby Christ now speaks to every faithful Christian, and stamps on him a character which enables him to understand the Divine voice.   The Benedictine rule and the traditional customs of a University act in a like manner in their own sphere.   Such is the machinery for the preservation of that *genius*, that *ethos*, which is felt but cannot be defined.   The rules and the liturgy, or *formulæ*, are not identical with the spirit behind them.   But they preserve it.   Personal intercourse in unbroken continuity passes it on, it is true, in direct line.   But tradition without a safeguard may fail. The innovating temper might find entrance.   The oral transmission might not be faithful.   Heresy might intrude under the pretext that it represents what is primitive.   Some strong personality might dominate the order or the Church, and revolutionise while professing to reform.

External *formulæ* and the external framework and rules prevent this.   They are an objective test ; a remedy for subjectivity.   In their measure they are the visible *umbra et imago* of the founder's invisible spirit.   They could not, it may be, create the spirit. But they give the language and the ether-waves whereby soul speaks to soul.   The living tradition passes from one to another, safeguarded from essential innovation by the external framework.   The burning torch kindles its fellow.   Christian, Benedictine, Jesuit, Dominican, each lives to-day with a spirit recognisable as largely that of the founders 300 or 1900 years ago.   And so, too, the tradition of culture is passed down from one generation to another in a great University.   The changes of form are here greater than with the religious corporations, but the habit and instinct whereby the best knowledge and thought of the time are assimilated remain the same.

We may observe several effects which were produced on Newman's philosophy by this recognition of the enormous extent of the work done by personality.

One was his own reverence for a man of genius. We remember his account of his own awe on first being told, " That is Keble ; " how he nearly broke down when Keble shook hands with him. We see the same feeling in his account of the first sight of Plato by the imaginary visitor to Athens.

"He goes to the Parthenon to study the sculptures of Phidias ; to the Temple of the Dioscuri to see the painting of Polygnotus . . . or let him go westward to the Agora, and there he will hear Lysias or Andocides pleading or Demosthenes haranguing. . . . He passes through the city gate, and then he is at the famous Ceramicus : here are the tombs of the mighty dead ; and here, we will suppose, is Pericles himself, the most elevating, the most thrilling of orators, converting a funeral oration of the slain into a philosophical panegyric of the living. Onward he proceeds still ; and now he has come to that still more celebrated Academé, which has bestowed its own name on universities down to this day, and there he sees a sight which will be graven on his memory till he dies. Many are the beauties of the place, the graves and the statues and the temple . . . but his eye is just now arrested by an object ; it is the very presence of Plato. He does not hear a word that he says ; he does not care to hear ; he asks neither for discourse nor disputation ; what he sees is a whole complete in itself, not to be increased by addition, and greater than anything else. It will be a point in the history of his life ; a stay for his memory to rest on, a burning thought in his heart, a bond of union with men of like mind ever afterwards. Such is the spell which the living man exerts on his fellows for good or for evil. . . . A Spaniard is said to have travelled to Italy

simply to see Livy : he had his fill of gazing, and went back
again home. Had our young stranger got nothing by his
voyage but the sight of the breathing, moving Plato ; had he
entered no lecture-room to hear, no gymnasium to converse,—
he had got some measure of education and something to tell
of to his grandchildren." [1]

Newman's sketch of the influence of Abelard on his
disciples, and his sermon on " Personal Influence as a
Means of propagating Truth," give the two sides of the
same view—the immense power for good or for ill of
a dominating personality. And he himself supplied an
object-lesson in his theory. " Credo in Newmanum "
was hardly a jocose formula. Shairp, Froude, Church,
Wilberforce, Lake, Gladstone, are only some of those
who have borne testimony to the personal magnetism
which left its mark on the whole of thinking Oxford.

This sense of the influence of one person on
another, given the attitude of the appreciative disciple,
with the electric sympathy it presupposes, coloured
his own theological views. " My sheep hear My
voice ; " " I know Mine, and Mine know Me ; " " I pray
not for the world ; "—these were favourite texts with
him. They speak of the doctrine of predestination
in the form in which Newman loved it. He tended,
as far as the Church would allow him, to divide the
elect from the world ; those to whom Christ's words
had a meaning—to whose hearts He spoke—from
those who heard not the voice from moral deafness
and hardness of heart. " The religious mind ever
sees much which is unseen to the non-religious," he
once wrote in a private letter. The passing of the
flame of faith from one torch to another held good
only for those of like nature, who were capable of

---

[1] See " Historical Sketches," iii. 41–42.

being kindled. Thus personal influence, from the same intangible cause which made it so strong, was also limited. The dialectic that all could understand was only a shadow : one listener could pass to the substance behind ; to another the words—the image or shadow—were all. The words were only φωνᾶντα συνετοῖσι. The spirit, the reality, could only be handed on between those whose hearts were in union. " Cor ad cor loquitur."

Another peculiarity—due to this general view— was that Newman, holding that the Real was the personal or quasi-personal essence behind the sensible framework, was constantly endeavouring in all fields of inquiry to find this Reality, and appeared some- times to dwell on it to an extent which would seem to an unimaginative mind almost fanciful. Not only does he treat of the genius of a University, the spirit of a religious order like the Jesuits or Benedictines, or of a secular congregation like the Oratorians or Oblates, but he detects the strong silent influence of the genius of an age, of a race, of a language.

In looking at history he sees living forces at work as much beyond the explanation of the mere recorder of facts, as the living force informing the human body is beyond the ken of the anatomist. Apparent chance and immense waste are overruled in the story both of nature and of man to produce an orderly result. In nature the type is preserved while individuals are recklessly destroyed. A thousand grains of pollen are wasted for one which fertilises. And so, under the apparently aimless chaos of history, some portion —limited, but unmistakable—of a purpose, to us as yet largely unintelligible, may be descried.[1] A national

---

[1] Similar is the view of Walter Bagehot, whose words are quoted by Sir M. E. Grant Duff (see *National Review*, January, 1900).

spirit works out a coherent result according to law. Its institutions express its spirit. So, too, the genius of a movement is shown in results in which purpose and meaning are ascertainable. And a language grows by laws which only the finest scholarly instinct can fully appreciate. Newman's views on this subject are somewhat similar to Hegel's as given in his "Philosophy of History," a work which Newman, I believe, had never read.

Once more, the recipient of personal influence, through channels only partially capable of analysis, gains in turn a power of perception defying analysis. Newman regards both the faith of the Christian and the grasp of the educated man as such a result. He compares each to the action of the mind on our sensible impressions, in converting a multitude of sensations, already to some extent unified by the aid of sight, into a coherent whole to which bodily unity is ascribed. Faith realises in the mass of religious impressions an objective whole.[1] The cultivated intellect in its *phronesis* regards a larger or smaller field of knowledge, as the case may be, not with specialists as isolated aspects, but as a combined unity. In each case the individual is made aware of something beyond the sum of impressions— namely, the organised and connected whole ; and further, he passes on to the Reality, of which the combined impressions give him the suggestion—of which they are the *umbra et imago*, but no more. The trained mind reaches out with masterly directness to the heart of the Reality. "Cor ad cor loquitur."

Now, all this explains the overwhelming preconception which underlies Newman's philosophy of faith.

[1] See the last of his "University Sermons."

It is the opposite to the assumption of the agnostic. "We have but faith, we cannot know, for knowledge is of things we see," says the poet. Allow this as a matter of terminology. But in that case faith is responsible for as much of our irresistible and indispensable certainty as knowledge. If the "things we see," the visible, sensible world, is found, the more we examine it, to be but the *medium* through which invisible forces and personalities act on one another, and carries no meaning to our intelligence on any other hypothesis, we have for *practical* purposes a very wide knowledge of the unseen. If voice, gesture, expression, fall on our senses only to convey to ourselves the thought, feeling, character, of our fellows ; if colour, sound, shape, come to our senses only to convey to us the abiding Reality behind them ; if social institutions are —much as the individual voice and gesture are—only media for the interaction of personalities ; if the Parliamentary system is only a rather clumsy mechanism enabling the will of the people to have some share in the process of legislation—and this by means of further machinery whose critical results are also due to personal intercourse in Parliamentary debate ; if law itself is but the machinery for ensuring just, orderly, and happy relations between the citizen and his fellows ; if religions and schools of thought are (at all events) the machinery whereby great minds and souls act on inferior ones ;—it follows that the invisible powers and factors are, *on any view of life*, all in all— the visible world being but their instrument. If we really face indubitable facts, the interaction of spirit with spirit, through the machinery of the external world (whatever that machinery may really be), is the most certain and general of processes. "Cor ad cor loquitur," which speaks of direct intercourse achieved when the machinery is so perfect that it is forgotten, becomes in a wider sphere the aspiration of all the working institutions of social and religious life.

And in the religious life itself to hold converse with the Highest Personality we can detect behind the vast *umbra et imago* supplied by the phenomenal world as a whole, is (in view of such facts as these) an aim strictly in accord with the nature of things. The presumption is not with the extreme agnostic, who denies that the spirit-world is knowable, but with him who frankly recognises that we assume it to be knowable every time we talk to our friends. The presumption is not with those who confine our rational knowledge to what we can logically justify, but with those who recognise that in all which is most important it transcends full analysis. Here we have the doctrine of the illative sense, and of explicit and implicit reason —of the " Grammar of Assent" and of the " University Sermons." Language falls far short of explicit thought, explicit thought of the mind's power of vision. Logic and dialectic are—in the deepest matters—calculated not for adequately defining, or even directly discovering truth, but for training the living mind to see more truly and accurately in regions into which the instruments of its training cannot themselves pass. *Primâ facie* the development of external rites and of dogmas is but the changed shape and position of the shadow, and we have to look for the Reality beyond. If the most highly trained minds detect behind the *umbra et imago* the voice not of man but of God, if they see in it the embodiment of the age-long tradition that God once spoke to man, all the presumption is in favour of their view, not against it. Such gifted spiritual minds are not imagining something new in kind. They profess to be carrying to a further point that power of passing from the seen to the unseen, of recognising Personality behind phenomena, which is in daily intercourse undeniable. If the verdict of the most gifted is that all religion is partly from God and partly reveals His Personality, but that the Christian dogma comes by a stream of special purity, then the religious insight of all the sages is more or less justified by common consent, while Christianity is accepted as the highest truth, as a more advanced stage of religious insight confirming the common knowledge by exhibiting it in a developed and purified form. Thus, Saint Augustine tells us in his "Confessions" that he found in Christianity all that truth concerning Divine things which had fascinated him in Plato and his disciples, and far more as well.

And this is, it seems to me, the outcome of Newman's position. He finds in the historical development of the dogmatic expression used by the Church, and in the fact that the acceptance of it has in all ages produced saints fashioned to the self-same image of Christ, and in the response of that image to the highest conceptions of conscience, proof at once of the abiding and unchanging Reality behind the developing machinery of the Church, and of the directly Divine origin of the faith. Mahomet speaks through the ages to Abdul, and there may be in his voice some faint echo of Divine law. Christ speaks to the faithful Christian through the Church, which is coeval with the Christian era, and the words of Christ, not in part but wholly, respond to the dormant revelation of holiness in the human conscience. The electrical directness of His speech is scarcely any the less that the revelation is of

1900 years back—for the dogmatic Church lived then ; she lives now. It is still almost as with the disciples themselves, "Cor ad cor loquitur."

The personal love of Christ, visible alike in an Augustine, a Loyola, a Fénelon, the simplicity and freedom with which they walk in the theological clothing which, to an outsider, seems so entangling and elaborate, are a practical witness that the dogmatic system is in fact what it pretends to be, an instrument whereby the unchangeable God, of infinite simplicity, has ever communicated, in the changing and complex conditions of human history, with finite man. It is like the infinitely complex machinery of a pipe organ, which may yet play to a child the simplest melody.

Dogmas relating to the infinite God remain, as I have said, but shadows of that truth which it is beyond us to know directly. We accept the Christian mysteries, we do not understand them. This limitation must remain while we see "through a glass" and "darkly," and until the day in which we "shall know as we are known." It was to that day that John Henry Newman looked for philosophy exercised on the shadow to be turned into direct vision of the Reality. And we who remain still read this hope of his life in his own words on his memorial tablet : "Ex umbris et imaginibus in veritatem."

IX.

NEWMAN AND RENAN.

On October 6th, 1845, Ernest Renan went down the steps of the Seminary of St. Sulpice, "never again to remount them," he tells us, "in priestly dress." Two days later, in the little village of Littlemore, near Oxford, John Henry Newman fell at the feet of the Passionist Father Dominic, whom he besought to receive him into "the one fold of Christ." I propose briefly to compare and contrast these two remarkable men, both eminently the products of nineteenth-century culture, and to inquire why it was that ideas characteristic of the century had a large share in leading one of them to that very Catholic Church from which they drove the other.

Both were men of rare mental endowment. Both were strongly characterised by the historical mind. The one was pronounced by his contemporary, Döl-linger, to be the most thorough of living masters of the Christian history of the first three centuries; the other was a close student and brilliant exponent of modern German Biblical criticism, and a considerable Orien-talist. Both were by intellectual temperament philo-sophers of history as well as its critical students. Both were, moreover, avowedly life-philosophers, or world-philosophers, rather than mere specialists. Both writers, within a short time of the great change in religious profession which each made, gave to the world some account of the world-philosophy and life-philosophy to which their studies had led them—Newman in his "Essay on the Development of Christian Doctrine," Renan in his "Future of Science." Each, later on, deepened some of the broad lines of his treatment, and supplemented it by exhibiting the personal equation, in autobiographies which were widely and eagerly read— the "Apologia" and the "Souvenirs de ma Jeunesse." Each of them showed himself in his writings to be eminently (as I have said) a child of his age in intellectual tendency—of the age which has striven to unfold the story of the evolution of the universe, inorganic, organic, sentient, ethical, rational, social. Renan, in "The Future of Science," maintains that in every department of knowledge the true philosophical explanation lies in the story of its evolution and development. "Its science means its history" is the epigram in which his conclusion is summed up.[1]   A dogmatic system which professes to be in its nature unchangeable cannot be true. Its science must constitute its disproof. Its profession is false to fact. The Catholic Church makes this profession. Therefore no reasonable man can adhere to it. It professes that its dogmas are identical with those doctrines which Christ taught. But history shows that they are not so. The Church professes that as they have never changed in the past, so they cannot change in the future. But criticism shows that the present teaching of the theologians on the Bible must change if it is to command the assent of reasonable men, as it is incompatible with facts which critical science

[1] "The Future of Science," translated (Chapman & Hall, 1901), p. 162.

has ascertained. Therefore, the Catholic theology is doubly incredible.

Newman, like Renan, finds in history the law of development. But the principal sphere in which he finds this great key to the understanding of the world, is the very department in which Renan denies its existence—namely, dogmatic theology. To Newman it was Protestantism and not Catholicism which contradicted the philosophy of the nineteenth century; which denied the necessity and the possibility of dogmatic evolution. However little Catholic theologians had analysed "development" in dogma, the Church had in practice (he held) admitted it. It was Protestantism and not Catholicism which strove to test the accuracy of Christian dogma in these latter days by its not going beyond the primitive Apostolic and Biblical forms of expression, which denied to it that history and that development the records of which constitute its true science; which claimed for the expression of the revealed Word absolute immobility—as though an idea could live amid everchanging civilisation without expressing itself anew in response to the innumerable other living ideas which press upon it and attempt to influence its course. Catholicism, no doubt, affirmed the *semper eadem* of revealed dogma, but this identity of dogma has never been treated by the Church as an unchangeableness of theological forms. The Scholastic form differed widely from the Patristic. New definitions were admitted to meet new emergencies. Plato aided the Fathers of Nicæa in their terminology; Aristotle was used at Trent. St. Vincent of Lerins, the early prophet of the unchangeableness of dogma, in his "Quod semper, quod ubique, quod ab omnibus," had also indicated the complementary truth which Protestantism denies. He had compared the progress of religion to that of a living man, from boyhood to maturity—a progress in which identity is preserved not by a stationary fixity of form, but by its growth. The single abiding soul of a man expresses itself through bodily organs which grow and change. Newman embodied St. Vincent's two positions in a profound philosophy. Religion "changes," he said, "in order to remain the same." This is the condition of all that *lives* on this earth. With the fossil it is not so. In another world, too, it may be otherwise. But on our earth "to live is to change, and to be perfect is to have changed often." The Catholic dogma is Divine truth in human language. As Divine truth, it is now what it was in the time of Christ. But the human philosophies and language whereby it has been conveyed in *formulæ* have been applied gradually, have had in them the element of growth. Defined propositions are final; but they are not exhaustive, and do not preclude further development. Thus development and identity are no antithesis. They are correlative. History was indeed (according to Renan's phrase) the science of theology—but it was the science, not (as Renan would make it) of nothing, but of something. And that something lives and abides.

Whence this difference between the two men? Why did they come to opposite conclusions in respect of Catholic dogma, when their general philosophy of knowledge had so much in common?

The answer, I think, to the difference in the conclusions of their philosophy is to be found in their autobiographies. The "Souvenirs" is the key to the "Future of Science," the "Apologia" to the

"Development." Long before Renan had left the Church, before he had even left Issy for St. Sulpice, or entered on those Biblical studies which were the ostensible intellectual cause of his abandonment of Christianity, a holy priest, M. Gottofrey, broke off a conversation with him, in startled accents, with the words, "You are not a Christian." His remark, Renan says with characteristic candour, had "a boldness and precision which" the young student "did not appreciate until afterwards." The whole of the remarkable chapter in the "Souvenirs" in which this incident is related—a chapter which deals throughout with the period antecedent to the special studies the result of which Renan found incompatible with the Catholic theology—goes to show that the ethical attitude and the ethical convictions proper to Christianity were already absent in him, and that intellectualism and sentimentalism were the beginning and the end of his intense interest in religious studies. Up to this time he had not met with anything in his theological reading which presented an insuperable intellectual difficulty. He found his masters kind and sympathetic. Yet he stands before us as almost the embodiment of the mere man of culture as *contrasted* with the Christian in Newman's famous Dublin discourse [1]—in whom the moral sense does duty for conscience, and who substitutes the subjective creed of a gentleman for the objective creed of a Christian ; duties to self for duties to God ; the creed of refinement, honour, self-respect, for the creed of responsibility to and dependence on an external power, with the correlatives of the sense of sin and of the necessity of self-denial. "Everything tended," Renan

See "Idea of a University," pp. 187–191.

writes, " to lull me into a state of fancied security.   I
thought that by copying the politeness of M. Gosselin
and the moderation of M. Manier I was a Christian."
The terrible words of M. Gottofrey shook this repose.
They "sounded all night in my ears," he writes, "like
a clap of thunder. . . . I never felt such terror as
that which this phrase awoke in me."

The more gentle and sympathetic M. Gosselin,
however, reassured his pupil for the time.   Yet Renan,
looking back in later years, held that M. Gottofrey
was right.   " He was right a dozen times over. . . .
It needed the transcendent lucidity of this martyr and
ascetic to discover what had escaped " M. Gosselin
and M. Manier.   The temper, indeed, of the martyr
and ascetic had in Renan no counterpart whatever.
I think it was Monsignor D'Hulst who, years ago,
described Renan's mind as "living among cushions."
The love of pleasant intellectual sensations, the intense
frivolity, the want of religious depth in the Frenchman
meant an almost total absence of the inner forces
and principles which lay at the root of Newman's
earliest convictions, and led to his final conclusions.

Let me endeavour to make plainer the contrast in
this respect between Renan and Newman, and its
consequences.   The presence of God and the sense
of sin were, as we see so vividly in the "Apologia,"
the deepest and most unyielding convictions in the
mind of the English Oratorian from first to last.
Christianity is, to him, a revelation, answering to the
needs of our sinful nature, deepening, explaining, and
further developing our apprehension of the initial
truths of natural religion.   Dogmatic propositions
and theological science are the gradual systematic
attempt of the human intellect, overruled by God's

providence, at expressing and analysing the truths of revelation. The dogmatic history of the early centuries is mainly concerned with the efforts of the Church to keep from heretical alloy the primary beliefs on which the Christian life must ever depend, the belief that God is one, that Christ is true God and true man, that man is sinful and dependent on God's grace. These are the truths assailed in one way or another by Arianism, Nestorianism, Eutychianism, Pelagianism. At the same time, the theology thus evolved is not commensurate with the Divine truths it protects. The Trinity remains beyond human conceptions, though Arianism is known to be false. So, too, the great truths concerning free will and predestination remain in their mutual adjustment mysterious, not fathomed by Augustinianism or, later on, by Molinism—although the excesses of Pelagius were condemned. These truths are, and must remain, mysteries, exceeding human expression and human reason. Newman never forgets St. Thomas's doctrine of "analogical predication"—that all expressions by human ideas or words of truths concerning God are but analogies to the reality.

Thus, throughout, Newman is deeply sensible that the "Divine fact" which remains ever the same is not *identical* with the *formulæ* whose human words analogically represent it.[1] The realities, which theology can only partially express, constitute on the objective side that truth which is *semper eadem* to the Catholic mind. And they are precisely what is from the nature of the case beyond the speculations of the brilliant but frivolous Frenchman. The symmetrical, tangible, definite *formulæ* of contemporary theology

---

[1] "University Sermons," pp. 332, 350.

are self-sufficient for Renan. You may take them or leave them. But to regard theology as the living, growing body, with a soul of Divine truth informing it, is alien to his intellect, his character, his history.

Newman finds in each age of the Church a wonderful similarity in the ethical character of the Catholic—amid all the differences in the ecclesiastical polity, and in the various stages of doctrinal development. The one identical Divine truth, the one Christian revelation is in each age acting on the faithful soul, and with the same ethical result. The two are correlative. The character arises from the apprehension (albeit partial) of revealed truth which presupposes the truths of natural religion. In Renan they are both absent. To Newman the *semper eadem* of Catholicism is a *depositum fidei*, a revelation of truth beyond complete human expression, deepening and supplementing the intimations of conscience, gradually secured at many points by fixed dogmatic propositions, but far exceeding those propositions, as the Divine necessarily exceeds the human. The Frenchman's brilliancy and quick perception of all that lies at the surface are equalled by his inability to apprehend those deeper facts in the soul, those phenomena of the human "conscience," which Newman had so carefully analysed, and of which he has spoken as the " shadow " of God, testifying to His existence as the shadow is a proof of the substance—phenomena which are essential to the latter's view of revelation itself. With a keen, emotional sensitiveness to the beauties of Catholic worship, Renan appears to be almost without any sense of the abiding realities between which that worship and the dogmatic system form an imperfect link—the sinful human soul, and the

everlasting God, Creator, ever-present Sustainer, and
Redeemer. Consequently, to him the *semper eadem*
to be looked for in Catholicism is simply the visible,
tangible object with which he has been in contact
from his youth. It is hardly an exaggeration to say
that he looks for it in the candles, the vestments, the
altars, the flowers, as well as in the symmetrical
details of the Scholastic propositions learnt by him
at St. Sulpice, and in the French Catholic surroundings of his youth, in Paris and Brittany. This
Catholicism satisfies his feelings (to which he gives
the name of his "moral nature,") but the theological
details which it involves cannot be reconciled with
the conclusions of his reason. He presents to us, as
unalterable parts of Catholic dogma, positions which
are now taught in no ecclesiastical seminary of any
reputation. His strongest invective is directed
against the "neo-Catholics"—Montalembert, Gratry,
Dupanloup—who would so develop theology as to
make it credible to their generation. He regards
them as apostles of "the vague" and the worst
enemies of truth. "There is nothing so mischievous,"
he writes, "as the vague. It is even worse than the
false." No. Let us have, he says, either the beautiful, symmetrical, and absolutely incredible details of
the system of the old Sulpicians ; or let us have
complete rationalism. With characteristic frivolity
he suggests that we may "amputate" the critical
faculty, and then our feelings will find rest in the
ancient incredible forms of orthodoxy. If, on the
other hand, we give the critical faculty fair play, we
must arrive at the other alternative of rationalism.
Those who deny his dilemma—who hold that reasonable and sober criticism is consistent with the deepest

conviction of the mysteries of Christianity are to him intolerable.

Apostles of "the vague"—this is the limit of his comprehension of those earnest Catholics who, like Newman, had the culture and intellect of their day, and whose consciences were penetrated with Christian truth. Of "the vague," presumably because what was to them most undeniable and most definite—an unmistakable beacon-light—was for him non-existent or an uncertain *ignis fatuus*. It is true that some of the "neo-Catholics" (as he calls them) differed from Renan in training or antecedents. Some had early been under the influence of the *bête noir* of St. Sulpice —De Lamennais. Montalembert was a layman, Newman an Englishman. But no mere difference in early training or circumstances, between the intellectual habits of an Englishman and of a Frenchman, between a lay and a clerical education, will account for the divergence of which I am speaking. Another Frenchman, who had gone through Issy and St. Sulpice, whose training was precisely similar to Renan's—Henri Dominique Lacordaire—offers here precisely the same contrast to Renan which we see in John Henry Newman. Lacordaire had been a sceptic in religion. His mind was alive to many of the critical problems which exercised Renan. But, like Newman, he had the deep sense which Renan lacked of those realities on which religion depends for all its meaning—God and the responsible, sinful soul. Readers of Père Chocarne's "Inner Life of Lacordaire" will appreciate the distinction between the men—the friar, the apostle of an austerity which seems terrible to weaker mortals, and the easy-going devotee of the beautiful and the cultured. Lacordaire, like Renan, was regarded by

Sulpicians as an innovator, an intellectualist, of doubt-ful orthodoxy. They both presented on the merely intellectual side those qualities which appear dangerous to the representatives of routine. The contrast is therefore the more remarkable and the more in-structive. When Lacordaire can speak, as death draws nearer, of his faith as becoming gradually some-thing like sight,[1] he realises the beatitude awarded to the "pure of heart." To "see God" was to grasp the Reality underlying theological development. To Newman and to Lacordaire, the long sequence in Church History thus witnesses to a *semper eadem* in a sphere insensible to Renan—for it exhibits on every page those whose dogmatic belief was, like their own, based on what were to them realities, to what had for Renan no existence. The Sulpician theologians were dealing, in Renan's eyes, with a tangible and visible something, though it was intel-lectually incredible. But these other men were beating the air, holding on to nothing, philosophising about nothing—as in the story of the Barmecide feast the gestures of mastication are laboriously performed, while there is nothing to eat. Consequently, no school of writers arouses Renan's anger more than Lacordaire and his friends. He speaks of the great Dominican's apologetic as "theological buffooneries which, by force of impudence and eloquence, enlisted admiration in Notre Dame," but which "had no such effect on serious-minded Christians." Dupanloup's exposition of Catholicism was one in which "all its doctrines are toned down, contorted, blunted . . . a thing without

---

[1] "Chocarne," p. 356. "The light becomes so lively, so sweet, so pene-trating in proportion as we approach death under the auspices of faith and of a virtue which takes its root in the Gospel ! We no longer believe —we see."

frame or bone, with all its essence taken from it."
Montalembert comes forward only to exhibit "dogmatic ignorance and very weak reasoning powers."

Cardinal Newman, although little familiar with
modern Biblical criticism, had early been alive to the
fact that the new sciences, critical and physical, must
as they advance lead to further changes in theological
exposition ; and he found in the genius of Christianity
that which was especially adapted to make such
changes bearable. As early as 1826, he preached a
sermon in which he pointed out that in spite of the
points of opposition between the new scientific
synthesis of the Universe and the mediæval synthesis
to which Christians have in times past been accustomed
there is a very important point in which a true understanding of scientific method confirms the lessons
which Christianity has taught us.[1] Patience under
the seeming contradictions between appearance
and reality, between sight and faith, the hope to
understand *ultimately* by reverent and humble inquiry
the consistency of what now seems contradictory—
these are the virtues which Science preaches to her
true devotees. " Things are not what they seem," it
tells them. The need for patience is based on the
infinite complexity of the world of fact; and on the
present limitations and very gradual development of
our own powers of knowing. Humility and patience,
in the face of apparent contradictions, trust that the
reward of these virtues will be a fuller understanding
of the truth, are, then, what Science preaches in its own
domain. And they are an essential part of the true
philosophy of Christianity. The impatient theologian
who is prematurely positive that the speculations which

_____

[1] I refer to the first of the Unversity Sermons.

he has framed, or which others have framed, are final and irreformable, is doing in the case of religious science precisely what led the old Greek philosophers into the wildest absurdities in physics—namely, making his own present limited understanding the measure of a mind far greater than his; reasoning over-confidently on a few apparent data and on the *prima facie* appearances, instead of striving gradually to accumulate sufficient accurate data to justify hypothesis, and thus to penetrate below the surface. The mind of Nature is far vaster than the mind of its student. The mind of God is infinitely beyond the mind of man—even of the greatest theologian. The philosophy of induction —the key to modern science—recognises that we must reverently explore the greater mind, instead of drawing positive conclusions from a few of its more obvious exhibitions. Impatience at man's ignorance of Nature which made him theorise, impatience at the inadequacy of his theories which made him subsequently reject them, have both yielded to a patient faith, not in the adequacy of first attempts, but in the reality of the quest. And, in like manner, a deep religious philosophy counsels a reverent study of all the relevant phenomena, of the relations between God and the soul, as well as of the facts given us by the positive sciences, in place of over-confident theorising. In both cases rationalism is the foe to true philosophy.

Here we have, I think, the moral of the distinction I have been pointing out, between Renan on the one hand and Lacordaire and Newman on the other. If we believe deeply in the subject-matter of knowledge, and in the possibility of some science gradually emerging, this patience and humility are possible. Without such belief they are not. If we have confidence in the Christian revelation as containing objective truth, the limits of which are susceptible of a gradual approximate definition, to witness patiently the gradual revision of theological speculation in its relations with the development of other sciences, is natural and easy. If we have little or no faith in revelation, the detection of error or contradiction in those speculations which have in the past seemed to make revelation more concrete and tangible, which have given an artificial support to the little faith we have had, is easily regarded as the disproof of revelation.   To withdraw this symmetrical support seems to leave us self-sustained, *in vacuo*, or to launch us on the ocean of "the vague" without chart or compass.   It is faith in an objective truth behind theology, as in an objective truth behind scientific conjecture, which enables us patiently to bear with the failure of the moment.   It was the first glimpse of the possibilities of knowledge opened out by induction which substituted the Baconian patience for the Greek impatience.   It gave the scientist a new faith ; and so with religion.   Contrast Huxley's patient observation in physics with his restless, intermittent, impatient disquisitions on theology.   He believed in the one case and disbelieved in the other in the reality of the subject-matter in question.

With Renan, too, we find no sign of any disposition for patience and humility in his theological inquiries. And it is not surprising.   What motive had he for patient inquiry into a subject-matter of which he did not deeply believe the reality at all ?   To be patient means in such a case that we recognise, without any shock to our faith, that some things appear contra-dictory, for the time, just because we believe deeply that objective truth is really harmonious, and that

time will solve many present antimonies. A belief in
the reality of the subject-matter with which the science
is concerned is the motive for patience. And it was
absent from Renan. Not believing deeply in any
reality below the surface, he looks only at the contradictions on the surface. And he denounces
the philosophy that bears with them as " the vague."
He identifies Catholicism with the most rigid expressions of theologians who are repeating, in matters in
which natural knowledge and supernatural are both
concerned, phrases which were used in the prescientific
period. For this teaching is what was before his eyes
in his youth. He gives as its alternative pure and
simple rationalism. The view that the Church is
guarding a "deposit" of Divine truth given at first
not in fully defined form, and that critical science is
leading to new secular truth ; that the weapons of the
theologians are in great part those of human language
and human reason ; that consequently theologians as
well as critics are likely at times to betray human in-
firmities, and to go beyond the warrant of their
science ; that time will show more and more clearly
the true limits of each department ;—this is at least
an intelligible view, and historical fact does not
simply give it the lie. Copernicanism established the
falsity of what Dante spoke of as part of the teaching
of the Church, yet it is at least not obvious that it
thereby disproved Christianity. It is conceivable that
the speculations of theologians connected with the
locality of heaven, which Dante speaks of as the
belief of the Church "which cannot tell an untruth,"
have been shown by science not to be, as they were
once supposed, a part of Christian truth. Yet this
general view Renan never seems to contemplate in its

bearing on his own critical researches : and all suggestion of it he dismisses with apparent irritation. Had he indeed had the patience which comes of a deep faith, he would have lived to find it in a large degree justified. For we now see universally discarded many of the anti-Christian positions in Biblical science which men like Baur and Volkmar maintained to be established, while other positions which Renan regarded as demonstrably incredible and yet as inseparable from the Catholic theology, have passed away from the teaching of the Catholic schools,—just as our forefathers saw the disappearance of the belief that hell was in the bowels of the earth, and of the belief that *terra in æternum stat* proved the falsity of Copernicanism.

This peculiarity of Renan's attitude comes vividly before the readers of the " Souvenirs de ma Jeunesse," from which I may extract the following passages, in which I have italicised some sentences :—

"A single error proves that a Church is not infallible ; one weak part proves that a book is not an inspired one. Outside rigid orthodoxy, there was nothing, so far as I could see, except free-thought after the manner of the French school of the eighteenth century. My familiarity with German studies placed me in a very false position ; for upon the one hand it proved to me the impossibility of an exegesis which did not make any concessions, while upon the other hand I quite saw that the masters of St. Sulpice were quite right in refusing to make these concessions, inasmuch as a single confession of error ruins the whole edifice of absolute truth, and reduces it to the level of human authorities in which each person makes his selections according to his individual fancy.

"For in a Divine book everything must be true, and as two contradictories cannot both be true, it must not contain any contradiction. But the careful study of the Bible which I had undertaken, while revealing to me many historical and æsthetic treasures, proved to me also that it was not more exempt than any other ancient book from contradictions, inadvertencies, and errors. It contains fables, legends, and other traces of purely human composition. *It is no longer possible for any one to assert that the second part of the Book of Isaiah was written by Isaiah.* The Book of Daniel, which, according to all orthodox tenets, relates to the period of the Captivity, is an apocryphal work composed in the year 169 or 170 B.C. *The Book of Judith is an historical impossibility. The attribution of the Pentateuch to Moses does not bear investigation,* and to deny that several parts of Genesis are mystical in their meaning is equivalent to admitting as actual realities descriptions such as that of the Garden of Eden, the Apple, and Noah's Ark. *He is not a true Catholic who in these matters departs in the smallest iota from the traditional theses.*

" *Orthodoxy calls upon us to believe that the Biblical books are the work of those to whom their titles assign them.* The *mildest* Catholic doctrine as to inspiration will not allow one to admit that there is any marked error in the sacred text, or any contradiction in matters which do not relate either to faith or morality. *Well, let us allow that out of the thousand disputes between criticism and orthodox apologetics as to the details of the so-called sacred text there are some in which by accident, and contrary to appearances, the latter are in the right. It is impossible that it can be right in all the thousand cases, and it has only to be wrong once, for all the theory as to its inspiration to be reduced to nothing.*"

I will not here attempt a full examination of this passage. I will content myself with saying that to identify orthodoxy with the belief that every book in Scripture is written by its nominal author would be, I suppose, to place in the ranks of the heterodox nine-tenths of living Catholic students of the Bible : to reject the mystical interpretation of much of the Old Testament is to make heretics of some of the greatest Fathers and Schoolmen alike ; while to regard as fatal to the Catholic claim a single triumph of the representatives of science or criticism over the orthodox apologists, as to a fact which the orthodox may regard at a particular time as involving error in the Bible, is, at the very latest, to date the failure of the Church from the decree of the Inquisition in 1616. The researches of modern criticism are quite superfluous. They only slay the slain.

Thus the conclusions of M. Renan at St. Sulpice only confirm our anticipations from his career at Issy. He did not cease to be a Christian because his Biblical studies disproved Christianity, but he found the Bible incompatible with Catholic theology because he was not a Christian.

X.

THE LIFE-WORK OF CARDINAL WISEMAN.

It is now more than sixty years since Macaulay struck a note very unusual in English periodical literature, by his article in the *Edinburgh Review* on Ranke's "History of the Popes." Readers of the *Edinburgh* were accustomed to Sydney Smith's kindly plea for Catholics that they were not dangerous conspirators but harmless fools. But Macaulay's announcement that the Church of Rome was fast gaining ground on the Continent, and that she had in her organisation an extraordinary secret of vitality, conveyed a new idea to his readers. Since then the Catholic revival or reaction has been a subject of interest to various Englishmen—to Matthew Arnold and Mr. Morley, as well as to many persons of a more ecclesiastical type.

Not long after the revival had first taken form in Germany, Augustus Schlegel prophesied that Christendom would soon return to the Roman obedience. Yet Schlegel himself never did join the Church of Rome. Many of the *élite* of the German intellectual and artistic world went over—nearly sixty, according to Jannsen's computation. Stolberg, Overbeck, Frederick Schlegel (the brother of Augustus), are names which occur to the memory at once. But many stayed. Such men as Novalis and La Motte Fouqué shared in the Catholic sympathies of their friends of the Romantic school (the brother of Novalis became a Catholic), but they did not themselves take the great step. A similar phenomenon was visible in England thirty years later (though with a difference of motives), when Newman and Faber went, and Pusey and Keble stayed. In France, too, where the revival was equally noticeable, there were those for whom it meant a life of almost saintly devotion to the cause of the Church—as it did for Montalembert and Lacordaire—and those like Chateaubriand, whose æsthetic sympathies were affected, but not, permanently at least, their lives. Thus, while we can speak without hesitation of a remarkable movement on behalf of Catholic ideals, literary, artistic, and even directly religious, its practical outcome still remains somewhat undetermined.

Let us for a moment consider some of the ideals which were expelled with contempt from England at the Reformation, and discredited in the last century almost throughout Europe, and which are now winning assent, or at least respect, not only by reaction from the irreligious excesses of the eighteenth century, but in the name of a deeper philosophy.

Authority went out as the slavery of the reason : it comes back in the writings of De Bonald and Lamennais, and in Schlegel's " Philosophy of History," both as the expression of the knowledge first committed by God to the human race, and as the embodiment of the accumulated experience of society. External forms and ceremonies went out as superstitions opposed to the inward religion of the heart; they return again in the writings of Möhler, Newman, and

Cardinal Wiseman as symbols of great truths, as the very means whereby the heart and mind are roused to some apprehension of realities they can never fully grasp. The centre of Catholic devotion, the Mass, and the correlative doctrine of transubstantiation, went out, notably in England, as the *ne plus ultra* of intellectual degradation. The Mass was blasphemed in words not to be repeated. Transubstantiation was taken to involve the ridiculous conception of carnal presence in a multitude of places, and the reality of paying Divine honour to a piece of bread. The metaphysics of the last century, however, have brought home to an increasing number the thoughts—that of what substance is in itself we know nothing; that space is conceivably subjective; and that in affirming transubstantiation and the presence of the same substance in many places, we are saying what is, indeed, of great import to the devotional life, as it affirms a *præsens Deus*, but what, philosophically, has the unprovable but unassailable character of all affirmations concerning the unknowable.

And along with this deeper view of Authority, of Symbolism, of the Real Presence, has come a new reverence for those lives and characters which have been formed by the Catholic system. The Sister of Mercy or of Charity, who tends the sick and dying, is no longer the "popish" nun of Exeter Hall associations. The saint is acquitted of being a mountebank or a formalist when the external rites of his religion are viewed as a means of realising the unseen. Hence we have had thinkers of various schools writing with admiration of St. Teresa, St. Bernard of Citeaux, St. Francis of Assisi, St. Vincent of Paul. To take one case alone, St. Francis of Assisi : he has been an inspiring theme to the Protestant Minister, Paul Sabatier; to the Spanish Republican orator, Castelar; to the German Broad Churchman, Hase; to the Italian agnostic poet, Carducci; to the French *libre penseur*, Ernest Renan.

Such a phenomenon, be it observed, must not be taken as more significant than it is. Its significance probably varies in the case of each writer I have named. At most it may lead to the thought, in those who are eagerly looking for one ray of light from the unseen, that the system which fashioned such devoted men and women has round it a special aureole : more commonly it secures for the saint only the privilege claimed for him by Comte, of a seat in a large and somewhat mixed pantheon.

I propose here to deal with a chapter in the Catholic revival connected especially with one who, though almost unknown to the rising generation, was once a very prominent figure in England and on the Continent,—the late Cardinal Wiseman. Whether or not he was the chief instrument of the Catholic revival in England—as some of our German friends maintain— he was so beyond all question among those born in the Roman Communion. And the story of his work is that of a critical turning-point.

In England the work of winning respect for the Catholic ideals was complicated by the fact that these ideals had become almost exclusively associated with the detested English "papists." Ever since the reign of Charles II. the "papists" had been objects of popular contempt and detestation. The idea that they were conspirators against the nation, bent on striking a blow at Protestant England, and on restoring their own religion by foreign aid,—an idea which

had never been extinct from the days of the Armada,
—was rapidly developed after 1666, when they were
charged with being authors of the fire of London.
Plot after plot was invented and laid to their charge,
the story of Titus Oates being the most systematic,
but only one of many. "Hatred" of the Roman
Catholic religion, says Macaulay, "had become one
of the ruling passions of the community, and was as
strong in the ignorant and profane, as in those who
were Protestants from conviction." The House of
Lords echoed with applause when one of the speakers
said, "I would not have so much as a Popish man or
a Popish woman to remain amongst us; not so much
as a Popish dog or a Popish bitch; not so much as a
Popish cat to mew or purr about our King."[1] This
national sentiment, a combination of hatred of the
plots of the papists, and of the superstitions which
made them papists and plotters, was still a very
powerful force in the country in 1780. Two hundred
lives were lost in the riots of that year, brought on by
the mild Catholic Relief Act of 1778; and the property
of many a Catholic was destroyed. Meanwhile their
numbers had dwindled rapidly. Many conformed to
the Established Church, their faith sapped by the
doctrines of Voltaire and of Hume; others gave up
their religion, worn out by fines and disabilities—the
esprit de corps of the remnant grew cold. "The
splendour of the party," writes Mr. Berington in 1780,
"by such means vanished."

Moreover, the English "papists" had at the end
of the eighteenth century become isolated from their
friends at home and abroad. Since the beginning of the

---

[1] See Berington's "State and Behaviour of English Catholics from the
Reformation to 1780," p. 62. (London, 1780.)

wars between Charles I. and his Parliament, they had been a factor of importance to the Jacobite cause, but from the failure of the rising of 1715 onwards, their Jacobite friends gradually grew shy of them, and from the rest of the nation they had long been estranged. "We are brought up in a strange land," writes Sir John Throckmorton, in 1790,[1] "ignorant of the laws, manners, and customs (I had almost said the language) of our native country, strangers to those with whom we are to live. We pass our lives in struggling with the disadvantages of our education." And in an influential group of English Catholics loyalty to Rome, for which they had suffered so much, was abating. Just as the Gallican Church was becoming more national and less papal, as the Emperor Joseph of Austria was cutting off communication between the Austrian Bishops and the Holy See, as Tuscany was becoming Jansenistic, and German Catholicism Febronian, so also a group of the English Catholics were claiming to be members of a National Church exempt from Roman interference. Sir John Throckmorton urged the clergy to reject the Vicars Apostolic as "emissaries" of a "foreign power" —namely, "the Bishops of Rome," and to elect their own Bishops without referring to the Pope at all. The Catholic devotion to Our Lady was disappearing. Bible societies were being founded as a bond of union with English Protestants. The Catholic committee and their friends wished to call themselves "Protesting Catholic Dissenters." They minimised all practices repugnant to their Protestant brethren. They were prepared for almost any compromise to secure the repeal of the penal laws, which had become

[1] In his "Letter to the Catholic Clergy of England," p. 13. Second Edition, 1791.

their one fixed idea. Thus at once rejected and despised by their own countrymen, and themselves, in many instances, half ashamed of their religion and of too close a fellowship with their brethren in Rome, the English Catholics had reached a degree of isolation which, in a body insignificant in numbers and wanting in zeal, made them almost a negligible quantity.

How the arrival of the French *emigre* clergy softened English anti-Catholic prejudice, how Bishop Milner rallied a section of the Catholics and restored their self-respect and loyalty to the Holy See, how the publication of Lingard's " History of England," as well as the writings of Milner himself, awakened among the educated few some respect for the Catholic remnant, how O'Connell and the Irish Catholics finally won emancipation in 1829, has often been told. The work of Milner and O'Connell was that of Wellington's squares at Waterloo. It prevented the situation from getting worse, it made it a degree better, until the arrival of powerful allies,—Newman from Oxford, Wiseman from Rome.

When Nicholas Wiseman came, in 1835 (as Campion had come two hundred and fifty years earlier), to preach in England, from the Collegio Inglese in Rome (where he had been educated, and of which he was Rector), Catholic emancipation had been won with Irish aid, but the English Catholics still retained the traditions and habits of a proscribed sect. The average Protestant still shuddered at the sight of a Mass-house.[1] Wiseman used to relate how a priest who wished to trace a cross on the façade of a

---

[1] This paragraph is contained in the " Life and Times of Cardinal Wiseman."

chapel at this time was warned by the police authorities that the probable consequence would be the destruction of the building by the mob. The worst of the penal laws had been put into execution within living memory. Men were alive in 1835 in whose childhood Mr. Molony was imprisoned for life for no other offence than saying Mass. Lord Shrewsbury could tell Dr. Wiseman, when he visited him at Alton Towers, how his own great-uncle, Bishop Talbot, was informed against for the same offence and brought to trial. There were surviving personal friends of the saintly Bishop Challoner, who related the story of his last days and of his death soon after a night of terror spent in hiding from the Gordon rioters. Old Dr. Archer (who only died in 1835) would describe the days when Challoner, forbidden to preach publicly, although he was allowed to say Mass under the protection of the Sardinian Embassy, would assemble a knot of the faithful at the " Windmill " public-house, each ordering a pewter pot of beer, and then, when the waiters had left the room, would preach one of his earnest discourses in comparative safety. Clay pipes were added as an additional precaution when the more dangerous experiment of a meeting of the clergy was attempted. Dr. Archer used to describe a similar stratagem when he himself preached at the " Ship " public-house in Turnstile. Some of the tables were preserved as relics of those days, bearing still the marks of pewter tankards. Catholic chapels had not been legalised at all until 1791. A retired room in a back yard in Warwick Street, the Neapolitan Chapel situated in a stable-yard, and another room at Moorfields, with a spy-window, so that friend and foe could be distinguished before admission, had been the chief "Mass-houses" for London Catholics in those days of Archer's and Challoner's preaching. Men who were only elderly in 1835 could remember the warnings of the Catholic Directory to gentlemen returning from abroad, that in spite of the Relief Act of 1791, the "importer or receiver of such things as crosses, pictures, ladies' missals, rosaries, breviaries, etc.," alike incur the penalties of *præmunire*. Bishop Bramston would describe the Tenebræ office on which they secretly ventured in his younger days, in Castle Street, Holborn, the fourth house on the right hand, on the second or third floor. The party consisted of the Rev. Mr. Lindow, Bishop Douglas, Charles Butler, and Bishop Bramston himself—then a lawyer. After the office they "separated to thank God that even this much was done, and hoped for better days." The Catholic country houses were haunted by the older traditions of martyrdom and priest-hunting, which had been their pride. At one country house the Missals and Breviaries had their disguises, "Horatii Opera" or "Opera Virgilii" being printed on the outside. Mr. Constable Maxwell still paid the double land tax. Lord Arundell would relate to the visitors at Wardour Castle how, when he was a boy, his father was compelled by a Protestant neighbour to sell the four horses of his carriage for five pounds apiece, for such was the law up to 1778.

Such documents as the following—among the old manuscripts at Everingham—kept alive the remembrance of the priest-hunters of sixty years back :—

"To Mr. Watkinson at Middleton : Whereas you have taken upon you the office or function of Popish Priest, as I am credibly informed, therefore do I hereby give you notice that unless you do immediately quit this country you will be prosecuted as the law directs.   From yours, etc.,

"ELLIS CUNLIFFE.

"October 18th, 1770."

As of the penal laws, so too of the Gallican estrangement from Rome and its devotional ideals the tradition remained in 1835.   And the isolation of the English Catholics was increased by the fact that no very close relations existed between them and their Irish fellow-Catholics, though they had united to win emancipation.   Nay, disunion existed even among themselves.   They had no organic unity, no hierarchy, no synods.   The lay patrons had long been at vari- ance with the Vicars Apostolic.   The Vicars Apostolic had been at variance with each other, notably Bishops Poynter and Milner, as to the attitude to be taken up with reference to emancipation.

It is absolutely essential to bear these facts in mind to understand the work done by Cardinal Wiseman.   "He has done a great work," wrote Cardinal Newman, a week after Wiseman's death,[1] "and I think has finished it."   "It is not often," he adds, "that this can be said of a man."   This life- work was to give unity and organisation to the English Catholics; to make them among their countrymen no longer the proscribed "papists," the embodiment of hateful superstition, but men who had a right to be listened to like any one else when they gave their views on the supreme problems of religion ; to make them realise on their own side that they were not an isolated English sect, but members of the great international Church ; to make them no longer men

[1] In a letter to Dr. Russell of Maynooth.

ashamed of the ideals for which they had sacrificed so much; no longer speaking with contempt of the monastic life, with disparagement of the poetry of the Liturgy, but proud of their inheritance; no longer a body largely disaffected and disunited and almost worn out, but a Church with its due measure of discipline and of religious zeal; no longer confined in view to the political well-being of their own party, but capable of appreciating and uniting with such great movements as the Catholic revival in Germany and the Oxford Movement in England.

Such were the intention and direction of Wiseman's work. And for such a work he was in some respects almost a *deus ex machinâ*. He had spent twenty-two years of his life in Rome, free from all the discouraging traditions of the English "papist." He had already won unquestionable distinction in countries where "Popery" was no bar to fame, as it had been to Milner and Lingard in England. When only twenty-six he had gained a European reputation as a philologist and a Syriac scholar by his 'Horæ Syriacæ'" —not, perhaps, a great book, but one derived from original sources: and at that time Syriac studies stood in need of such works. Lachmann, Tischendorf, Tregelles, Scrivener, and Bishop Westcott, cite Wiseman's authority as weighty in matters of philology— in some cases as decisive. We may even lament, with Mr. Scrivener, that such "precocious" promise proved "deceitful," [1] for Wiseman never became the great Orientalist he promised to be. But during the ten years of his constant association with Cardinal Mai, as curator of the Arabic Department in the Vatican

[1] "Plain Introduction to the Criticism of the New Testament," Fourth Edition, p. 34.

library (in which capacity he discovered the Karka-
phensian Codex), he had all the advantages of one from
whom much was expected. He became the friend and
correspondent of very many eminent scholars who
visited the Eternal City—Englishmen among them.
He was a frequent contributor to and member of our
Royal Asiatic Society, and was more or less intimate
with such men in various countries as Bunsen, Tho-
luck, Abel Rémusat, and Frederick Schlegel. At his
lectures on "The Connection between Science and
Religion," in the spring of 1835, all the best intellect
of Rome was present and applauded. He was well
known, too, to Lacordaire and Montalembert, of whose
brilliant conversations with Wiseman in 1831 Lord
Houghton has left a record in his monographs. With
Döllinger and Möhler he frequently stayed at Munich
on his way from Rome to England. He was acquainted also with such of our own countrymen as
Gladstone, Archbishop Trench, Newman, Froude,
Manning, and Moncton Milnes. He had known
three Pontiffs and had been intimate with two, notably
with Gregory XVI., who was his friend of some
years' standing before he was made Pope.

Thus he came to England in 1835 not, like the
typical English "papist," a stranger to his countrymen and out of sympathy with the Roman authorities,
not an unknown man who had to win respect from
a population which inherited an almost insuperable
prejudice, but the host and friend of many an Englishman who had been glad of an English welcome in
the Eternal City, and was ready to return his hos-
pitality. He arrived a trusted counsellor of Pope
Gregory, with friends and a good name already won
in many countries. The cosmopolitan character of his

antecedents was suggested in a German review of his
" Horæ Syriacæ," which polysyllabically described him
as an "in-Spain-born,-from-an-Irish-family-descended,-
in-England-educated,-in-Italy-residing, Syriac scholar."

And he arrived at a peculiar time. There were
special opportunities of winning a hearing; and yet
there were many rocks ahead. Two years earlier Dr.
Arnold had positively stated that no power on earth
could save the Established Church of England. Mr.
Mozley has said that " the Church of England was
folding its robes to die with what dignity it could."
Newman had started his movement at Oxford, and
was holding up the Catholic devotional ideals as the
one hope for the future of Anglicanism. " There is a
great progress of the religious mind," he wrote,[1] " to
something deeper and truer than satisfied the last
century, and most unhappily the one religious communion among us which has of late years been practically in possession of that something, is the Church of
Rome." He was urging the Church of England to
claim for itself many of those very ideals which the
Papists had so long maintained. Liberal thought,
again, was manifesting the kind of readiness to hear
all sides, to be just and fair to " Popery," as to all else,
which Sydney Smith, Macaulay, and Hallam in
different degrees represented. On all hands, from
Newman to Macaulay, from Cobbett to Arnold, the
Reformers were receiving scathing criticism. On the
other hand, the old English Catholics, whose turn had
at last come to claim that they had for centuries been
saying amid imprecations many things which their
countrymen were advancing as new discoveries, were
not in a position to take advantage of the situation.

---

[1] In his letter to Dr. Jelf on the occasion of Tract 90.

They were profoundly mistrustful of the Oxford school. O'Connell and the Puseyites interchanged civilities of a very peculiar nature, and, to put it plainly, detested each other. To the Liberals, on the other hand, the English Catholics were too grateful and obsequious ; and their joy at a contemptuous toleration on the ground that they were no more unorthodox than Unitarians, angered Newman, and for the moment lessened the dignity with which his imagination invested the old Church.

Wiseman's object was to fuse all these diverse elements—to utilise them in order to strengthen the alliances of the Catholics, and yet not to be carried away by them. He thus hoped to win serious and general consideration for the whole view of life which Catholicism represents.

He went to England on a visit in September, 1835, halting *en route* at Munich, and conferring with Möhler and Döllinger, halting, too, at Paris, where he saw Lacordaire, who was in the midst of his conferences at Notre Dame. From London he went to stay with leading English and Irish Catholics, beginning with Lord Shrewsbury at Alton Towers, with the object of arousing them to enterprise. His lectures at the Sardinian Chapel and at Moorfields were attended by crowds of all religions, and he appealed to the fairness and common sense of Liberal Englishmen in favour of the Catholic creed—Lord Brougham being one of his constant auditors. The lectures found their way to Oxford ; and Newman reviewed them in the *British Critic*. "We hear with great equanimity," he wrote, "of the impression Dr. Wiseman's lectures have made on the mixed multitude of London. Romanism has great truths in it which we of this day have almost forgotten, and its preachers will recall numbers of Churchmen and Dissenters to an acknowledgment of them." A controversy with Mr. Poynder in the same year (1836), in which Wiseman emphasised the appeal to fair play, and deprecated sectarian bitterness, had also (as Mr. Gladstone has said) a very marked effect on the English mind. Then, before returning to Rome, he persuaded O'Connell to join him in founding the *Dublin Review.* Thus in this reconnoitring visit of a year's duration he had taken the first step in securing sympathy with his views from English Catholics and from the mass of liberal opinion, from Puseyites and from Irish Catholics.

How from 1836 onwards his attention was more and more drawn to the Oxford Movement; how he followed its every stage in the *Dublin Review;* how his article in 1839, comparing the Donatists with the Puseyites, made Newman write that he had had " his first real hit from Romanism ;" how Wiseman removed from Rome to be President of Oscott in 1840, nominally as coadjutor-Bishop, but really to watch more closely the opening prospect, cannot be told here. At Oscott, with Pugin and Father Ignatius Spencer for fellow-workers, he developed the Catholic Liturgy, and aroused the zeal of the future priests. Then he dreamed the great dream of reunion between England and Rome, depicted in the letter which he wrote to Lord Shrewsbury after the appearance of Tract 90. His argument was—if (as all say) Newman really represents the genius of the movement, and if the movement represents the only possible future for the Established Church, then reunion should be a probability. The false premise was just what seemed the most incontrovertible, and its falsehood was no more than an ambiguity. Newman did in one sense represent the genius of the movement; the movement did represent the future of the Anglican Church; but that Newman's logical conclusion, opposed as it was to a mass of national prepossession, could be as effectually imparted to others as his spiritual enthusiasm, was too much to hope. What in 1841 was the most anxious and uncertain question, "Will Newman go over to Rome?" was ultimately answered in the affirmative; the question, "Will the corporate movement follow in Newman's steps?" has hitherto received an emphatic negative.

But when in October, 1845, Newman came over, and every day the news of a fresh secession followed, the very height of the unexpected appeared to have been attained. After such wonders, no wonder seemed too great to follow. The paradox before the average English mind of that date was tremendous. The man whom the rising generation regarded as the greatest spiritual genius in England had become one of the proscribed "papists." The national amazement and anger found vent five years later when Wiseman was made Cardinal-Archbishop of Westminster, and wrote his pastoral from the Flaminian Gate. For six months the Cardinal was constantly burnt in effigy all over the country.

The restoration of the hierarchy itself had been, as Mr. Gladstone pointed out in the House of Commons, desired by Pitt to lessen the influence of Rome on English Catholics. It was first proposed by the English Gallicans. And though this anti-Roman intention soon passed away, the plan had been steadily kept in sight ever since. It had already been mistakenly announced in the papers as an accomplished fact, without provoking any adverse comment. But, coming as it did in 1850, with the entry into England of a Roman Cardinal, and with Newman's secession still a recent memory—the "blow" from which, as Disraeli said, the Church of England "reeled"—it was a very different matter. Wounded feeling found vent in an agitation all the more extraordinary because it issued in absolutely nothing. The language used in public suggested all the hatred of Popery which had existed under Charles II.; the impotent issue showed that even since the Gordon riots a great modification of the old hostile feeling had really taken place. Parliament, the bench of Bishops, the crowds of the London streets, the mobs of the country towns, made or listened to violent speeches, blaspheming "Popery" and all its works; but when action was called for, it took many months to pass the Bill making the new titles illegal. And even this measure was reduced to almost nothing in Committee, and what was passed was never enforced. Lord John Russell had written to the Bishop of Durham at the outset a wildly alarmist letter; but he was so irresolute over his Bill that *Punch* sketched him as the boy who chalked up "No Popery" on the wall, and ran away. Lord Campbell, speaking on Lord Mayor's Day at the Mansion House, quoted, amid thunders of applause, the lines—

> " Under our feet we'll stamp thy Cardinal's hat,
>   In spite of Pope and dignities of Church,"

words for which, fifteen years later, his son made silent reparation at Wiseman's death, attending the requiem at Moorfields and the funeral at Kensal Green. Most remarkable of the demonstrations of

1850 were the remnants of the old " No Popery " phrases in the charges of the Anglican Bishops. " The slough of Romanism," " Rome clings to her abominations," " The sorcerer's cup," " Crafts of Satan," " England is defiled by her pollutions," " We are not so degenerate as to be beguiled by the snare which Rome's ever-wakeful ambition is plotting for our captivity and ruin,"—these are a few extracts from speeches of Archbishops and Bishops, referring largely to practices which are now widely prevalent in the Church of England itself.

Of the Ecclesiastical Titles Act, which was to express by decisive legislation the deep feelings of the nation, Döllinger wrote at the time : " It appears to me a very harmless thing, notwithstanding the big words in which it is couched,—in fact, to be meant only as a sop thrown to the Cerberus of public excitement. For, if I mistake not the meaning of phrases, the position and authority of the Bishops will be after the passing of the law precisely what it was before."

The most permanent consequences of the agitation were, perhaps, the delightful cartoons which *Punch* published with Cardinal Wiseman in some new character nearly every week, and *Punch's* legend of " The Decline and Fall of the British Empire," to be read by Macaulay's New Zealander, in which the conversion of England by St. Nicholas and "the prodigies he did work" are duly set forth. Dicky Doyle forthwith, in the anger of that time, resigned his connection with *Punch*. The skits can now be read by all the world with no feeling but that of amusement.

After the outbreak of '50 the rest of Wiseman's

life was spent in getting rid of the newly aroused prejudice, and in organising the newly formed body of English Catholics with its heterogeneous elements, —Oxford converts, hereditary Catholics, and the Irish element, which had so largely grown in England in the present century.

Of his work in restoring and making again familiar to Englishmen the monastic life, and forwarding such good works of the nuns as hospitals and orphanages, it is enough to say that in London alone in the year of Catholic emancipation there was but one convent; there were no monasteries, or Catholic hospitals or orphanages. In 1863—two years before Wiseman's death—there were fifteen monasteries, twenty-five convents, and thirty-four hospitals and orphanages. The numerous churches built and missions founded by him, the transformation in the lives of the clergy and in the devotion of the people which he effected are still remembered; but it would carry me into too lengthened detail as to the past, and too technical as to the present, to say more of this.

Perhaps a still greater work was involved in the persevering efforts whereby Wiseman lived down popular prejudice. How completely he did live it down was made evident by the general demonstration of sorrow at his funeral, which the *Times* compared to the feeling at the burial of the " great Duke." He disarmed prejudice largely by the width of his secular interests. He showed, again, his early taste for scholarship, litera-ture, and art; he evinced, as occasion offered, his philanthropic and national sympathies. From the day when, as the *Times'* report tells us, an un-precedented crowd assembled at the Society of Arts

to hear his lecture on the " Home Life of the Poor "
in 1854, to the last year of his life, when the Royal
Institution invited him to lecture on Shakespeare for
the tercentenary, he was constantly delivering what
are called unsectarian lectures.   They were delivered
in the great centres, London, Manchester, Leeds,
Liverpool, and elsewhere—in London chiefly at the
Royal Institution, the Society of Arts, the Royal
Society of Literature, the Marylebone Institute.
Some of the titles chosen will give an idea of his
subjects : " On the Way to Hang a National Portrait
Gallery," " An Account of Explorations made in
Sta. Sabina, Rome," " A Lecture on the Future
Historian's View of the Crimean War," " On the
Points of Contrast between Science and Art," " On
the Influence of Words on Civilisation," " On the
Prospects of Good Architecture in London."   He
would also, it is true, champion convents against the
Exeter Hall bigots, as he did at Bath in 1851 ;
or defend the Pope's political action, as in the
lectures on the Austrian *Concordat* of 1855.   But
in these more religious lectures he took the strong
position of being purely on the defensive.   He
carefully avoided the risk of once more wounding
English susceptibilities unless duty obliged.   " He
came in a storm," wrote a popular journal at his
death, " he passed away in quiet.   We do not say
that the manner of his coming was free from offence,
but once installed it cannot be denied that he so
demeaned himself as to discourage the revival of ill
feeling in the country.   Despite the strange blending
of nationalities represented in his parentage, birth,
and education, Cardinal Wiseman was essentially an
Englishman at heart.   He was indeed thoroughly a

man of the world, a courteous and polished gentleman
. . . an accomplished linguist. He was fond of
society, and made friends and intimates among
men of all parties and creeds. He loved art and
the elegant branches of literature. He represented
the Church . . . as she is when she mingles with
society. . . . Protestants, as well as Catholics,
can afford to bear to hear cordial testimony to the
great abilities, the varied acquirements, the high
character, and, where private intercourse was concerned, the entirely liberal sentiments of Cardinal
Wiseman."

The interest taken in the Cardinal at the time
of his death is now forgotten. The *Times*, his
first assailant in 1850, made ample amends to his
memory. "In learning, in ability, in piety," we
read in its obituary notice, "it will be long ere the
English Roman Catholic Hierarchy can expect again
to find the like of Nicholas, Cardinal Wiseman. . . .
His memory will be looked back on with feelings of
greater interest, and even admiration, than might have
been thought possible, from the part he took in
arousing one of the keenest religious discussions of
this generation."

And now I feel that this meagre summary of
Cardinal Wiseman's life-work gives really no idea of
the effect on his contemporaries of the personality
of the man. It is but the outline, which cannot give
the colouring of face and figure. It was in the
mixture of his gifts that lay alike his influence and
its limitations. The infectious energy and enthusiasm,
the vivid imagination and love of symbolism, which
were so stimulating and attractive, are not presented

in the summary of results. The simplicity which made his Vicar-General say that "he was a school-boy all his life;" the mystic sense of the symbolism of the Liturgy which made him say himself "a great function is to me like the Apocalypse;" his attractive, though sometimes trying, impulsiveness; the loving sympathy with distress which made Newman write [1] that his was "one of the tenderest hearts in the world;" the love of children, which made them idolise him—and many of us can recall Christmas presents chosen carefully to suit our taste; the hours given to writing plays for his children-friends and superintending their rehearsal; his enjoyment of fairy stories (sleepless nights were soothed by Kingsley's "Water-Babies");—these things were an inseparable part of the man. They showed him to be eminently human. And, on the other hand, he never ceased, in spite of constant ill health, from unresting, manifold, and energetic work,—preaching, writing, lecturing, and directing the labours of others.

Let us glance, almost at haphazard, at some of the traits noted by those who knew him. He loved a progress in mediæval state, as when he reached Douay, *en route* for Rome in 1859, posting with four carriages, containing chaplains, doctors, librarian, and servants as well as a brother Bishop: and yet the overawed Douay monks were astonished when they found that his greatest pleasure there was talking to the school-boys and securing treats and holidays for them. He preached at the London Oratory with the intention of giving the Oratorians a grave warning against foreign practices of devotion, which were unsuitable for England, and changed his mind in the

---

[1] In a letter to Wiseman in the year 1855.

middle of the sermon—delighted at the perfection of ritual and music—and burst into an unmixed panegyric. He sketched out able and splendid designs for St. Chad's Cathedral, Birmingham, and was disappointed at finding that the architect did not mean to pay for their execution. His private journals reveal a spiritual ideal worthy of St. Ignatius, and systematic endeavours to lead a life of self-denial; but he hated pretension and the unnecessary parade of good actions; and it was only an accident in 1839 which made his pupils in Rome aware that he had long been in the habit of secretly visiting the poor late at night. When entertaining guests he was careful to keep the table of a Roman Cardinal, and surprised his Puseyite friends by four courses of fish on a Friday, which they kept at Oxford on herbs and bread and water. One of the Puseyite wits remarked that the Cardinal had a "lobster salad side," as well as a "spiritual side." He was an accomplished linguist. "He can speak with readiness and point," writes Cardinal Newman, "in half a dozen languages without being detected for a foreigner in any of them, and at ten minutes' notice can address a congregation from a French pulpit or the select audience of an Italian Academy." [1] He made great plans,—as for other things, so for Newman's work as a Catholic. Newman was given every help in founding his Oratory; to Wiseman it was largely due that he was named Rector of the Irish Catholic University; but much more was promised, and never carried out. Newman was to be a Bishop, to enable him to hold his own with the Irish Bishops. He never was a Bishop. He was to translate the Scriptures; the plan fell through.

[1] "Historical Sketches," iii. p. 256.

He was to lecture on Dr. Achilli in 1851 without fear, as Wiseman had documentary evidence of the charges against Achilli. Achilli sued Newman for libel, and the Cardinal could not find the documents. Such traits and incidents fill in some of the outline. An engaging and attractive fancy—as the author of "Fabiola" must have had,—an untiring zeal on behalf of a great cause, wide plans, quick perception of the lie of the land, great energy, varied personal accomplishments, a knowledge of detail on many subjects, were accompanied by an evanescence of impulse, and the absence often of power to accomplish. He could carry through a great effort, as he rose to the occasion at the "papal aggression," writing his impressive "Appeal" to the English people amid constant interruptions and with scarcely a single erasure ; but long - sustained labour was uncongenial to him. He could found a hierarchy and the whole polity it entailed, writing nearly every word of its constitution in the first Oscott Synod in 1852 ; and yet the financial difficulties which followed were never resolved or even fairly faced in his time. "Thou couldst a people raise, but couldst not rule."

Of the vigour and versatility which Wiseman did show in his active work, I will cite the verdict of one who was little given to hyperbole. Cardinal Newman, referring to the volume of speeches delivered by Wiseman during his journey through Ireland in 1858, wrote in the *Rambler* as follows :—

"The facts of the case are these : Cardinal Wiseman, complying with the invitation of an Irish Prelate, who requested his presence at the opening of a new church, went at the appointed time, without expectation of any call upon him for more than such ordinary exertion of mind and body

as the ostensible purpose involved ; but to his great astonishment, he found that his coming had struck a chord in the
heart of a Catholic people, whose feelings are the more keen
and delicate, because they are seldom brought into play. A
Cardinal of Holy Church was to them representative of the
Vicar of Christ, and nothing else ; his coming was all but the
advent of the Holy Father ; and he suddenly found that he
must meet, out of the resources of his individual mind, the
enthusiastic feelings and the acts of homage of the millions
who were welcoming him. It was an expression of trust
and loyalty manifested towards him, similar in its critical
character, though most dissimilar in its origin, to the panic
fear which, from time to time, spreading through the multitude, causes them to make a sudden run on some great
banking establishment which is reported to be in difficulties ;
and, however gratifying, both officially and personally, to
the high dignitary who called it forth, it would have been to
most men the occasion of no ordinary embarrassment.

"We venture to affirm that there is no other public man
in England who could have answered to the demand thus
made upon his stores of mind with the spirit and the
intellectual power which the Cardinal displayed on the
occasion. He was carried about, at the will of others, from
one part of the island to another ; he found himself surrounded in turn by high and low, educated and illiterate ; by
boys at school, or by the youth of towns ; by religious communities, or by official and dignified persons. He was called
to address each class or description of men in matter and
manner suitable to its own standard of taste and thought ;
he had to appear in pulpits, in lecture-rooms, at dinner-
tables, on railroad-stations, and always to say something
new, apposite, and effective. How he met these unexpected
and multifarious calls on him, this volume is the record ; and
though nothing remained of Cardinal Wiseman for the
admiration of posterity of all that he has spoken and written
but what is therein contained, there is enough to justify the
estimation in which his contemporaries have held the talents
and the attainments of the first Archbishop of Westminster."

One further point must be considered. I have

spoken of a definite work done by Cardinal Wiseman, and yet if we look at the scattered records of his life-work and at the impression formed of him by contemporaries, his career seems to be one of the most manifold and diverse activity, at first sight almost suggestive of the *dilettante.*

Browning sketched him in "Bishop Blougram," and apart from the fancy picture of Blougram's faith and doubt, we see the impression made on the Cardinal's contemporaries of the hospitable and somewhat magnificent entertainer who appreciates the dignity of the Prelate and loves the society of "Gigadibs," the literary man ; the antiquarian student who writes disquisitions on "the fictile vase." A chapter in Wiseman's life of great interest is his intimacy with Abbate Gioberti, the author of the bold scheme for placing the Pope at the head of the national movement in Italy. "Adventurous pilgrim of Liberty," writes Montanelli the republican, "he advanced to plant the tricolour on the Church of St. Peter." In this movement Wiseman was deeply interested; and when Pius IX. appeared to be making some attempt at its realisation in 1847 (an attempt which became more definite when Rosmini came to Rome in the following year), Wiseman was sent as unofficial envoy to the English Government, to gain English support against reactionaries and Austrians, who disapproved of a Liberal Pope. Lord Minto's mission was the result, which obviated the immediate danger from the Austrians, though it helped eventually to press on the Liberal movement beyond papal control. Again, in 1862, we find Wiseman at the Tuileries, on an informal embassy from Pius IX. to Napoleon. We have already seen how large a share in his early life was occupied by the special studies of a Syriac and Arabic scholar. One of the most popular works of religious fiction of the century, " Fabiola," was from his pen—" a good book," said the Archbishop of Milan, "with the success of a bad one. Translations of it were made into nearly every European language, and at least in Germany, Italy, and France its popularity continues to the present time. The establishment of the penny post greatly occupied Wiseman, and, at Sir Rowland Hill's request, he submitted to the Metropolitan Board of Works a memorandum of suggestions on the new postal arrangements. The Arctic Expedition of 1851 was another matter in which Wiseman took a lively interest, and he corresponded with some of the explorers. During his last two years he was greatly taken up with the study of the works of Darwin and Huxley, in which he was first led to take an interest by his friend, Professor Owen. One of his lectures— delivered in Ireland in 1858—contains an anticipation of Huxley's distinction between the "cosmic" process and the "ethical" process in evolution. Among guests at his house in York Place were such different persons as Charles Dickens, Mr. Stanfield the marine painter, Charles Kean the actor, besides French and German ecclesiastics such as the Bishops of Münster, Bayeux, Perpignan, and Amiens. " He was an all-round man," writes the late Lord Acton,[1] of the impression he made earlier at Oscott, "and we did not clearly see his drift." And yet there remained with his intimate friends a strong sense of the unity of his work and purpose, of devotion to one cause as the mainspring of his life, which entirely prevented any suspicion of *dilettanteism* among those who knew him.

---

[1] In a letter to myself.

The key to this apparent contradiction is, I think, found in a saying of Father Whitty, his friend, and for many years his Vicar-General, in a letter to Henry Edward Manning, written just after Wiseman's death. The cause of Wiseman's influence did not lie, he said, only in his talents and acquirements, considerable as they were, but in his being a faithful representative of the Catholic Church—*not*, he adds, as a saint represents her, solely on the ethical side, but as a national poet represents the all-round genius of a particular country in his various poems.

Cardinal Wiseman has himself pointed out, in his inaugural lecture at the opening of the Catholic Academia in 1861, his ideal of the Church in its relations with the world. While he resolutely maintained that, whether triumphant or depressed, in the Lateran Basilica or in the Catacombs, the Church has the great ethical ideals of the Gospel to teach, that these have been securely preserved only where the primitive traditions have been jealously guarded and handed down, and that if the world despises them so much the worse for the world; while he insisted that the saints were the seers and witnesses to the possibility and the value of the highest life; while in this sphere he held that whether men of intellect laughed with Voltaire or bent in reverence with Pascal, the Church was a *teacher*,—he was equally emphatic that in the sphere of scholarship, art, and secular civilisation, Catholics must be largely learners, and adapt themselves to the genius of the age or country in which their lot is cast. And in this spirit he urged them to be strangers to no phase of secular interest. He compared the Church to a large surface of wax, which, while remaining the same, receives the impress of the various phases of civilisation with which it comes in contact. And by another metaphor he pointed out that the Church cannot expect to be the source of the varied energy of the community ; all she can do is to turn it in the direction of those high ideals, of which she is the guardian, or in a direction which bodes no harm to those ideals, as the signalman does not give the force to the train, but only modifies its line of movement.

This, I think, gives the true meaning of Wiseman's very various lines of interest. He strove, partly unconsciously, to realise his ideal of the Church in contact with human activity. He wished to learn from the best artists and scholars of his time ; he was ready to take his place in all works of importance to the commonwealth. Like Richelieu, he was prepared to negotiate with Princes and to found an academy. The ideal Churchman should, he thought, be ready to work in every sphere, but not, in secular departments, in order to secure the domination of the Church, but to show only that the Church is not alien from any human interest, and that the priest can give and take, or if necessary learn from others in secular matters if he claims to teach in religion. In a touching letter before Newman's conversion, he shows this wish to learn where he feels himself in the presence of superior intellectual gifts, and declares that if ever the Oxford men should come, it will be fitting that they should take the lead ; that he himself will willingly work under a new leader. When delivering his lectures from 1854 to 1864 he repeatedly affirmed that his wish was to show the world that a Churchman can share all human interests ; that he can put off the cassock and mix freely with

representatives of art, science, or social life as one
of themselves.

In this, perhaps, he differed, partly in view, partly
in temperament, from his illustrious successor in the
early years of his rule, though the difference is less if we
consider Cardinal Manning's later career. Manning,
too, had a wide conception of his sphere of action as
representing the Church, but it was as ruler, guide,
originator. Wiseman wished to liberate the activities
of others, to set specialists at work, to learn from
them, to make them unite to achieve results for the
commonwealth. Manning no doubt tended rather to
direct personally all he undertook. To many he
appeared to mistrust activities which he could not
himself control. Thus while Wiseman was at first
eager that Catholics should gain the intellectual advantages of Oxford and Cambridge, Manning preferred
a Catholic University College in London with fifteen
students under his own eye and command. While
Wiseman, in his letter to Lord Shrewsbury, suggested
almost impossible concessions in order to encourage
the Anglican movement towards reunion, Manning
wished to check it by a clear Roman decision on the
mooted questions, preferring, as he said, a few immediate submissions to Rome to the larger but indefinite
movement which he could not guide. While Manning
sympathised in some degree with those who saw in
Montalembert's policy in 1862 a dangerous liberalism
against which the Holy See should be on its guard,
Wiseman wrote of it generously as of a view which
should be given fair play, urged as it was by one of
Montalembert's splendid loyalty to the Papacy.

Such contrasts are never absolute. But in some
degree these opposite tendencies were widely

recognised. It may, perhaps, be said that Manning loved the strict military discipline of a Church under fire; Wiseman's ideal was the genial and many-sided life of the Church at peace.

Broadly speaking, Wiseman was true to the ideals of his youth. When, as young men, he and Döllinger and Möhler and Montalembert and Lacordaire were first fired with the idea of a religious revival, there were two watchwords : " Freedom " as against Gallican tyranny; and " The Papacy " as the protector of religious freedom. The great ideal was that the aspiration for freedom, which is the genius of the nineteenth century, should be satisfied by the Church ; and that the Church should fuse with and purify modern civilisation.

But another ideal came athwart this. The age did not seem tractable. It was not disposed to fuse with the Church. Pius IX. tried to guide the Liberal movement, and failed. Lamennais had broken with the Papacy. Lacordaire found that a Catholic priest could not sit on the left of the French Assembly. A little later Froschammer's philosophy showed the obstinacy of intellectual freedom. The conception of freedom under the Ultramontane banner, and of fusion with modern civilisation, gave place to the antithesis between Ultramontanism and Liberalism.

The term "Liberal Catholic" became one of re-proach. The Church authorities retired behind the trenches, and ruled their own with a firm hand, lest all should be lost. The forces outside were alien or hostile, and were to be neglected or opposed. This phase was brought to an acute crisis by the attack of Victor Emmanuel on the Papal States, and by Napoleon's desertion of the papal cause. The great Powers, which had intervened with one accord in 1849, now stood aloof. As appeal after appeal proved useless, Pius IX. took up the position that Christendom had apostatised. The appropriate action of Catholics was intense loyalty to the central power, unity among themselves, and separation from the outside world. Such an attitude was the natural response to the Syllabus and Encyclical of 1864. And it was taken up by an influential section in France, in England, in Italy, and elsewhere.

It was the attitude of Cardinal Manning in the first years of his reign. It could never have been congenial to Wiseman. *Felix opportunitate mortis*, he died a few months after the appearance of the Syllabus. To the last, although, broken in health, in individual acts he failed to carry out his own earlier impulses, and followed the counsel of Manning in the matter of the English Universities, and of the reunion movement, his double devotion to the Papacy and to the ideal of a Church energising with various activity in harmony with the civilisation of the hour, remained theoretically unchanged. He could not see that in Europe at large it had been for the time defeated.

Since Cardinal Wiseman's time we have witnessed several transformations. There have been the Catholic revival in France after the war of 1870 : the subsequent irreligious movement and the Ferry laws ; later on the "esprit nouveau," represented by M. Spüller and M. Brunetière, which valued the Papacy, and the organisation of the Church as guardians of order and a protection against Anarchism and extreme Socialism. We have had the Kulturkampf in Germany, and its failure. We have now the violent anti-clericalism of M. Combes. We have had the fall of the Pope's civil sovereignty, and the new influence of the Papacy under Leo XIII. There still remain competing the two conceptions of the suitable action of the Catholic Church,—that Catholics should blend with the rest of the world, learn from it, and by this means become fitted to have their due influence on it; or, on the other hand, that they should form an army apart, with modes of thought and a language of their own.

And to conclude with the question which I raised at starting, it seems plain that, whichever of these two programmes is ultimately found to be best suited to the times which are to come, the exclusive programme can only be a painful necessity and the confession of defeat. If the increased interest in Catholic ideals— so far as there is interest in religion at all—is to benefit the organisation of the Church, Cardinal Wiseman's conception of the Church, touching and being touched by surrounding civilisation, must first be realised. If the organisation and the intellectual and ethical movement are not allowed to touch each other, we shall have many such as Augustus Schlegel and Novalis, and few Frederick Schlegels and Stolbergs.

XI.

THE LIFE OF MRS. AUGUSTUS CRAVEN.

IN spite of the vast amount of biographical literature which crowds our circulating libraries, it still remains true that really good biographies are welcome from their rarity. A large proportion of memoirs are written either by or about dull men and women. A man who is distinguished in public life dies; and forthwith we have memorials of him by surviving friends or relations. They forget Dr. Johnson's remark, " It is wonderful, sir, with how little real superiority of mind a man can make an eminent figure in public life." The letters of the person commemorated form the staple of the book, and they naturally prove dull. The incidents of such lives are mainly those belonging to official routine. The residuum, which may be a contribution to the political or diplomatic history of the day, and ought to be interesting if well told in a brief volume, loses all power of arresting attention if distributed through a lengthy series of heavily written letters. The most interesting events and figures become insipid if looked at through the medium of a dull mind ; and the letters of men of real practical ability, if that ability be unaccompanied by the gifts of insight and expression, may be as dull as those of simply stupid people. The special qualities to which a successful career has been due, and the really instructive features of the personality, which are seldom wholly wanting, need to be recorded by an onlooker who has had both exceptional insight and exceptional opportunities for observation ; and such a biographer is in most cases not to be found. Thus even great men may cease to live, until a Carlyle or a Walter Scott arises to breathe life into the scattered memorials. And those lesser public men whose gifts are practical rather than mental, remain for future generations even duller than they were in real life.

In ordinary cases, then, the only absolute security for a readable biography, even where the record touches public events and persons of great importance, lies in the endowment of its subject with remarkable powers of observation and expression.

If it were only for her possession of these powers in a high degree, and for her opportunities of exercising them on men and things of wide interest in the course of a long life of eighty-two years, the "Memoir of Mrs. Augustus Craven"[1] would be well worth reading. The daughter of a distinguished French Ambassador, the Marquis de La Ferronnays ; connected by ties of relationship and intimate friendship with many of the most prominent of the French and Italian great families; intimate with Montalembert, Ravignan, Cochin, Gerbet, Dupanloup; married to an English diplomatist; in frequent contact during many years with such English families as the Palmerstons and the Granvilles, and a constant guest at Holland House;

[1] "A Memoir of Mrs. Augustus Craven, with Extracts from her Diaries and Correspondence," by Maria Catherine Bishop. (London, 1894.)

seeing at different times the best life that was to be seen at Rome, Paris, and London, Mrs. Craven had opportunities as extensive and varied as her powers of turning them to the best account were exceptional. Her impressions of the world with which she came in contact partook of the character of the three nationalities to which she in some sense belonged. They give evidence of an artistic temperament which is almost Italian; her letters and journals are French in their *esprit*, candour, sense of the dramatic, and perspicuity of expression; yet her judgments are neither impulsive nor idealistic, but are marked before all things by sound English common sense, often accompanied by a touch of English humour. There are to be found in her journals and correspondence some records of her intercourse with Englishmen of whom we are always glad to hear. We have a masculine and very definite, though limited, estimate of Lord Palmerston. Her impressions of Mr. Gladstone vary to some extent, but gradually converge to a decisive condemnation both of his aims and of his methods. She was keenly appreciative of his personal charm, and of what has been called his "intellectual effervescence;" sensitive, likewise, like a true Frenchwoman, to the full effect of his earnest rhetoric. Yet she seems gradually to have realised, more and more, that his genius for making the worse cause appear the better, to himself as well as to others, not only led him astray, but had a disastrous effect on the national mind. Her opposition to his Irish policy came to be the absorbing feeling of her later years. He professed to defend Ireland from her "mortal foes;" he was himself, she said, her "mortal friend."

Mr. John Morley, whose acquaintance she made

at Sir Mountstuart Grant-Duff's house, comes in for a page of acute criticism ; Mr. Bright for a shorter panegyric. "He is to me," she writes, "the very personification of good sense, firmness, and honesty. These used to be rather common traits of the English character ; but Mr. Gladstone has done much to obliterate them." General Gordon seizes her imagination and holds it captive. " I believe in Gordon with the most undoubting faith," she writes ; but she adds, in frankness, " I can well understand [however], that for practical English statesmen (like Lord Granville) it must be difficult to put entire confidence in one who looks for guidance in political and military affairs to the Book of Isaiah."

These and many other prominent Englishmen pass across the scene. And we have descriptions of political and religious crises—as, for example, of the various stages in the unification of Italy, of the Irish Home Rule Bill of 1886, of the Vatican Council—all marked by the same emotional sensitiveness to all the characters and features in the drama, and the same strong sobriety of judgment as to the practical outlook.

Such characteristics are enough by themselves to make these Memoirs a readable book,—the record of the impressions left by noteworthy events and persons on one of whom M. Taine remarked, "Elle est la femme la plus spirituelle que j'ai jamais vu." But it is something more than this. "C'est par l'esprit," Madame Swetchine has said, "que l'on s'amuse ; c'est par le cœur qu'on ne s'ennuie pas." The saying is true of a book also. Something more than brilliancy is needed in it to give its reader the sense of permanent satisfaction as distinct from passing amusement ; and Mrs. Craven's Life has that "something." Readers

of her beautiful work, "Le Récit d'une Sœur," will
look in the biography of its editor and part-author for
certain characteristics very distinct from that *esprit*
which fascinated M. Taine when he met her; and
they will not be disappointed. This clever Frenchwoman, so shrewd in her judgments of men and things,
so capable of political enthusiasm, so sensitive to all
the pleasures of art and of intellect, an excellent
amateur actress, and for years delighting, apparently,
in the whirl of social amusements, was living throughout a deep inner life of the mind and the affections,
which she describes with the same vividness, the
same realism, the same intense eagerness, and the
same strong practical and unsentimental judgment
as to its import and true direction, with which she
chronicles her impressions of Mr. Gladstone or her
views of the Italian revolution. The work before us
is indeed a combination of a volume of social and
political " Reminiscences " and diaries, with a *journal
intime*. This latter aspect occupies a comparatively
small space; but to many the pages devoted to it will
be the most interesting ; and they reveal a personality
which adds greatly to the interest of the purely secular
portion of the work. Mrs. Craven was powerfully
affected by the wave of religious reaction which took
its rise in France after the Revolution, and grew in
the middle of the century to be so great a power. It
was the vividness of her faith in God, the firmness
of her belief that religion was the one hope for the
stability of civil society, which gave her much of her
eagerness and zest, even in matters political and
social. It gave a greatness of scale to the drama of
contemporary history as it passed before her. So
critical a mind might without it have tended, perhaps,

to cynicism and pessimism, and to what Mill has called "the disastrous feeling of 'not worth while.'" Her faith in religion made her, on the contrary, earnest and hopeful. It made her view public life, not as do so many of the unconscious sceptics of our own generation, as a source of pleasurable excitement or an avenue to success, but as something involving sacred and far-reaching issues, as a great battle of various forces, one of which was the Christian Church, whose very presence in the strife was a reminder that the cause of right and truth was at stake. Thus it was in the religious issues, involved in so many of the political struggles of her time, that her deepest interest centred. Hence her passionate delight in the victories of the Church over the hearts of men in infidel France, which she witnessed in the conferences of Lacordaire and Ravignan, and her passionate regret when the clergy in Ireland or in Italy took a line which she held to be in one case unprincipled, in the other retrograde and narrow—a deeper regret than the persecutions of Paul Bert aroused, because the cause of the Church was in her eyes more seriously injured by the errors of its own ministers than by the attacks of its enemies.

Let it be added that the reality of feeling which made the fortunes of the ecclesiastical world so vital to her, likewise kept her free from the slightest touch of what is invidiously known as professional clericalism. We see this throughout her correspondence and her journal. She is as sensitive to the faults of Churchmen as she is impressed by the genius of Christianity. And the peculiarities typical of a religious caste or sect are foreign to her whole conception of the Church Universal. Her letters on secular subjects are entirely free from "religiosity;" although we see throughout them a nature for which the claims of religion are paramount. There is no anxiety to introduce a moral in and out of season, or to speak for edification. Unreality was her *bête noire*, and even the Puseyites, in whom she naturally took a deep interest, came in for a share of criticism, from a tendency which she thought she saw in them to avoid looking frankly in the face the special characteristics of their position, and to use Catholic language without realising its import or submitting to Catholic authority. "In her many-sidedness," wrote a shrewd observer, one who differed from her both in politics and in religion, "she threw her soul into all she had to do, whether politics, religion, or social life;" and thus, while we have pages on the love of God and the spiritual life which might have come from Fénelon or St. Francis of Sales, her appreciations of social and political life are as free and natural and untrammelled by theological bias as those of Lord Macaulay or Mr. Greville. The Church indeed, as a power in society and in politics, is something to her which it is not to them; but she is able to measure men and things by the standard to which the man of the world appeals, while she neither suppresses her own conviction that there is a higher and more spiritual standard, nor obtrudes it out of place or season.

In attempting to place before my readers this personality with its two aspects,—that of the *femme du monde* and that of the Catholic *dévote*,—both so intimately part of herself and yet so distinct from one another, I shall touch first on the more external and superficial side, although this is more fully represented in the later than in the earlier part of the Memoir. I

may cite, to begin with, some of her estimates already
referred to of English persons and things of political
prominence. Here is an account of Lord Palmerston
after a visit to Broadlands in the sixties :—

"Lord Palmerston has been extremely kind and cordial
to us during this visit. I have talked with him very often,
and always found him the same—that is, quite other than
his reputation. I should be almost tempted to say, above it;
but he seems unlike it rather than unequal to it.

"He is not a great party leader, as his friends represent
him to be, and as the position he holds would indicate ;
neither is he the evil genius which the greater part of Europe
will have him to be. In fact, he is in no way a genius, and
he is nothing great. His nearest approach to greatness is in
his imperturbable good temper, which remains unshadowed
whether he is in or out of office, beaten or triumphant, violently
attacked or unduly praised. He is always the same, always
ready to do justice to his adversaries, never embittered against
them, never even impatient. In 1852 I was at Broadlands at
the time when he resigned office under Lord John Russell's
Government. I saw no traces of resentment in him : he did
not say a word of recrimination or bitterness, nor did he
assume affected moderation. The only perceptible difference
appeared in a greater elasticity of spirits in his conversation.
He was less reserved and more playful, and gave more time
to society."

More noteworthy is the judgment of a cosmopolitan
like Mrs. Craven, as to the sources of Palmerston's
unpopularity on the Continent, and of the mistakes in
his foreign policy, which the march of events is now
bringing home to an increasing number of his own
countrymen. Mr. Bagehot, many years ago, maintained that Palmerston's genius lay in his retentiveness
of the lessons of experience ; his weakness in his
inability to reason in the abstract or to form correct
conclusions outside the sphere of his personal observation. The innumerable cases in which he could bring

forward his " I knew a man who," etc., and cover the
facts of the case by a precedent, gave him a great
hold on the people of England, the land of his experiences; but when he touched on Continental matters
this intimate personal knowledge was no longer there
to guide him.   Consequently he blundered often and
seriously.   Somewhat similar is the verdict of Mrs.
Craven :—

" He is," she writes, " in England, generally master of his
hearers, because he knows them so well, while his ignorance
about foreigners is extreme, and his tolerant spirit towards
his fellow-countrymen becomes coloured by the strangest
prejudices when he has to do with other people.   That
explains some of his mistakes and the dislike felt for him
outside his own country; and yet this dislike is unjust.
Notwithstanding his misconceptions, nothing is less true
than that he has the wish attributed to him to revolutionise
Europe for the benefit of England.   He loves justice as
sincerely as he hates oppression.   He thinks it is for the
interest of all nations that they should be governed as well
as possible.   He has the right to think that the political
experiences of his country have been fortunate, but he is
wrong not to see that elsewhere the risks of English methods
might be greater than their advantages, and that though it
is easy to mimic English institutions it is not easy to imitate
them."

The misconception of Continental politics here
attributed to Palmerston was, in Mrs. Craven's
opinion, common among English Liberals.   This
view—less evident in the early days of her Italian
enthusiasms—gained ground with her in later life.
Forces which on the Continent were really tending
towards a practical atheism, destructive of public
order, were often regarded with genial approval by
those whose estimate of practical results was due to

experience of the slow-moving English temperament. Liberalism was supposed by Englishmen to be naturally allied with liberality rather than with licence. The shortsightedness of this view, as applied to Continental politics, once it became apparent to Mrs. Craven, was insisted on by her strongly. Thus, when her friend Mr. Grant-Duff met Gambetta on friendly terms, she openly expressed her opinion that he did not really know what tendencies he was encouraging. "I object," she wrote, "to a man like Mr. Grant-Duff —an advanced Liberal, certainly, but a gentleman, utterly incapable of tampering with such social doctrines as are . . . those of Gambetta's party—I object to such a man conversing with him as if they belonged to *à peu près* the same camp."

And similarly, when she met Mr. John Morley at Mr. Grant-Duff's house, she felt that, in his views of the revolutionary party in France, he was dealing with his own ideas and not with facts.

"Mr. Morley, the celebrated writer, one of the notable men of the advanced party, was there. He is agreeable and unaffected. He converses well and knows everything, or nearly everything. Like all ultra-Liberals, he is mistakenly *Francomane*, and he judges his favourite eighteenth century, with which he is in love, as I think, very incorrectly. I could measure the distance between our ways of thinking when since our meeting I read his volume on Burke. His style as such is almost equal to that of Burke himself. He is, for the most part, just in his appreciation of that great man's talent and personality, and he rises to the height of the noble character he describes. But when he comes to the point in which Burke so shines by his clear foresight,—his judgment on the French Revolution,—all changes, and the writer takes the colour of that system which governs Liberal free-thinkers, of whom he is one. The crimes of the Revolution are represented as momentary exasperations of sentiments in themselves just. Burke's previsions, which received such terrible confirmation, are but the exaggerations of his party spirit, etc. In England there is in Radicalism and Atheism a certain good faith, which makes their professors, if not less dangerous, less odious than elsewhere, because they are not possessed, as in other countries, by special hatred of Catholicism. Their indignation against the persecution of Catholics equals our own ; and on that subject John Morley is nobly eloquent."

By far the most characteristic, however, of Mrs. Craven's political estimates are those relating to Mr. Gladstone and the Irish crisis. And these are given in her letters to English friends, which, although written in English—a language in which to the end she did not habitually think—are certainly such as to deserve a place of their own as specimens of that class of literature. An old woman of seventy-eight when the Home Rule Bill was brought in in 1886, not a resident in England, but only an occasional visitor, her intense eagerness and public spirit on this subject are indeed noteworthy. It must be remembered that she had already met Mr. Gladstone on several occasions and had been attracted by him, although she did not fail to see in his temperament something which did not inspire confidence. These earlier meetings are recorded in her letters, and are very characteristic. She sits next to him in July, 1881, at a dinner-party at Holland House, and thus chronicles the impression left upon her—

"He was most pleasant, talkative, brilliant, eager, full of poetry and earnestness, and yet, to my mind, how visionary on some points, and how unpractical ! We talked of everything, and it certainly was most interesting. One thing he said with an energy which added to the feeling he expressed, that the growth of infidelity was the one evil to be resisted

before all others, and that whoever served the cause of Faith
and Christianity was doing the greatest of all the deeds
to be done. 'In comparison with that, nothing whatever
signifies much in this world.' I said it was a good thing for
England that her Prime Minister should utter such words."

She meets him again at Lord Lyons's house in Paris,
in 1883.

"I found him in good health and spirits, pleasant as ever,
and altogether very much like himself. What is particularly
like him is this: after dinner we had a long conversation on
those subjects (not political) in which he is ever the most
interested, during which an article I have just published
in the *Correspondant* (on the Salvation Army) was mentioned, and he expressed a wish to read it. He was
leaving for London the next morning (Friday), so I sent it
him at once; and—would you believe it?—in the midst of
the ocean of work into which he must have had to plunge on
his return to town, he found time to write me a long and
interesting letter about that article, which reached me here
on the Sunday morning."

From the moment when the Tory Government
went out in February, 1886, Mrs. Craven's letters are
full of the Irish crisis. "What is to happen now?"
she writes. "The whole game is in the hands of
Parnell." She saw in an instant the full significance
of Mr. Gladstone's attitude. On February 16th she
writes as follows from London to Mr. Grant-Duff,
who was living in India, being at the time Governor
of Madras :—

"You must wonder indeed at what is going on here, and
Mr. Gladstone is, I hope, as great a puzzle and a trial to you
as he is to us. I doubt of your approving the nomination of
your friend Mr. J. Morley, and altogether England never was
in such a position; at all events not since I have belonged
to it. The hesitation and vacillation of the Liberals, the

dreamy nonsense they talk in the presence of an organized conspiracy like that of the National League, is perfectly astounding. . . . I often keep wondering what other proof of weakness and imbecility we are to expect from that dear old foolish great man who is now (even now) asking people to tell him what is going on in Ireland. I hope I am not hurting your feelings. Mine are, I own it, much roused, and it is as well that I should go away. I leave England on the 23rd."

A month later she continues the subject.

"When one sees Englishmen rushing to the support of such Irishmen as are the leaders of this movement, it seems as if a spell had fallen on the two countries to work the destruction of both. . . . How any gentleman, how any statesman, can be found to treat seriously with such men as Parnell, seconded by Biggar, Healy and Co., after reading their Irish speeches, is just one of those incomprehensible things only to be explained by the spell I speak of. When a French Republican wrote, 'Fusillez-moi tous ces gens-là,' even French Republicans felt ashamed of him; but Mr. Biggar says, 'I don't *advise* you to shoot your landlords; in the first place, because you often miss them, and kill other people instead of them;' and Mr. Gladstone thinks it not unworthy of the policy of England to attempt to satisfy the man of whom Biggar is but the *alter ego.*"

Mrs. Craven characterises Mr. Gladstone's policy of granting Home Rule because it is inevitable, as "the policy known in France as that of *Gribouille*, who, because it was raining, *s'est jeté a l'eau pour ne pas être mouillé.*"

Gladstone's great speech in April, 1886, is described with a keen sense both of its power and of its evil effects—

"Our 'sometime friend' has now spoken his best and said his worst. The words can no longer be recalled; his splendid and fatal eloquence has not failed him. There they are—the 27,000 of them, already under your eyes, at this moment probably, and giving you, I dare say, much my own feeling of present and future certain mischief as their result. It is an astounding speech in its beauty and in its folly. However, I again say, it can't be recalled, and who can foresee what will happen? There is danger in rejecting these insane measures, almost as great as in passing them. Anarchy and civil war on one side, dynamite on the other, bloodshed anyhow. It is certainly not a cheering prospect."

A month later she writes—

"It really looks as if Lord Hartington and Mr. Chamberlain had flung themselves efficiently at the heads of the runaway horses which Mr. Gladstone was whipping so furiously down-hill. If so, it is a brave and useful act of strength and courage."

The news of the rejection of the Bill came to her while, by a coincidence, Lord Granville's brother-in-law, Mr. Fullerton, was staying in Paris and seeing her constantly. Her intense exultation, which she longed to express to every Englishman she saw, had to be kept within the bounds which civility pre-scribed. The situation touched her sense of humour. She writes, however, to her friend (afterwards her biographer) Mrs. Bishop with ecstatic delight of the " great event," and adds—

"Think of my lips being absolutely closed on the subject at such a moment as this. But Mr. Fullerton is still my daily guest, and we get on amicably and comfortably, but on condition that Irish politics are never to be mentioned. I could not help, however, saying (with great composure), 'The Bill is rejected, and by a large majority.' He said, 'Yes, indeed, and it is an awful calamity; we are now plunged into revolution.' To this I replied, that 'if the Bill had passed, that would have happened still more surely, I thought.' He then said, 'Don't you remember Lord Beaconsfield's answering the Irish Bishops in a very insolent manner?' . . . I dropped the subject in a hurry."

A racy letter to Mrs. Bishop in July expresses on the whole a hopeful view as to the future, and she can still afford to see the humorous side of things. Mr. Gladstone's intensely earnest explorations of the history of Irish wrongs, and his discovery that Cromwell had once been to Ireland, delighted her.

"It looks as if really 'the harp was not to be uncrowned,' nor 'the Shamrock parted from the Rose,' and so far hurrah. But I don't feel easy at all yet, unless dear Mrs. La Touche is also quite right in thinking that the Irish themselves wish to be 'aisy,' and have had enough of all this fatiguing agitation. If not, if in that way they are indefatigable and insatiable, I am afraid that Mr. Gladstone . . . will still have it in his power to do us a great deal of harm, except that in his fury he oversteps the mark, and people may realize more and more that he is not a safe man to have at the helm in stormy weather. Have you read his letter to G. Leveson? It looks as if he had never read till quite lately anything about Ireland, and reminds me of the Bishop of Orleans [Dupanloup], who all of a sudden, not many years before his death, discovered the frightful ill-usage to which Marie Antoinette had been subjected, and astonished everybody by advising them to *read her history*. He seems to have been, at that time, the only person in France who did not know all about it."

I must reluctantly break off from this piquant commentary on the successive phases of the situation. My readers will do well to pursue it for themselves. Mrs. Craven's indignation at the action of the French clergy, her horror at the *Freeman's Journal*—("Don't send it me any more," she writes; "it makes me sick with disgust and alarm")—her pained surprise at the policy of such men as Lord Aberdeen, Lord Spencer and Lord Ripon, her delight at Leo XIII.'s attitude on the Irish question, are all given with a keenness in her joy or in her anger worthy of a rising English politician in his twenties, and are truly remarkable in this Frenchwoman, born in the days of the First Empire and now in her eightieth year. It should be noted, however, that, though she looks on the crisis as one calling for the strongest expressions, her language is not that of the partisan, but conveys the sense of measured and deliberate, as well as severe, judgment on the merits of the case. Nothing can be more intense than her feeling on the policy of the Irish leaders — it is as though they were doing some personal injury to those nearest and dearest to her. "I cannot conquer what I feel about it," she writes; "it is such a frightful connivance at lawlessness, that it seems to me that nothing like it has ever been seen." Yet, when she reads Charles Greville's "Past and Present of Ireland," there is no lack of sympathy with the oppressed.

"Oh, what a story it is!" she writes. "But what a terrible thing it is, too, that all the pity and indignation it must arouse are now useless—indeed, dangerous feelings to indulge in! It is dwelling too much upon those recollections that has turned Mr. Gladstone into the mortal friend of Ireland he now is. Of course, that past is detestable, and can never be sufficiently abhorred, but it cannot turn a socialistic revolution into a remedy; it cannot turn the present leaders of the Irish into wise, safe, honest (giving that word its usual meaning) men and rulers. No, there is nothing to be done, but for England, who has done so much harm to Ireland, to do her best now;—patiently, persistently, and firmly to do her all the good she can."

I have been led to exhibit Mrs. Craven's sustained

commentary on one important crisis of English political
life more or less fully, because it belongs to the time
at which the biographer's epistolary material is most
abundant. But it was evidently only a typical instance.
The eager interest in public affairs revealed in her
letters appears to have been almost universal, where
she had the opportunity of knowing the facts of the
case. And it was the same with matters ecclesiastical,
and with literature. A new book or a new article is
sent for at once, read thoroughly, discussed eagerly,
its effect on the public mind—if it is serious—weighed,
its artistic value, if that be the true standard of appreciation, duly appraised.

The judgments given both on public affairs and
on literature are fearless and independent. The
great majority of mankind are, as Mr. Balfour has
reminded us, strongly affected by various "psychological climates"—by the opinion of the age, or of
their neighbours. There is *some* public opinion,
whether of their co-religionists or of their compatriots, or of those among whom they are living,
or of the would-be representatives of the intellect
of the day, which affects them deeply. They
are normally either carried with it, or in a state of
protest against it. Mrs. Craven appears to me to
have been free from both extremes. She gives to
each phase of public opinion its weight, considers it,
decides upon it. Generally she discriminates—finds
part true, part false, part doubtful. Yet she is not
afraid on occasion to identify herself with one party,
with a thoroughness which a philosopher would
condemn beforehand as unintellectual and indis-
criminating. In the war for Italian unity she goes
on the whole against the majority of her co-religionists

and with the Liberal school. Yet we have distinct reservations, in her clear recognition of the dangers of modern Liberalism, and strict regard for the rights of the Holy See. In Irish matters, even before the public opinion of the educated classes had declared itself unequivocally, she opposed vehemently the slightest tampering with democratic ideals; and when the Unionist party was formed, she identified herself unreservedly with its programme. In the case of the Vatican decrees she professed from the first sympathy with the minority, but at the same time her readiness to bow to the final decision of Authority; and after the Council, with prompt and frank logic, she carried out her determination. She had an obvious scorn of the habit, perhaps especially characteristic of modern England, of thinking and judging by fashion. And yet she was entirely free from that unwise insensibility to the signs of the times and to the inevitable future which marks the stubbornness of a blind reactionary. "La faiblesse tremble devant l'opinion," says Madame Roland; "le fou la brave, le sage la juge." I do not go so far as to say that Mrs. Craven's knowledge of the facts and breadth of mind were always sufficient to guarantee the unerring judgment of "the wise:" but she *did* keep her head and judge; and she was never either timid or foolhardy. This remark applies to her interesting estimates, not only of politicians and persons, but of such books as " John Inglesant," the "Journal of Marie Bashkirtseff," Mrs. Oliphant's " Life of Montalembert," Montalembert's own " Essay on St. Simon," and many other works referred to in the course of her letters.

The inner personal life which underlay this

incessant and vivacious mental activity appears to have been mainly determined by two influences. The first was a personality characterised in some respects by great intensity—an intensity evinced especially in the extraordinary vividness with which her early life remained ever present to her. An English philosopher has named memory as the chief mark of personal identity. And it may be said, somewhat analogously, that what Tennyson calls the "abysmal depths of personality" may be in great part gauged by the strength of that sense which binds the past and present together. The life of an intense personality is one marked by deep impressions. And impressions can scarcely be deep if they are readily forgotten. Pauline Craven has given us the story of her early sorrows, so wonderfully blended with spiritual hopefulness, in the "Récit d'une Sœur." One after another, brother and sisters were taken from her before their time, bound to each other and to herself by an ideal of family affection which could scarcely be surpassed. They had gone, full of that religious hope which is nowhere more definite than it is among religious French men and women, as it is nowhere more scoffingly set at nought than among the compatriots of those who in the days of the Terror tore the crucifixes from the hands of the dying, and took a pleasure in substituting ribald blasphemy for the last prayers of the priest. These memories and these hopes became in Pauline Craven an inseparable part of herself and of her own personal religion. She lived over again each word and act of the past as anniversaries recurred, or scenes of bygone events were revisited. The wounds were never healed ; the early feelings never became dim. Later scenes and

persons were not to her new gifts replacing what
was gone, and helping her to forget; they were the
supplement and continuation of the earlier. The
deepest friendship of her mature life was hailed as
intimacy with one who would understand her past,
and prolong for her those sweet interchanges of
sympathy which death had cut short. Madame
Swetchine was the *confidante* of the story of the
beloved dead—of Albert and Alexandrine, of Eugénie
and Olga, of all that Pauline herself had hoped, of all
she had lost, of all that religion still gave her to hope
for in the future. " I have always had a passionate
love of memories," she wrote in her journal, " and
felt the need of connecting what is past with what is
present. I have for long had a profound dislike for
all that can end as well as for all that can begin."

The other determining element in her *vie intime*
was the great religious movement in France, which
was brought into such close connexion with her life.
Montalembert and Père Gerbet were two of her
most intimate friends, and they had drunk in at La
Chesnaie the intense enthusiasm with which the
famous Abbé Félicité de Lamennais inspired his
followers. To work for the regeneration of French
society through the instrumentality of a purified
French Church,—a Church inspired by a new devotion
to the Apostolic See, and absorbing into itself all that
was generous and true in modern liberalism,—was an
idea which in these men amounted to a passion. The
irreligion of the eighteenth century was in their eyes
responsible for the horrors of 1793. "The old state
of society," says Père Lacordaire, "perished because
it had expelled God. The new is suffering because
God has not yet been admitted into it." The religious

movement, then, so intimately blended with the idea of social regeneration and reconstruction, naturally affected at its outset the statesmen and diplomatists of the time. The very earliest pioneers of the movement — Chateaubriand and Vicomte de Bonald in France, Joseph de Maistre in Savoy, Leopold von Stolberg in Germany—all held prominent positions in public life.

The family of the Marquis de La Ferronnays was a noteworthy instance of this influence. Readers of the "Récit d'une Sœur" need not be reminded how closely the atmosphere of the religious revival surrounded its members. It was an atmosphere full of bright and imaginative enthusiasms, and with none of the gloom of English Puritanism. It blended with the love of art, of intellect, of Catholic symbolism. With this atmosphere Pauline Craven was ˚impregnated. It underlay all her other interests, even in the days when society had the greatest charm for her.

In her forty-ninth year, however, its hold on her visibly deepened; and the change, so far as I can see, lasted until the end of her life. Up to this time the war between intense French impressionableness, a certain native waywardness, and all the temptations of a brilliant success in society on the one hand, and on the other the fixed ideal which she shared with the friends of her youth, and which she had never allowed to be obscured for long, had apparently lasted. The cause of the Church was ever to her the one great cause, the life of devotion the one real life; and yet her imaginative sympathies and her aims were scattered in various directions. The great effort to sum up and appraise the value of conflicting attractions, the effort which was needed to give unity of purpose, had yet to be made. We gather that it was made in 1856, and made once for all. And yet what gives to my mind a special character to this "conversion," as contrasted with many others, is that her eager interest in external events and persons, her freedom and spontaneity of mind, her downrightness and independence of expression and judgment, continued after it as before. The extracts already given from the letters of the last decade of her life are sufficient testimony to this fact. Indeed the element, which in different forms so often gives opportunity for an effective sneer at religious conversions, which enabled ill - natured persons to call Dr. Arnold's pet sixth-form boys "prigs," which gave Mr. Toole his typical Quaker in the "Serious Family," which filled the soul of Charles Dickens with disgust, and created Pecksniff, Chadband, Stiggins, and a host of others, was completely absent from Mrs. Craven. These latter instances are no doubt the broadest caricature, but they are the caricature of real features in human nature; and of these features not the least rudiment was apparent in Pauline Craven. She was as delightful, racy, *spirituelle* a companion after as before her religious change; but her life was more consistent, her purpose more definite, her affections even deeper and more constant. She gained in weight of character without losing in lightness of mental movement, or in any way impairing its freedom or contracting its range.

The change came, as in so many cases before and after St. Augustine's "Tolle, lege," from reading something which came home to her as apposite to her own life. Père Gratry had lent her a manuscript containing the private record of the struggle and conversion of another. Mrs. Craven notes the result as follows :—

"I mark September 29th and 30th as the days on which I read a certain manuscript. I pray that its effect may be lasting on me.

"In the first place, amid a thousand differences of circumstance, there was an extraordinary similarity at least of aspiration to mine, if indeed I may compare desires which have borne no fruit with unconquerable resolve and heroic sacrifice. There, too, was clear to me the only evident means for me—means which I have fully understood, but which I have never really adopted. To overcome love by love, what is perishable by what is eternal, the visible by the invisible, the human by the Divine, and this not by the extinction, but by the full development of our faculties. Never have I read anything that so corresponded to my inner consciousness. My heart tells me that herein is truth.

"Is it for nothing that God has given me this narrative to read, and has shown me these manifestations of His perpetual presence, and has made known to me these accepted prayers—these petitions and the answers to them?

"Is not all this truer than what we see with our eyes? —stranger, sweeter, and more limitless than all we could dream?

"I know not what will come of all this. Nothing, perhaps. Nothing! Great God, that is impossible! I shall have seen and heard and tasted all this, and make no further steps along the path Thy grace has shown me? It may be so, for so it has been a thousand times with me. Ah, that indeed is to be feared and grieves me, and there is nought else in the world that need be feared. I should never again feel sorrow or alarm if I could be, and knew that I was, faithful. But such as I am, it is no wonder that I am trembling and troubled, and that I live uneasily between earth's delights, which no longer please me, or are not for me, and that heavenly peace which I have not known how to attain."

Ten days later she goes to see Madame Swetchine at her house at Fleury. She notes with her usual

candour, both then and a little later, that the vivid
impression which the manuscript had made has by
this time passed away; but her resolution that it shall
take effect is fixed.

"It is strange. Since that flash of fervour, that momentary
view of an entirely different order of things which suddenly
revealed to me this world and its affairs in their absurdity;
since that day and in spite of the resolves I have made, and
to carry out which I again renew my determined intention,
the impression of which I spoke has absolutely disappeared.
I know that what I felt was true, both as regards my real
desires and my real needs—true, in fact, about myself, and
the true light in which things of this world should be seen.
I do not express myself clearly, but I understand myself,
and I have noted this here, so that if that flash of light never
again illumines my life, I shall still remember what it has
made clear to me. I shall still train my rebellious will in
that direction. Even when this breath of enthusiasm may
possibly be quite over, my will will remain fixed, I am sure."

Almost smiling at herself for the minuteness and
triviality of the rules in which what had seemed to
her a burst of heavenly light resulted, she begins to
practise early rising, and regularity in attending daily
mass and meditation. Such apparently small practices
seem to lead steadily upwards, as little things lead
fast downwards. We read between the lines that
there *are* occasional failures to carry out her resolves,
and that these failures are, on their side, due often to
trifles. She quotes her Dante—

> " O gente umana, per volar su nata,
> Perchè a poco vento così cadi ? "

Still the change appears to have been on the whole
permanent, and we are conscious of the new strength
which it brings increasingly as time advances. It

was at this time that she began her "Journal of Meditations," a part of which was published in her lifetime.

The habits and thoughts belonging to this period of inward reflection blended themselves with memories of the past. On February 10, 1857, she writes : "Yesterday and to-day are days for me of dear remembrance, of sad and sweet thoughts which lie deep in my life—thoughts which are ineffaceable and always present." She recalls the companions and scenes of earlier days, and the hopes which belonged to them :—

"We did not desire this world's splendours, nor anything which is counted earthly prosperity. We wished to love and be loved. We wished for life in which there should be affection, and duties transfigured by affection. We wished for busy but private lives, spent among our friends, and given to religion and study and love. Albert, Alexandrine, Eugénie, Olga, were not those our dreams? They are the dreams of many another, and they are righteous dreams ; and if God does not let us realise them on earth, it is that by well-endured privation we may hereafter earn their complete fulfilment.

"And yet, when the bolt falls on our youth, which destroys our faith in happiness, it seems for ever dead ; and when I recall the time and the way in which all those dear ties were broken, and all those pleasant forecasts proved illusions, I confess that even now I feel deeply the pain of that loss. Yet in all I acknowledge that every one of us has to bless God. During these last days I have for some moments felt a living sense of that heavenly happiness which is most within our conceptions—that of reunion. I must altogether doubt God's mercy, or believe that those dear souls are saved and are together. My father, my mother, Albert, Alexandrine, Eugénie, Olga—have they not all believed, suffered, loved, hoped, and worked the works of faith ; some in the strength of their innocence, others in that of their repentance, and of

their perfect and unmurmuring faithfulness to the law and
the will of God?

"Dear, dear souls, I cannot fear for you. I hope and I
believe in your happiness. What would mean faith and hope
if it be not that you have reached the height of all these joys,
by the lapse and loss of which we were once so grieved?
Past sufferings have become but faded dreams; and for you,
awaking for eternity will be the realisation of all perfection.

"Their lives and their deaths allow me, as I believe, to
think thus of them without presumption. There is such
happiness in the thought, that 'joy,' and not 'sorrow,' is the
right word to use on the day of their entrance into their
true life."

The next two years are years of peace and tranquillity. They were probably her fullest realisation
of the inner life of peace for which she had learned to
pine; although the higher purpose continued through
later times of trial. She put aside as a religious duty
the sense of anxiety, which the circumstances of her
external life even then suggested, and her natural
sensitiveness fostered; and she reaped her reward in
great inner tranquillity. "There are sufferings," she
writes, commenting on the text, "Be not solicitous,"
etc., "which our Lord has named Beatitudes, but
there is one suffering forbidden to us. It is one
which can so possess my soul that there is hardly an
instant of my life in which I do not feel it, and that is
anxiety in all its forms."

Madame Swetchine, who had been so great a support to her resolutions and affections, had passed
away in 1857. Pauline Craven mourned her loss;
but it seemed only to help to consecrate afresh her
resolution to lead an inner life of devotion and of
retirement from worldly thoughts and temptations.
We have the picture of this life, amid the lovely
Italian scenery of Castagneto, early in the year 1858.

"At this moment I believe I have all I need for calm and progress—solitude amidst this enchanting scenery, work to do which I love, interesting and improving books, long hours, and even days of blessed silence which are necessary to my peace. For never, if I talk for long, do I fail to regret something that I have said. I have far greater spiritual resources than at Naples, or, indeed, than I can have in the country anywhere else. I have a chapel so close by that it seems to belong to the house—Mass every morning, and every evening the Benediction of the Blessed Sacrament. I have an unexpected happiness in finding a confessor in one of the Benedictines of the fine Monastery of La Trinità. Often in this silence have I heard that dear voice which used to speak to me not a year ago. Often have I visited Fleury in thought, and listened here to what she used to say to me there. Her words made, two years since, such an impression on me that, notwithstanding a thousand failures and through all the occupations of the world, it has never been effaced. A little more than a year ago, during the last day I spent there with her, what tender and good advice she gave me! With what wise and trenchant sayings did she make me understand and accept it!

"She was witness, as no one else was, of the anxieties my life occasioned me. Often she said that I must make a refuge in my heart to which I could retire in times of uncertainty; she said that I needed an immovable central point in my soul whatever were its external agitations. . . . 'Il vous faut l'assiette dans ce repos intérieur.' She often repeated and wrote the phrase, and sometimes she hurt me by so doing, because it did not seem applicable to what I was suffering at the moment—painful anxiety, anxiety about circumstances independent of my will. Sometimes she said almost harshly to me, if the epithet could be applied to her sweet and gentle words, 'You suffer because you are wanting in calm.' And yet it appeared to me that I was not calm just because I suffered. Sometimes I wept as I listened to her, and looked at her in dumb appeal that she would console me in a different way. How I remember her sweet smile at such moments! and I see her now especially as she was one evening. It was not at Fleury, but in her Paris drawing-room. I had given my thoughts free course as I never did but with her. Neither my mother, whom I loved so tenderly, nor my sisters, to whom my heart was open, had known how to read it as she did. I would not appeal to their affection, which was too ready to sympathise in my troubles and to excuse me. I felt that their tenderness might have enervated me, and I knew that I required strengthening. For this reason my dear friend could help me more than any other, for, however tender might be her love for me, I did not fear weakness in her. For that reason I hid nothing from her. That same evening I was kneeling by her side and crying. She gently shook her head and stroked mine so tenderly, so lovingly, and the expression of her countenance remains so vivid in my memory, that I feel certain that her love for me endures, and that her prayers for me are still offered in heaven. Then she laughed a little, and said to me, 'You look at me with your great suppliant eyes as if I had said something very cruel to you. Yet what I said is truth, believe me. Of course, I ardently wish for you all external help from a tranquil life ; but whether we have that or not, there is a complete interior stability which you ought to acquire.'"

Again, with the candour with which she ever marks the limitations of her spiritual progress, Mrs. Craven notes the human satisfaction which the new life of calm has brought to her, and which she seems to record as a set-off against any claim to heroic self-conquest in her comparative abandonment of the pleasures and excitements of wordly life. " Quite independently of its spiritual advantages," she writes, " I love this uniform and peaceful life. It pleases my taste, and it really would be my ideal of happiness, not only for a few months, but at all times, if now and then the society of two or three good friends could be added to it, as well as some possibility of hearing good music. I crave for music sometimes, and feel the need of it and poetry."

In perusing this minute record of impressions, sensations, aspirations, noble ideals, in Mrs. Craven's Journal as in the "Récit d'une Sœur," one point of contrast between the English and the French or Russian mind becomes apparent. Alexandrine and Madame Swetchine, no less than Mrs. Craven and her own brothers and sisters, express each thought and sensation with an unreserve which appears to an Englishman almost inconsistent with the deepest feeling. When Alexandrine writes down the record of her grief and prayer, placing the sheet of paper on her husband's yet unburied coffin, and when Pauline depicts the vivid glimpses of a higher world which remain to her imagination as a beacon light after they are withdrawn, there is to some English minds a suggestion of shallowness, or of self-consciousness, or even a little of both. Englishmen are in the habit of contrasting words with deeds, volubility with reality, profession with execution. The minute record of one's own aspirations reads to them like mere wordy profession ; and the story of their fulfilment, even if balanced by that of incidental failure, belongs to no category they know of except the utterances of the self-conscious poser, even if they hesitate to qualify it by an epithet so distinct. I have heard such judgments passed upon the self-revelations in the " Récit d'une Sœur."

And yet to the present writer such a verdict appears quite unjust,—an instance of the deep and almost impassable prejudice which separates races or even persons of opposite temperaments, and prevents them from being fair to one another. I believe that the French habit of self-analysis and self-expression really belongs to a stage of self-realisation radically different from self-consciousness, and which is characteristic in some respects of a higher advance in purely mental civilisation than our own countrymen have yet reached. That it may be occasionally accompanied by some of the undue flexibility, tending to instability, which highly civilised minds, from the Greek to the Gallic, have been wont to exhibit, I am not concerned to deny. But neither unreality nor self-consciousness is necessarily involved in it. It is in fact a habit of dramatic self-realisation which makes each man at once actor and spectator in his own life. He instinctively loves to express fully for himself a drama which interests him so deeply. He does it not with the self-consciousness of an Englishman,—to whom the attempt does not come naturally, who hesitates, fails to concentrate his attention and to see truly or candidly, and looks back at his attempt in the pause which ensues, is half ashamed of it, and thinks to himself, " How will such interest in myself appear to others ? " It is this very pause and hesitation of mind which, like something which interrupts the illusion in a play and reminds you that it is not real, opens the door to English self-consciousness. The Frenchman is too deeply dramatic for this. He may remain in totally unself-conscious concentration on the phenomena of his own mind and on their interest as the scenes of a drama.

In extreme cases of this attitude he may appear to the Englishman to be *simply* bragging, and talking for effect, or, again, playing a part with a purpose, until he astonishes his Saxon critic by some deed of heroism, or of brutality, or of daring, in which he acts out his idea, and shows thereby that, whatever his " wordiness " was or was not, it at least corresponded to something which was wonderfully or terribly real. I have known readers derive from the early part of Père Chocarne's "Vie Intime" of Lacordaire the impression of a self-conscious and almost vain Frenchman, and they have been amazed to read in the sequel of the mediæval austerities by which Lacordaire actually shortened his life.

I believe, then, that such an outcome of the dramatic temperament as we have in the reflections of Pauline Craven or of Alexandrine de La Ferronnays is compatible with the intensest reality; and while some possibility of self-consciousness remains, even amid deep reality, its extent and prominence are far less than an Englishman would suppose. The drama of life occupies a far larger, self a far smaller, space, than would be the case in similar circumstances with one of our own countrymen. The candour of the French nature is a form of mental eyesight which is generally wanting in the Englishman. Consequently, contemplation of the phenomena of their own minds becomes a true and, it may be, an absorbing occupation to those who can see so much and so accurately : and the record of it is not *rhodomontade*, but an exact register of observations. The average Englishman has not this power of vision, and he is therefore, when trying to fancy himself in a similar position, much like a man devoid of artistic perception placed in a picture-gallery amid a company of artists. While time passes for them in unconscious absorption in the interest of what they are studying, he looks about him and becomes self-conscious, because what is an occupation for the eye of an artist is none for him.

Hitherto I have dealt almost entirely with the

personality of Mrs. Augustus Craven as revealed in these pages. Yet a biography is naturally the story of a life, and not merely the exhibition of a character. What is to be said of the book from this point of view?

In truth there is much less to be said of it. Mrs. Craven's life was not a public life; her husband's career as a diplomatist was not greatly distinguished; his ambition to be a great statesman was never fulfilled. "Le Récit d'une Sœur" did, no doubt, bring fame to Mrs. Craven when she was approaching sixty; and that fame was due, not only to the unique interest of the materials at her command and the story of love and devotion she had to tell, but to her own supreme powers of literary expression and selection, her penetrating sympathy and delicate appreciation of the drama she set forth. Yet notwithstanding this, any expectation of a career of public interest, even in the same sense as George Eliot's or Thackeray's life could be so characterised, remained unfulfilled. The brilliant success of "Le Récit d'une Sœur" naturally led its author to write again. She wrote several novels; they were well written, and in some cases well received at the time, but hardly one of them can be said to have taken a permanent place in literature. She remains, and will remain, known as the author of the "Récit d'une Sœur."

Her perfect sense of literary form and expression, her acute judgments of intellectual character and of political and religious movements, even her deep appreciation of the drama of life as it passed before her, did not involve the creative genius which is essential to the really great novelist. She was a critic rather than an originator. Keenly sensitive to dramatic incident when it occurred, she had no proportionate power of inventing it. Her insight into character even in real life did not touch those deepest springs which give the great novelist his inspiration. Her appreciations of Palmerston, Bright, Gladstone, Gordon, are wonderfully vivacious and acute, and true so far as they go; but their scope is most definitely limited. The effect of the policy of these men, their impact on the world about them, the broad features of their method, are very exactly estimated, but we do not find anywhere the finest analysis of personal character or detection of the inmost sources of human motive. The "Récit" succeeded because the characters were ready made and were revealed in their own letters and journals. All that was needed was the highest sympathy of the dramatic critic, as distinguished from the creative dramatist, and the sense of literary form and proportion. And these gifts Mrs. Craven had in a very high degree. When she had, in addition, to create the characters herself, she had not the special genius required for work of the first class.

Thus the only public distinction Mrs. Craven attained to she failed completely to sustain. And yet if her eminence was not sufficient to ensure her Life being written in the history of the times, assuredly some of the history of the times is written in these pages. Of the passing glimpses we find there of events of political interest I need say no more. They are not perhaps considerable enough or sustained enough to call for further mention in this connection. But this Life, like the "Récit d'une Sœur" itself, contains a chapter in the history of the religious revival of the nineteenth century which cannot be overlooked by its historians. This aspect of the book

may seem at first sight to promise comparatively little
that is of interest to English readers, from its apparently exclusive connection with the fortunes of the
Papal Church.   And yet I believe that such an
anticipation will be agreeably disappointed.   I do not
propose to deal with this subject at length, but
will briefly indicate what appears to me its significance.

Mrs. Craven was born four years after Napoleon
was crowned Emperor.   The French Church was
feebly attempting its own reconstruction after the
frightful scenes of the previous years, during which,
in Lacordaire's words, "the Church presented to men
and angels the appearance of nothing but a vast
ruin."   Chateaubriand's "Atala" had already been
published when she was born.   Joseph de Maistre's
"Du Pape" and Lamennais' "Essai sur l'Indifférence"
appeared in her early girlhood.   In one shape or
another, thinking minds in France were beginning
to urge on their fellow-citizens that the destructive
philosophy of the eighteenth century had left them
without rudder or compass; that it had ignored the
accumulated experience of ages, to which in reality
we owe so much more of our practical knowledge
than the individual critic can hope either to justify
or to discredit; that Christian tradition must be once
more invoked to rescue society from anarchy and
individuals from pessimism.

De Maistre and Lamennais were impressed by the
difficulty of trusting the fortunes of the restored
Church to a more or less infidel State.   They
urged the enfeebled French Church to cast itself
unreservedly on the Apostolic See as the protector
of its liberties against the encroachments of the civil

power. This was its one chance of restoration to health and strength. The religious life, which began to revive in earnest soon after the Revolution of 1830, gradually acquired the special *esprit de corps* which personal loyalty naturally breeds, and centred round the Apostolic See and the Ultramontane cause. The same phenomenon became apparent in Austria, in Belgium, in Bavaria, in Prussia, in Tuscany. Churches which had formerly developed on the National side, and resented the interference of the Papacy as an encroachment on their liberty, now welcomed its protection as the best security for necessary freedom. Catholics realised their weakness and became penetrated with the sense that union is strength. German Febronianism and Austrian Jansenism, as well as French Gallicanism, gave way before the new Ultramontanism.

But this movement which, to Englishmen, may appear at first sight to be significant politically, almost as much as religiously, can only be understood in its true moral bearings by studying the men and women whom it fashioned and the type of religious character it fostered. And this study can nowhere be pursued more vividly than in the "Life of Mrs. Craven" and in the "Récit d'une Sœur." These works deserve to be read with the pages of Montalembert, the lives of Lacordaire and of Ozanam, by those who care to understand the inner as well as the outer aspect of a remarkable revival. The combination of sympathy with all that is best in the spirit of the times, including a genuine love of liberty, with the tendency to ecclesiastical centralisation and loyalty to the Papacy, remind us that, at the outset, Liberalism and Ultramontanism were, as religious movements, one and the same, and were opposed to Gallicanism and to the narrower forms of Nationalism.

It does not fall within my scope to trace the successive phases of the movement itself. They are abundantly illustrated, alike in Mrs. Craven's own character and in the side-lights which her letters throw upon it. It moved onwards with rapid strides —in France especially—between 1830 and 1857. In 1830 a priest dared not venture into the streets of Paris in his *soutane*. In 1848 some twenty priests were elected members of the Assembly. In 1857 Cardinal Newman avowed that " France professed Catholicism with an ardour unknown since Louis XIV.'s reign." The share in this transformation borne by Lacordaire's conferences at Notre Dame recalls the fact that it was essentially a change, not merely in religious practice, but in the public attitude towards the Church. Even those who remained free-thinkers were deeply influenced by his contention that religion was necessary for society.

But the conferences did also bring back to numbers the faith they had lost, and fill the churches which had been so long emptied. And in this respect, as in others, their effect was to a great extent lasting. When Père Félix preached in 1857, his audiences were as large as those at the earlier conferences of Lacordaire. Mrs. Craven gives us a characteristic glimpse of her own feelings,—intensified no doubt by her memory of the days when what she now saw had been only an aspiration and a hope,—at the sight of Frenchmen gathered together once more in prayer. Here is her account of a visit to Notre Dame in the Holy Week of that year.

"To Notre Dame. Strong and profound emotion was caused by the scene, both as it was then and as memory recalled it to me.

"Nothing has ever, in my eyes, surpassed the general effect of what is to be found in that place, and at that hour, during those holy days. The crowd of men was greater than in the days of the finest sermons from Père de Ravignan and Père Lacordaire; yet Père Félix does not at all equal either of them. The compact mass of listeners is all the more edifying. But what gave me one of those spiritual shocks, rarely felt, but which strike from the soul a living spring of urgent and fervid prayer, was the anthem ' Parce, Domine,' which followed the sermon. Without having heard it, it is impossible to imagine the effect of the cry, first uttered by one voice and then by the five or six thousand voices of the men who overflowed the vast nave of Notre Dame. ' Parce, Domine, parce populo tuo.' Never were words and music in such accord. Never did the impression of unanimous prayer—the prayer which obtains—strike me so strongly.

"The men of Paris, so powerful alike for good as for evil —when I remembered that it was their voices I heard, I could not help joining them with confidence and hope and faith in the future of our sick and troubled commonwealth, which is yet so full of the vigorous sap by which national prosperity may be always resuscitated.

"It is when I remember this that I love France, and that I feel I still belong to her. In no other country does one feel so happy, so pure, and so full of energy in the presence of evil. Fighting it at close quarters, not disguising it by specious names, not yielding to it ; keeping our souls at their highest level, using the words ' self-abnegation ' and ' devoted-ness ' in a sense that is more thorough than the meaning in which they are understood elsewhere—a sense that is the highest, and which is forgotten by other nations. Of such Frenchmen I am the fellow-citizen and the sister."

It is instructive to see how a religious revival, which had so profound an influence on the French people, and which remained throughout more or less homogeneous in its effect on their ethical ideals, nevertheless eventually became separated, in the intellectual temper of its representatives, into many divergent and even conflicting streams. In this respect Lacordaire's conferences may be compared to Newman's sermons at Oxford. They imparted an unworldliness and spiritual enthusiasm to many representing entirely different schools of thought. And although in France the divergence of intellectual position was necessarily limited by doctrinal union and by the common deference of so many to the Papacy, the contrast of intellectual temper was hardly less than in England. Matthew Arnold and Clough, Jowett and Stanley, drank deeply of the same stream from which R. W. Church and Pusey, as well as Oakeley and Faber, drew their inspiration ; and Principal Shairp and Mr. J. A. Froude have given us, in language the significance of which is not to be mistaken, records of the ethical transformation wrought at a time of life when impressions are lasting, by those Sunday evening sermons from the pulpit of St. Mary's.

And so, too, the religious movement in France— due, it is true, much less to one single influence— seized upon many who ultimately represented different schools, and it stamped them with its genius. We discern, both in Mrs. Craven's Life and in the " Récit d'une Sœur," features in the inner character of many different French Catholics, supplying illustrations of this unity in diversity which the historian cannot afford to neglect. The girlhood of Pauline de La Ferronnays was passed in the days when Frayssinous and De Quelen were reviving the better aspect of the pre-Revolution Catholicism, solid and undemonstrative

in its piety, Gallican in its creed, unenthusiastic in
its temper, rendering before all things to Cæsar the
things that are Cæsar's; her early womanhood and
the years of the most romantic interest of the " Récit
d'une Sœur" are full of the echoes from La Chesnaie,
where Félicité de Lamennais, no longer a Royalist
but by a sudden *volte-face* a Liberal of Liberals, was
urging papal absolutism and the democracy to combine in forming a Church which should consecrate all
that was noblest in the Revolution.   This phase
of thought, coupled with a new zeal and depth of
the spiritual life, and tempered by the sanctity of
Lacordaire and Gerbet,—both of them disciples of the
Master at La Chesnaie—determined once for all Mrs.
Craven's own aspirations.

But it was destined to be succeeded by others.
Papal absolutism and Lamennais' theory of freedom
first collided; Gregory XVI. refused to endorse
Lamennais' scheme, which would have invested the
Roman See with an inconvenient power under
inconvenient conditions.   Lamennais' journal, the
Avenir was condemned; the leader himself renounced allegiance to Rome.   Later on, the modified Liberalism—still one with Ultramontanism—of
Montalembert and Lacordaire separated itself from
the aggressive and, as it seemed to many, extravagant
Papalism of Louis Veuillot and the *Univers*.   And
at the Vatican Council came the apparent paradox
that Montalembert, the chief representative of that
Liberal movement which had defeated Gallicanism
and made France Ultramontane, was in alliance with
men who drew some at least of their inspiration from
the old Gallicanism of the France of Frayssinous
and De Quelen.

It will not, perhaps, be of interest to the general reader to follow this sequence of events farther. Its significance appears to lie in this fact, that, as I have said, amid all the differences which suggest that most irritating of all forms of prejudice, the *odium theologicum*, and which as appearing on the surface of things are the part of the story best known to the world, we find in the inner character of some of those who were furthest apart, the same breadth of religious sympathy, the same self-devotion, the same almost saintly type. And the two works I have named afford substantial assistance in enabling us to detect this, from the abundant indications they give, in letters and journals, of the spiritual temper of many different persons. We come, in reading them, to see a true unity amid divergence, and to understand how the Catholic movement had in reality that union which gives power. Abbé Gerbet, whose policy was in the main that of Louis Veuillot, excessive in its claims for the papal prerogative; Dupanloup, so considerably tinged with the Gallicanism of an earlier time; and, on the other hand, Montalembert, Lacordaire, and the family group which was so closely united with their aspirations and views, however different in intellectual temper and practical policy, are remarkably alike in that spiritual character which reveals itself in the story of their private lives, their letters and their other writings. It is startling to those who look on the "Syllabus" as the embodiment of all that was reactionary, and as especially directed against the followers of Montalembert and Lacordaire, to find in the letters of one of its chief promoters, Abbé Gerbet, that union of large-hearted tenderness with uncompromising maintenance of religious principle,

which made Abbé Lacordaire himself so great an
influence on the youth of France.   And Dupanloup
—although he figures less prominently than Gerbet
in these works—whatever he may have retained of
Gallican sympathies, had evidently imbibed just
that temper of ascetic zeal and hopefulness which
characterised the revival, and was almost conspicuous
by its absence in the French Church of the twenties.
The whole movement had one definite religious *ethos*
of singular spiritual charm, and we see this *ethos* in
very different persons, far apart alike in temperament,
in theological tendency, and in cast of mind.   The
historian who should note the theological differences
and omit to observe the inner unity, would give a
misleading picture of the time and of the men.

And this leads me to make two remarks in conclusion.   First, the whole book in its more serious
aspect suggests the lesson of unity of *ethos* and
principle amid theological division, as being applicable
beyond the limits of any particular time and place,—
as applicable to England in 1903 as well as to France
in 1850.   Mrs. Craven is devoted to General Gordon,
and says he is at heart a Roman Catholic.   Many
an English reader, who is far from having sympathy
with the Catholic Church, will feel, while reading
these pages, the truest sympathy with Mrs. Craven's
inner life and religion.   Men like Sir M. E. Grant-
Duff, the late Dean Church, and Mr. Matthew Arnold
are known to have been as deeply fascinated by her
spiritual experiences as any Catholic.   It is, I suppose,
important for us all to learn this lesson of comparative
unity amid divisions.   The cause of religion and the
cause of law and order are more and more felt to be one.
The feeling that all religious men must act to some

extent in concert if society is not to be dechristianised, and if the forces which are exhibited in terrible carica- ture by the Anarchists are to be successfully resisted, is unquestionably on the increase. A life, then, like Mrs. Craven's, which brings home to Englishmen how much sympathy may exist between them and members even of the " exclusive " Church, has great practical value.

Secondly, I would remark that Mrs. Craven's history brings home to us just that critical march of events which has so signally identified religion with the cause of Authority and of a rational Conservatism. We see in her life the dawn, the testing, and the failure of the attempt of the present century to fuse religion with what has proved to be a revolutionary and fanatically optimistic conception of social and intellectual progress. The enthusiasm of her youth was united Italy. The enthusiasm of her old age was Unionism in Ireland, or more truly anti-Radicalism. We pass with her through the remarkable era when civilisation was supposed to promise universal peace ; when it was hoped that an extended suffrage would perfect our Constitution ; when our Constitution was ex- pected, by transplantation to Italy and France and elsewhere, gradually to civilise the world ; when Science was promising to subdue the earth for men and quickly to bring the Millennium ; when Darwinism and German criticism were to widen the intellectual horizon to a degree of which our benighted forefathers could not have conceived ; when every change was regarded as a manifestation of the underlying Great Power, the Spirit of Progress, who was to bring us blessings which were only not described in detail because they were too vast for description; when all the freedoms—free-trade, free criticism, a free press, and many others—were invoked, and the one fear was lest man should fetter the action of this ideal controller of our destinies ; when the poet whose voice was that of the nation sang with triumphant gladness—

"Let the great world spin for ever down the ringing grooves of change."

I will not undertake the melancholy task of singing in full the threnody of these hopes. Reform Bills have extended our franchise, and yet the Progressive party have arguments to advance other than those from experienced results. France and Italy have the desired constitutions, yet they are not the envy of the surrounding nations. The horrors of war are not at an end. The advance of Darwinism has not been homogeneous,—indeed, it has illustrated the law of reversion as well as that of evolution. The various freedoms have done a good deal, but hardly with the stately march and ideal equilibrium for which the poet looked. The hero of " Locksley Hall" was not satisfied with the fulfilment of at least this part of his dream. "Freedom of destruction" was not in his programme; and yet it marched under cover of the great banner he raised ; and somehow, as the "great world spun," this perversion of "liberty" seemed to the poet to fuse with and corrupt the ideal freedoms. The disenchantment grew, and Tennyson lived to write another memorable line on Freedom. The years had changed enthusiasm to something less than indifference. If the Freedom of the first "Locksley Hall" was that of the "Star of the morning, hope at the sunrise," that of the second was equally characteristic of the " Gloom of the evening, life at its close." We remember the line—

" Freedom free to slay herself, and dying while they shout her name."

And the change which came to Tennyson and his hero came too, in its measure, to Mrs. Craven. Though she was less affected than the poet by the scientific enthusiasms of the day, its political ideals had moved her deeply, and her disappointment threw her all the more absolutely on the preservation of Christian principle as the great hope for the future.

THE END.